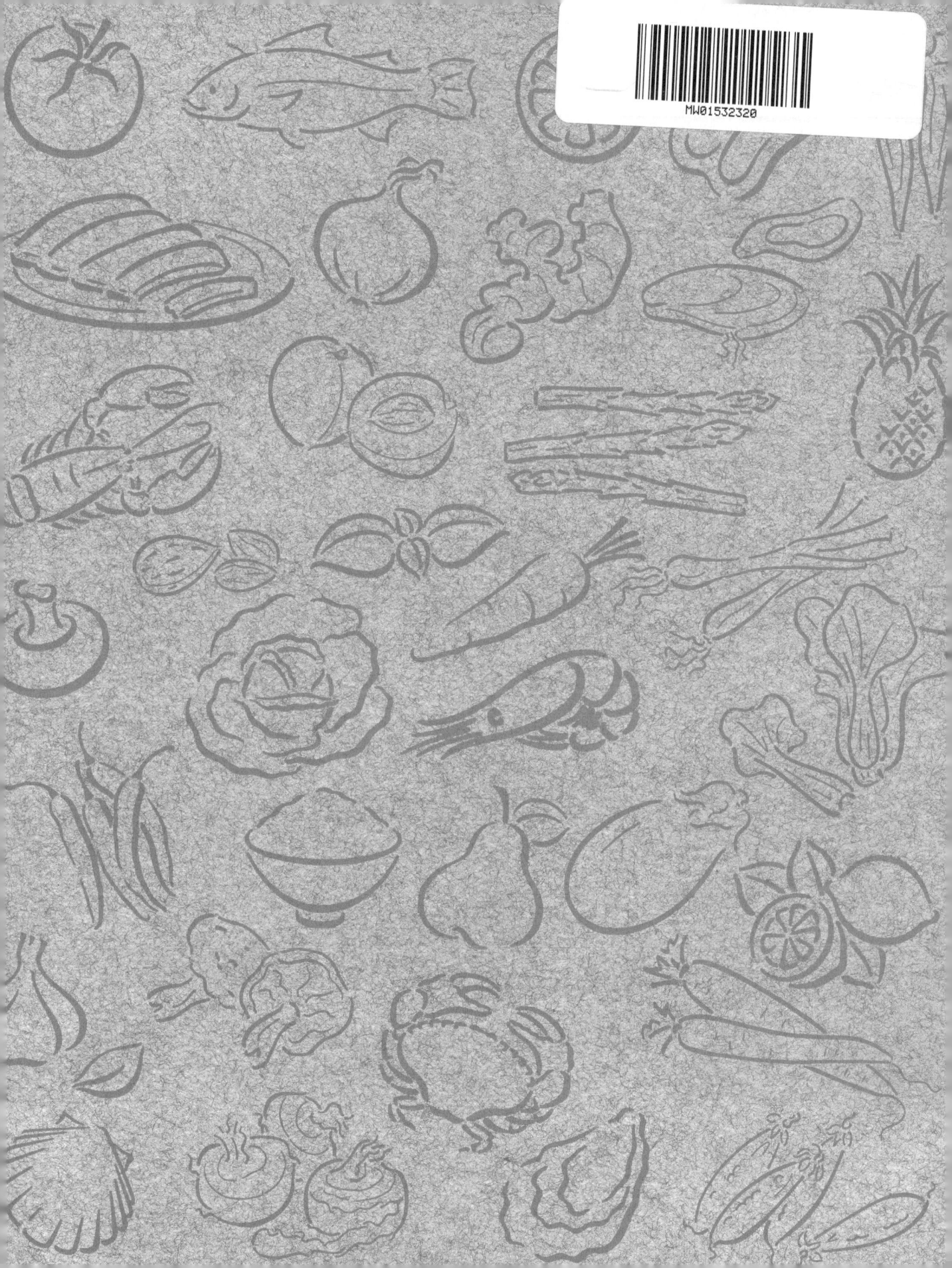

ASIAN COOKING

ASIAN COOKING

IRWIN GELBER

Photography by J. Gerard Smith

VAN NOSTRAND REINHOLD

I(T)P® A Division of International Thomson Publishing Inc.

New York • Albany • Bonn • Boston • Detroit • London • Madrid • Melbourne
Mexico City • Paris • San Francisco • Singapore • Tokyo • Toronto

I ⓉP® A division of International Thomson Publishing, Inc.
The ITP logo is a registered trademark under license

Printed in the United States of America

Food styling by Arno Schmidt

For more information, contact:

Van Nostrand Reinhold
115 Fifth Avenue
New York, NY 10003

Chapman & Hall GmbH
Pappelallee 3
69469 Weinheim
Germany

Chapman & Hall
2-6 Boundary Row
London
SE1 8HN
United Kingdom

International Thomson Publishing Asia
221 Henderson Road #05-10
Henderson Building
Singapore 0315

Thomas Nelson Australia
102 Dodds Street
South Melbourne, 3205
Victoria, Australia

International Thomson Publishing Japan
Hirakawacho Kyowa Building, 3F
2-2-1 Hirakawacho
Chiyoda-ku, 102 Tokyo
Japan

Nelson Canada
1120 Birchmount Road
Scarborough, Ontario
Canada M1K 5G4

International Thomson Editores
Seneca 53
Col. Polanco
11560 Mexico D.F. Mexico

1 2 3 4 5 6 7 8 9 10   VHP   01 00 99 98 97 96

Library of Congress Cataloging-in-Publication Data

Gelber, Irwin, 1933–
    Asian cooking / Irwin Gelber.
        p. cm.
    Includes bibliographical references and index.
    ISBN 0-442-31942-8
    1. Cookery, Oriental.   I. Title.
TX724.5.A1G45   1996
641.595—dc20

95-48014
CIP

To my wife, Peg, with gratitude

for accompanying me through so many journeys.

CONTENTS

Asian Cooking seeks to provide the professional chef and the serious student of the culinary arts with a representative sampling of dishes reflective of the culinary heritage of Asia. I must, at the outset, emphasize the word "sampling." As one might expect from such a vast geographical area of the globe, home to so many diverse cultures and subcultures, the number of recipes and variations of recipes is positively staggering. Add to this the regional preferences and personal inclinations of individual cooks and the number of possibilities becomes astronomical. Consequently, choices, at times difficult ones, had to be made in order to deal effectively with this abundant source of culinary ingenuity and creativity. To help narrow the selection process, the recipes chosen for inclusion had to meet the following objectives:

1. They must have a strong association with a specific national cuisine;

2. They must use basic raw and processed ingredients that are readily available in the United States market; and

3. They must be within the culinary realm of a broad spectrum of western diners and therefore, be marketable.

The preparations presented in this volume are rooted, for the most part, in the cuisine of the common people, comprising a collection of representative appetizers, soups, rice and noodle dishes, vegetables, as well as fish, poultry, and meat entrees. Since dessert, as we in the West know it, does not really play a major role in the every-day Asian diet (where fruits often enjoy the final place on the menu), I have chosen to include a small, representative selection of possible menu items that might be useful, rather than the hybrid concoctions like green tea ice cream, et al., which have been created for the Western consumer.

The recipes, on the whole, reflect a commitment to the use of fresh, easily obtainable ingredients and a straightforward, uncomplicated method of preparation. Some of the ingredients essential in the preparation of these dishes may not be familiar to some western cooks. These include certain fresh produce items, dried, fermented and pickled products as well as other kinds of processed foods. Fortunately, the influx of immigrants from Asia to our country within the last several decades has created a demand for many of the ingredients needed to prepare the dishes described in this book. The most essential products are now readily obtainable in our wholesale and retail markets.

We owe a large vote of thanks to the waves of immigrants who came to our shores to work, and eventually, settle. They brought not only the culinary traditions of their native lands along with other rich aspects of their native cultures, but they also brought the techniques and skills honed over thousands of years of culinary practice. Their needs, in turn, brought about the development of a network of producers and purveyors to provide the raw materials necessary to prepare the dishes of their native lands. These factors have combined to give us a gastronomic treasure of tastes, aromas, and textures. They have greatly enhanced our choice of edibles and have provided us with a uniquely exuberant, multi-cultural marketplace. The foods of Asia are now an integral part of our diets. The prepared products, fruits, and vegetables, once considered exotic, have taken their rightful place on the shelves of our markets and on the menus of our dining rooms, enabling us to enjoy much of the world's culinary traditions while remaining comfortably at home.

Our own curiosity about and fascination with a diverse diet has also played an important role in helping "foreign" food preparations become firmly rooted in the dietary practices of our country. Naturally, whenever a culinary transplantation takes place, one can expect to find modifications, substitutions, or even the inclusion of non-authentic ingredients. This has probably held true whenever people have moved from their native soil to settle elsewhere. Despite these modifications or, in some cases, amplifications, the essence of the cuisine, which is central to the survival of its cultural identity, has always been preserved. Adaptability usually goes hand-in-hand with survival. And nothing is more basic to the survival of a culture than a healthy supply of foods that nourish the body as well as the soul.

After the arrival of the Chinese, whose labor helped to push the country westward, other groups of immigrants from Asia followed: Koreans, Thai, Cambodians, Burmese, Vietnamese, as well as others from what we now call the Pacific rim countries. They too brought with them their own culinary preparations as well as new foods for us to enjoy. They introduced us to their cooking techniques, kitchen implements, herbs, fruits and vegetables, along with a host of new of sauces and condiments. Asians have not only given us an unusually broad spectrum of public eating places, they have also greatly influenced the kinds of foods we eat at home, pack for lunch and purchase from street vendors for snacks.

This fact of life has not gone unnoticed by American and European chefs who have now begun to incorporate ingredients and methods of presentation that were formerly exclusively used in Asian cuisine. As local chefs have begun to present more "globally conscious" menus, a "fusion cuisine" has emerged, which seeks to create a synthesis between the foods of the West and those of our Asian neighbors. Such preparations have begun to appear on menus throughout the world and could very well be the subject of another book. But for now, it is hoped that through this book, a familiarity with a small slice of the foods of Asia will provide a stimulus for the Western cook to learn more about the culinary techniques and ingredients used to prepare foods from this part of the world. It is also hoped that those who use this book will continue along the long culinary tradition that combines experimentation and creativity with a healthy respect for the untold generations of cooks who made these dishes possible.

ACKNOWLEDGMENTS

I would like to express my gratitude to the countless, nameless cooks, whose creative efforts over the centuries resulted in the recipes, cooking techniques, and methods of preparation referred to in this volume. I would hope that their achievements in the culinary arts are not viewed as the final word, but rather, as a guide to further culinary inspiration. That being said, I would like to also thank a number of more contemporaneous individuals who helped me in preparing this book. First, my thanks go to Myriam Gelber, who served as my research assistant, and Margaret Bachelder, who offered valuable editorial assistance and constant encouragement. A very special thanks to my colleagues, Chef Charles F. Leonardo, C.E.C., Director of dining services at Clark University, and Executive Chef Ennio Vespa, C.E.C., A.A.C., for providing me with valuable research materials; to Walter Neuhold, C.E.C., for sharing his personal collection of recipes gathered when he served as Executive Chef at the Westin Hotel in Seoul, Korea; to Charles Rodriguez, Northeast Regional Sales Manager, the Kikkoman Corp.; to Kachane Marutan, chef/manager of Thai Kitchen, Boston, MA; Bela Tong, cook extraordinaire; and to Kenny Chan of the Joy Luck Cafe in Needham, MA. I am greatly indebted to all of these individuals for graciously sharing their vast knowledge of the Asian kitchen with me.

I would also like to acknowledge the following chefs who took time from their busy schedules to review the manuscript and offer valuble and constructive advice: Michael Acker, Michael Black, Brian Clark, Ann Cooper, Linda Hierholzer, Dory Kwan, Christoph Leu, Gerard Lewis, Daryl Notter, Emiliano Sotelo, and Otto Weibel.

And lastly, my thanks to Melissa Rosati, Amy Shipper, Jackie Martin, and Sharon Cornell of Van Nostrand Reinhold for their patient efforts in bringing this volume into existence.

RECIPE CONTENTS

CHAPTER FOUR
VEGETABLES

CHAPTER FIVE
FISH AND SEAFOOD

CHAPTER SIX
POULTRY

CHAPTER SEVEN
MEATS

CHAPTER EIGHT
FLAVORINGS AND CONDIMENTS

CHAPTER NINE
RICE AND NOODLES

CHAPTER TEN
DESSERTS

RECIPE LIST BY COUNTRY

RECIPE LIST BY COUNTRY

Introduction

Our increased awareness of good nutrition and other concerns relating to a healthful diet have stimulated a growing interest in the foods and eating practices of Asia. Rooted in what are essentially agrarian societies, the Asian diet is based on an abundant use of grains, legumes, and fresh vegetables, and a limited consumption of fish and other seafoods, meats, and poultry. Because of this particular balance between vegetable and animal products, we view the Asian diet as being a healthy one. But it is not only the health benefits that attract us to these cuisines. The complex, often exotic, flavors; the attractive, contrasting textures and colors; and the mouth-watering aromas are even more seductive. The popularity of the Asian kitchen in its many guises is evidenced by the ever-growing number of restaurants serving the foods of China, Japan, Korea, Thailand, India, and other Asian countries that have been cropping up in cities and towns throughout the world.

Serving their distinctive national and regional foods, the cooks of Asia have brought many new ideas to our table. Their cooking methods have had a pronounced influence not only on the way we cook and what we cook, but also on the manner in which we arrange and present our dishes when serving. Rapid cooking of vegetables, for instance, not only helps to preserve the nutritional value but also creates a more colorful and therefore more pleasing and appetizing presentation. Such cooking techniques, mixed with the ingenious use of spices, herbs, and other flavoring agents and a wide range of marinades to tenderize and add texture and flavor, have strongly influenced our own methods. Possessing what many believe to be the world's greatest inventory of ingredients, these cooks have placed great emphasis on the relationship between foods and the well-being of the diner. Insistence on freshness of product with a commitment to maximize inherent flavors has resulted in food preparations that have found market acceptance throughout the world.

Replicating this cuisine in our western kitchens with a good degree of authenticity is not especially difficult in a well-equipped kitchen, although large-scale production on a daily basis might pose some challenges. While some utensils, knives, and some other tools might differ to a degree, the basic techniques required are quite similar to those that are familiar to us. How these techniques are put to use, however, will greatly affect the end result. We will discuss this in some detail later in the chapter; but first we will explore the origins of this cuisine.

ASIA Asia is the largest continent on Earth. This vast territorial expanse encompasses more than 17 million square miles, which is more than four times larger than the European continent. Its northern boundary very nearly touches the North Pole; it then reaches southward to the equator and beyond. The topography of this great continent embraces all of the world's extremes: its highest mountains, deepest valleys, arid deserts, and high plateaus. Its range of climate is also extreme, with some of the world's hottest, driest, wettest, and most frigid climates. More than two-thirds of Asia's total land mass lacks the necessary resources to support all but a relatively few inhabitants. The northern regions contain vast stretches of permanently frozen ground and large swamplands. Central Asia, equally hostile, has many arid deserts, high mountains, and plateaus where human life can be sustained only at irrigated oases. Aridity also prevails in much of southwestern Asia from Turkey to Iran continuing on to the Arabian peninsula. Viewed on average, settlement of this large continent is surprisingly sparse—only 100 inhabitants per square mile.

The popular image of Asia, however, as a place teeming with humanity, is a highly accurate one. More than 90 percent of its total population—more than half the world's inhabitants—dwell in a crescent-shaped area that occupies little more than one-third of its total land. Known as "monsoon Asia," this area extends from West Pakistan to northern China and Japan. It enjoys a climate that is humid, tropical or subtropical, containing broad, fertile deltas and flood plains. These regions have an abundant annual rainfall, creating conditions which are ideal for the intensive agricultural production needed to support the large number of inhabitants. Two of the greatest population concentrations on Earth are found in this confined region: in east Asia, whose center is China, and in south Asia, home to India and Pakistan. Each of these areas contains more inhabitants than the total population of the European continent.

Given these realities, it is not surprising that the distinctive culinary characteristics peculiar to each of these very densely populated regions would develop around the vegetable, grain, and legume crops that could be easily and efficiently cultivated. These crops, combined with foods that could be taken freely from the seas, rivers, lakes, and forests, shaped the character of the Asian diet as we know it today: copious use of grains and vegetable products enhanced by small servings of meats and fish. As in other parts of the world, the products of animal husbandry came to play an increasingly important role in the diet as the various societies advanced and became more numerous. The more efficient usage of the land through agriculture, however, constrained this production to smaller animals such as swine and poultry. While modern means of land and air transportation have greatly accelerated the movement of foodstuffs from region to region and country to country, the food products utilized in these geographically defined zones are still determined to a great degree by local conditions—the fertility of the soil, the proximity to the sea and forests, and the restraints imposed by the climate.

In China, for example, there are four, arguably five, primary gastronomic regions. In the northern provinces, wheat, millet, and barley, not rice, are the staple grains. Noodles, steamed buns—both savory and sweet—and steamed dumplings provide the starch component of the menu. Barbecued and roasted lamb and mutton, brought by the nomadic tribes of Manchuria and Mongolia, are also commonly found. Savory fermented bean paste, dark soy sauce, onions, and rice wine are the preferred flavoring agents. The renowned Beijing Duck and Mu Shu Pork, with their pungent sauces and use of raw scallion, originated in this region. The southern provinces, with their long seacoast, feature a wide variety of fish and other seafood dishes which call for more subtle sauces and flavorings. These southerly areas also produce an abundance of vegetables. Steamed and quick cooking stir-fried dishes are prevalent. The eastern regions also are noted for their delicious seafood and fish dishes which feature a variety of freshwater species not available elsewhere. Some of China's finest teas come from these regions, which are known also for their "red-cooked" dishes: those prepared by slow simmering in soy sauce mixtures to impart a reddish color to the food. Sweet and sour concoctions, so popular in the West, are said to have originated in this region. And finally, the foods of Szechwan, whose distinctive, hot and pungent flavors have found an appreciative audience in the West. Strongly influenced by the fiery spices emanating from India, Thailand, and Burma, the Szechwan kitchen has brought us hot and sour soup, and duck or chicken smoked over tea leaves. Similar regional distinctions, based primarily on geographic conditions, can be found in most of the major cuisines of Asia.

The Asian diet is rich in grains such as rice, wheat, millet, and numerous varieties of fresh vegetables, while meat, poultry, and fish are generally consumed in modest quantities. The creative utilization of spices, herbs, and contrasting textures also figures prominently in the distinctive dishes of various Asian societies. Foods preserved through pickling, drying, and smoking that are needed for use when fresh foodstuffs were not readily available continue to figure prominently in the diet. Nowadays, seasonal dependencies are lessened to a degree by the use of canning and other modern means for preserving foods. Less than ideal growing conditions have also been somewhat enhanced by modern farming techniques. In most regions of Asia, however, the methods of production still rely heavily on the intensive use of human and animal labor, and the dietary preferences continue to seek out the freshest foods available. In some Asian cultures, a rich philosophical, medicinal, or quasi-religious system of beliefs still governs the daily preparation and ingestion of food. Tenets prescribe the "proper" use of spices and herbs and the healthful benefits of planning the correct relationship of one dish to another. Societal traditions as well as religious proscriptions have served to encourage culinary creativity. The interplay among these diverse factors with all of their subtleties and complexities, plus the time-honored ingenuity of the cooks of Asia, has created what many believe to be the world's largest inventory of culinary delights.

THE COOKING PROCESS

Western cooking techniques can be described under two broad categories: those that use dry heat and those that use moist heat. Asian cooks view the categorization of cooking techniques from another perspective. The Chinese, for example, identify three categories: cooking with water, cooking with oil, and cooking with neither oil nor water. However, roasting, grilling, and broiling, three techniques in the "neither oil nor water" category, are not commonly found in Chinese cuisine. Chinese cooks feel strongly that foods should have an intermediary substance such as oil or water to serve as a buffer between the food to be cooked and the source of heat. Fortunately for us, other Asian societies, such as the Korean, Vietnamese, Mongolian, and Thai, do not share this aversion for foods that are cooked by applying fire in a very direct manner. Many of the recipes, therefore, do reflect a particular cultural bias stemming from the beliefs of the people who created them. Since this book is primarily designed to serve the needs of cooks who may not have a familiarity with Asian cuisine, I too will invoke a cultural bias and will categorize the needed cooking techniques using a frame of reference that is more familiar to the western cook.

In preparing foods of any culture, it is fairly common to use more than one process to complete a particular recipe. For example, stir-frying (a dry-heat technique) is often followed by an additional process—steaming (a moist-heat technique), to complete the preparation of a particular recipe. Certain deep-fried dishes require that some of the ingredients be blanched initially in oil or other liquids, reserved, and then deep-fried at a later stage in the process. It is also fairly common for steamed or poached dishes to be first deep-fried briefly or seared, adding texture, color, and flavor to the product which the basic moist-heat technique alone could not provide.

COOKING WITH DRY HEAT

STIR-FRYING

Stir-frying is the most fundamental cooking process used throughout Asia. Dishes that are properly stir-fried are succulent and retain the colors, textures, and natural flavors of their ingredients. To stir-fry successfully requires a thorough knowledge of how to perfectly cook a number of disparate ingredients, more or less at the same time, using the same pan. Stir-frying is an extremely fast, extraordinarily versatile way to cook. This technique is capable of producing a myriad of satisfying dishes, yet is the most fuel-efficient method of cooking ever devised. Despite obvious similarities with the western technique of sautéing, stir-frying is done at slightly higher temperatures and requires a more vigorous approach since foods must be kept in constant motion. Many western cooks have incorporated this Asian technique not only because it is efficient, but also because it conforms to contemporary practices of cooking with reduced amounts of oil and other fats, it preserves nutrients, and it produces very satisfactory results. Prior preparation to stir-frying will include:

1. Precise and appropriate cutting to size of all meat and vegetables;

2. Assembly of all other necessary ingredients: stocks, sauces, herbs, spices, condiments, and binding mixtures; and

3. Convenient placement of all of the above to the cooking area so they may be incorporated quickly.

Ingredients to be stir-fried are cut into small pieces of uniform thickness to help ensure an even degree of cooking. Meat, poultry, and seafood products are usually marinated for varying lengths of time prior to cooking, which serves to tenderize, impart flavor, and provide a light coating. When stir-frying, foods are kept in constant motion with a spatula and a rocking motion of the pan. In the initial moments, constant motion brings every surface of the food into contact with the hot oil, sealing in natural flavors and juices. Since the ingredients have been cut into small pieces and the temperature is very high, the cooking time will be very short. If additional cooking is necessary, for example hard vegetables that have not been previously blanched, a sauce or binding mixture is usually added, the heat lowered, the pan or wok covered, and the preparation quickly finished by steaming. Because some ingredients require different cooking times, meats, poultry or seafood are often removed from the pan after an initial, quick stir-frying in order to cook other components of the dish. They are then returned to the pan along with a sauce or binding mixture for an additional and final cooking period.

Stir-fried dishes are prepared "a la minute," a term that implies "made-to-order." While it is not absolutely necessary to use a wok for stir-frying, this utensil is probably best. Well-seasoned skillets of all sizes, however, are also used for stir-frying. Whichever you use, the pan should first be brought quickly to high heat before adding the oil, which is done by swirling it over the surface of the pan as the pan is returned to high heat. Vegetable oils are usually preferred when stir-frying for two reasons: They are capable of reaching a very high temperature before smoking or burning, and they impart the characteristic flavor associated with many Asian foods.

Deep-Frying

Deep-frying is another very popular cooking method used in the Asian kitchen. It requires a substantial quantity of hot oil, sometimes lard, so that the foods to be cooked can be completely submerged. Deep-frying produces cooked foods that are not oily, as one might suspect. When properly done, foods emerge crisp and dry, nicely browned on the outside and well-cooked and moist on the inside. It is important to keep the temperature of the oil as constant as possible—around 350°F (175°C) for seafoods and 400°F (200°C) for most meats and vegetables. Keeping this in mind, foods that have been prepared in advance and refrigerated should first be brought to room temperature before placing them in the hot oil. This may not always be practicable or advisable because of stringent health and sanitation regulations and genuine concerns regarding consumer safety. It is therefore recommended that deep-frying be done in relatively small batches to avoid the possibility of lowering the temperature of the oil too much. Deep-frying in oil that is not hot enough will result in foods that are oily and heavy, not crisp and light as desired.

Foods may be cooked in this manner with or without a coating. Common coatings are cornstarch, flour, whole egg, egg white, egg yolk, used either singly or combined, depending on the coating desired. Some dishes require that certain ingredients first be blanched in hot oil, then removed while other parts of the recipe are completed. These "oil-blanched" ingredients are usually returned briefly to the hot oil and deep-fried until crisp and cooked through. Whole fowl and larger cuts of meat are sometimes deep-fried for a short period before they are steamed or poached. The first stage of this double cooking process greatly enhances the color, texture, and flavor of the food. A wire strainer or basket is used to remove small deep-fried foods from the oil. To absorb excess oil, deep-fried foods should always be drained on paper or clean kitchen towels before serving.

Grilling/Broiling

Grilling and broiling, while not used greatly by Chinese cooks, are methods that are very commonly used by the cooks of other Asian cultures. These techniques have become increasingly popular not only because of the characteristic flavor imparted by the slight charring of the foods, but also because foods prepared in this manner do not usually require additional fats or oils and are, therefore, perceived as being more healthful. Grilling and broiling have many similarities. The primary difference between these two methods is the placement of the heat source: Grilled foods are placed over hot coals while foods that are broiled are placed directly under the flame. Since both of these methods expose the food product directly to the heat source, care must be taken not to let foods dry out through excessive exposure. Heat may be regulated by increasing or decreasing the distance between the food and the heat source or simply by lowering the flame. Familiarity with the distinctive cooking characteristics of the product is essential to successful broiling or grilling.

Foods to be grilled are usually marinated prior to cooking. Many times, to further enhance the flavor, the same marinade is used to baste the foods while they are cooking. It is important that the grill or rack be well heated in order to sear the foods immediately upon contact. The distance between the source of heat and the food is also crucial. If placed too close, the food will char; if too far from the heat, it won't cook quickly enough and may become dry. When grilling, it is very important to allow the food to remain on the grill long enough for it to release itself from the cooking surface without sticking or tearing. Grilled foods are usually turned once during cooking. If large quantities are needed, foods may be partially cooked on the grill, then placed in a hot oven to finish the cooking process.

ROASTING

Western-style roasting techniques do not play a significant role in the traditional Asian kitchen. Since most household kitchens lack the necessary equipment—an oven—roasted dishes were traditionally relegated to the province of commercially oriented food establishments, which possessed the necessary oven capacity. In many Asian cuisines, therefore, roasting and baking processes play virtually no role. Despite this, the Chinese and Indian kitchens have given us a number of outstanding roasted dishes which have become very popular: Beijing duck from China and Tandoor roasted fowl and meats of India. These dishes are usually prepared in special ovens. The clay tandoor oven, which originated in Persia (modern-day Iran) and has come to be closely associated with the breads and skewered roasted meat and poultry dishes of India, has the ability to bake, roast, and grill at the same time. Another special oven is the commercially available "barbecue" or "smoke house" oven found in most modern Chinese restaurants which enables foods to be roasted, suspended vertically on hooks. Dishes prepared in these specialized ovens can be done in our standard ovens with some degree of success.

Roasting requires that foods be surrounded by dry heat. If not carefully attended, this method of cooking can eliminate much of the natural juices from the food being cooked. To compensate for this tendency, foods to be roasted are usually marinated for an extended period of time in order to add more moisture and flavor. Regardless of the particular marinade or frequency of basting when roasting foods, it is important to cook them just to the point where they are perfectly done, and no further.

PAN SMOKING

Marinated or other foods that have been previously cooked by simmering or steaming are sometimes smoked to add color and flavor. Tea leaves or moistened wood chips are placed in a wok that has been covered with several layers of heavy-duty aluminum foil cut large enough to hang over the rim of the wok by five or six inches. The food is then put directly on a rack which has been placed several inches over the tea leaves or chips to ensure that the food does not come into direct contact with the smoking agent. A tight-fitting lid is then placed over the wok and the overlapping aluminum foil is crimped around the edges of the lid to create an airtight seal. (Alternatively, one may use a wire rack and two roasting pans of the same size, one to hold the smoking agent and the other as a cover.) The smoking is done over medium to high heat, 200–250°F (93–121°C). The length of time needed depends on the thickness of the product and the degree of smoky flavor desired. If a lighter "smoke" flavor is desired, the products can be removed from the pan smoker and finished in the oven. If a slow or cold smoking is desired—50–85°F (10–30°C)—foods should first be cured with a brine solution or salt rub to prevent spoilage. Smoked foods usually require additional cooking either before smoking or after since the primary purpose of this smoking process is to enhance color and flavor.

COOKING WITH MOIST HEAT

STEAMING

Steaming—a common cooking technique that is found throughout Asia—cooks food quickly while retaining the natural flavors and aromas. It requires very little oil or added fat, thereby making it one of the most healthful methods of cooking. It is best to place food in a steamer after the steaming liquid has been brought to a full boil in order to surround the food immediately with the hot vapors. Keep temperatures high while steaming meats, poultry, fish, or vegetables. Custards or egg dishes are best when steamed over lower heat. Cooking time will vary considerably depending on the density and nature of the product. Steaming usually requires a longer cooking period than boiling. Food can be placed on a heat-proof plate or bowl, or put directly on a parchment, cheesecloth, lettuce or other leaf-lined steamer tray, which, in turn, is placed on a rack about an inch above the boiling liquid. Bamboo steamer trays are made to "nest" together so that several can be used to prepare different products simultaneously. There are also steamer sets available which are made of metal that consist of a container for the water topped by two or three perforated trays and a lid. These sets, as well as the more traditional ones made of bamboo, come in many different sizes, up to two feet across. If using more than one tray at a time, reverse them occasionally to ensure even cooking. If these utensils are not available, a steamer can be improvised by using a colander or a steamer basket placed in a sauce pan containing boiling water filled to approximately one inch below the level of the steamer tray. A tight-fitting lid to contain the steam will complete the steamer. Foods prepared in this manner are often wrapped in leaves or other green leafy vegetables to create firm, small parcels.

BOILING/POACHING/SIMMERING

These three moist-heat techniques are probably best understood through commonly agreed upon temperature gradations: 160–180°F (70–82°C) for poaching; 180–205°F (82–96°C) for simmering; 212°F (100°C) for boiling. All of these techniques require that the food be submerged in a liquid. Since the liquid has a strong influence on the taste of the finished product, aromatics and other flavoring agents are usually added. Poaching is most often used for tender foods such as eggs, fish or other seafood, and poultry breasts since they do not need a very long cooking period. Tougher cuts of meat, whole fowl, grains, and vegetables can be simmered since they require a higher temperature and a longer cooking time. Boiling uses larger amounts of liquid, usually water, and cooks foods very rapidly. Not very many foods are cooked this way, however. Most boiled products, such as meats or even eggs cooked in the shell, are really simmered after brief exposure to a boiling temperature. Noodles are among the few products that are cooked completely through the boiling process.

BRAISING

Foods that are braised are usually larger pieces of meat or older fowl that need a long, gentle cooking. This process serves to tenderize the food and—depending on the liquid used—to add flavor to the product as well. Braised foods are usually seared in hot oil first, then finished in a heavy pot along with enough liquid to immerse the food by half.

Various liquids such as meat, poultry stock, or soy sauce–based mixtures can be used. The liquids are heated slowly until they reach the boiling point. The pot is then covered and the heat lowered to a slow simmer, gently cooking the food until done. Maintaining a slow, gentle simmer is the key to braising. The cooking liquids can also provide the basis for the sauce, whose flavor and texture may be enhanced through reduction, the addition of other flavoring ingredients, and by adding a thickener such as cornstarch during the final stage of cooking.

THE IMPORTANCE OF BEING PREPARED

It cannot be too strongly emphasized that the most important aspect in cooking the foods of Asia is the advance preparation of every ingredient needed to complete a particular dish. All of the items contained in a recipe should be measured, marinated, blanched, sliced, diced, chopped, peeled, etc., in advance of the actual cooking. In most cases, the time needed for preparation will far exceed that required for the actual cooking. Since the cooking time is so short for most dishes, and the timely, rapid-fire addition of ingredients so essential to the cooking process, it is imperative that all preparation steps be done well in advance. The pre-prepared ingredients, along with all necessary sauces, herbs, spices and other condiments, must be kept handy and close to the stove, since they are usually added to the pan in quick succession. Most of the recipes in this book can be cooked in a relatively brief period of time, redefining, perhaps, the term "fast food."

MONOSODIUM GLUTAMATE

To Use Or Not To Use?

Monosodium glutamate, commonly called MSG, is routinely used as a flavor enhancer in many Asian countries. An integral part of the Asian cook's spice rack, it is used to bring out the natural flavors in foods. MSG is the sodium salt of glumatic acid found naturally in meat, vegetables, poultry, and milk. Glumatic acid is produced naturally by both animals and plants. Foods that are naturally high in glutamate, such as tomatoes, cheese, and mushrooms, have been used for centuries not only for their distinctive characteristic flavors, but also for the way in which they enhance flavors when combined with other foods.

The substance known as MSG was first isolated in 1908 by Professor Kikunae Ikeda of the University of Japan. Extracted from *Lamimaria japonica,* a variety of seaweed commonly used in the preparation of soup stock in Japan, it was identified as the primary substance responsible for the enhancement of naturally occurring flavors. Commercially prepared MSG is produced through a fermentation process similar to that employed in the manufacture of beer, vinegar, and yogurt. Food substances that are derived from corn, sugar beets, or sugarcane are used as a base in its manufacture. Its use is not generally perceived as having undesirable or adverse effects on health. Many people, however, have reported experiencing adverse reactions—from mild to severe headaches, attacks of asthma, and numbness of the lips, to various gastric symptoms after consuming foods prepared with MSG. Some of these symptoms may be allergic reactions to particular foods or combinations of foods. Despite these reports, MSG is considered safe for public consumption by regulatory and scientific agencies such as the United Nations World Health Organization/Food and Agriculture's Organization's Joint Expert Committee on Food Additives, the European Communities' Scientific Committee for Food, and the Council on Scientific Affairs of the American Medical Association.

While MSG may not have been linked scientifically to various adverse health reactions, I have elected to err on the side of consumer safety and not call for the use of MSG in the recipes contained in this book. My decision to do this was bolstered by the many Asian restaurateurs in the United States who also take this position, offering menus that list dishes made without the use of MSG.

Should you wish to use MSG, however, keep in mind that it is a self-limiting substance that can produce the opposite effect if used excessively. One-half teaspoon (3 g) can enhance the flavor of a pound (450 g) of meat or 4 to 6 servings of a vegetable, stew, or soup. Since MSG has the tendency to mimic salt while containing about one-third the amount of sodium by volume, recipes calling for salt can be modified, lowering the total sodium content by substituting MSG. MSG is most effective when used in savory rather than sweet dishes, where it seems to be of little consequence in enhancing the flavor.

Should you prefer to cook without the use of commercially produced MSG, keep in mind that flavors can still be enhanced by this substance in the time-honored way that cooks used before science gave us its extracted and concentrated form: by using products rich in high levels of naturally occurring free glutamate, enriching stocks and other flavoring agents, the freshest available food products, and fresh herbs and spices.

CHAPTER TWO

Appetizers

Crab Omelet

YIELD: 1 SERVING

Crab meat, cooked	2 oz	60 g	*Remove any pieces of shell or cartilage from the crab meat. Reserve.*
Eggs, beaten	2 large	large	*Combine ingredients and mix until the sugar and salt have dissolved. Add the crab meat.*
Soy sauce, light	1 tsp	5 ml	
Rice wine or dry sherry	1 tsp	5 ml	
Sugar	pinch	pinch	
Salt	pinch	pinch	
Oil, peanut	2 tsp	10 ml	*Heat a wok or skillet over medium heat. Add the oil. When hot, stir-fry the gingerroot briefly until it becomes aromatic. Add the egg/crab meat mixture and cook, stirring occasionally, over low heat until the eggs have begun to set.*
Gingerroot, minced	1 tsp	4 g	
Egg/crab meat mixture			
Scallions, white and green parts, sliced thin	1	1	*Add the scallions and cook for another minute or until the eggs are done as desired.*

Pork with Sesame Seeds

YIELD: 12 SERVINGS

Ingredient	US	Metric	Method
Scallions, white and green parts, chopped	5–6	5–6	*Combine ingredients. Reserve.*
Gingerroot, peeled and grated	3-in. piece	8-cm piece	
Soy sauce, light	2 oz	60 ml	
Rice wine or dry sherry	2 oz	60 ml	
Sugar	1 tbsp or to taste	15 g or to taste	
Salt	1 tsp	5 g	
Pepper, black, fine ground	1/2 tsp	1 g	
Pork, leg or loin, trimmed of all fat and skin	2 lb	900 g	*Cut pork into 1/4-in. (0.75 cm) slices, then into strips approximately 1 x 3 in. (2.5 x 8 cm). Place in a glass or stainless steel container with the marinade and toss to coat evenly. Refrigerate for 1–2 hours.*

TO SERVE

Ingredient	US	Metric	Method
Egg white	as needed	as needed	*Use one egg white per 2 level tablespoons (20 g) of cornstarch to make a batter. Dip the pork strips into this mixture, then into the sesame seeds. Deep-fry at 325°F (165°C) until well browned and crisp. Drain on towels before serving. To serve, place pork strips on a bed of shredded lettuce and serve with a small bowl of light soy sauce for dipping.*
Cornstarch	as needed	as needed	
Sesame seeds, untoasted	as needed	as needed	
Marinated pork strips	2–3 oz per serving	60–90 g per serving	
Oil, vegetable	for deep-frying	for deep-frying	

Spring Rolls

YIELD: APPROXIMATELY 80 PIECES

Cloud ear fungus	2 oz	60 g	*Soak cloud ears in warm water for 30 minutes or until the fungus has expanded to 4–5 times its original volume. Trim and discard any of the hard central stems. Rinse thoroughly, then chop fine. Place in a mixing bowl.*
Cellophane noodles	2 oz	60 g	*Soak the noodles in warm water for 15–20 minutes or until soft. Drain, then cut into 1-in. pieces. Add to the cloud ears.*
Pork, lean, ground twice	1 lb	450 g	*Add ingredients to the bowl and mix thoroughly. Reserve.*
Onion, minced	3/4 lb	340 g	
Crab meat, cartilage removed and shredded	8 oz	226 g	
Garlic, minced	2 tsp	10 g	
Scallions, white part only	3–4 depending on size	3–4 depending on size	
Black pepper, fine ground	to taste	to taste	

(Continued on next page)

Rice paper, round sheets or preferably in triangles*	as needed	as needed
Beaten eggs	3–4, or as needed	3–4, or as needed

If using rounds, cut each rice paper sheet into quarters. Lightly brush the beaten egg over the entire surface of the rice paper. When the rice paper has softened, place a scant teaspoon of the filling mixture along the curved edge of the quartered wrappers. Fold the curved edge over the filling, then fold the sides in and continue to roll until the wrapper completely encases the filling. The spring rolls should be finger shaped. Place the finished rolls on a sheet pan, seam side down, and refrigerate until needed.

To PREPARE

Spring rolls	4–6 per serving	4–6 per serving
Oil, peanut	for deep-frying	for deep-frying
Lettuce leaves, Boston or Bibb	as needed	as needed
Cucumber slices	as needed	as needed
Mint leaves, fresh	as needed	as needed
Nuoc Cham (see recipe)	as needed	as needed

Deep-fry in 350°F (175°C) oil until cooked through and golden brown. Drain on paper or clean kitchen towels. Garnish serving plate with the same number of lettuce leaves trimmed to size, cucumber slices, and fresh mint leaves. This appetizer is assembled by the diner at the table in the following manner.

To ASSEMBLE

Place spring roll on a lettuce leaf, add a small amount of cucumber and mint, then roll. Rolls are then dipped into small, individual serving bowls of Nuoc Cham (see recipe) just prior to being eaten.

Available in both forms through commercial sources.

Squid Stuffed with Pork

YIELD: 12   SERVINGS

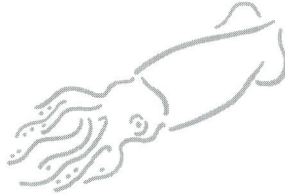

Squid, small to medium	24–36 depending on size	24–36 depending on size	Pull out the head and tentacles. Cut off the tentacles just above the eyes. Squeeze out the beak at the base and discard. Reserve tentacles. Remove the transparent back-bone and any other material from inside the body. Wash under running water, peeling off the purple skin. Place squid in a colander to drain.
FILLING			
Pork, shoulder, ground twice	1 1/2 lb	680 g	*Combine ingredients and mix thoroughly. Sauté a spoonful in a little oil and taste for seasonings. Adjust if necessary. Fill each squid two thirds full with the meat mixture. Do not overfill to allow for expansion during cooking. Close ends with a small wooden skewer or toothpick. Reserve in refrigerator until needed.*
Reserved tentacles, chopped fine	half of quantity reserved	half of quantity reserved	
Fish sauce	1 tbsp or to taste	15 ml or to taste	
Garlic, minced	2 tsp	10 g	
Shallots, minced	2 tsp	10 g	
Pepper, black, fine ground	1 tsp	2 g	
Sugar	1 tsp	5 g	
Salt	1 tsp	5 g	
TO PREPARE			
Reserved stuffed squid	2–3 per serving	2–3 per serving	*Squid may be fried in 1 in. of peanut or vegetable oil over medium heat for 4–5 minutes on each side or until cooked through. Or, they may be steamed in advance for 20–25 minutes, then reheated and lightly browned in hot oil just prior to serving. Accompany with a small portion of marinated carrot and sweet radish (see recipe).*

Braised Spareribs

YIELD: 10 SERVINGS

Chicken stock	16 oz	470 ml	*Combine ingredients. Stir to dissolve the sugar and reserve.*
Soy sauce, light	4 oz	120 ml	
Soy sauce, dark	2 oz	60 ml	
Rice wine or dry sherry	2 oz	60 ml	
Sugar	1 oz or to taste	30 g or to taste	
Pork spareribs, bone in, cut along the bone, then cut or chopped into 2-in. (5-cm) segments	4 lb	1.8 kg	*Prepare the ribs and reserve.*
Oil, peanut	2 oz	60 ml	*Heat wok or skillet over high heat. Add the oil and heat to just below the smoking point. Add the scallions and gingerroot. Stir-fry until they become aromatic.*
Scallions, white and green parts, cut into 1 1/2-in. (4-cm) pieces	10	10	
Gingerroot, peeled and sliced thin	1-in. piece	2.5-cm piece	
Reserved pork ribs			*Add the ribs and stir-fry until they begin to brown.*
Reserved flavoring mixture			*Add the flavoring mixture, stir well, and bring to a boil. Lower heat and simmer, covered, for 20–25 minutes. Degrease the cooking liquid and serve in small amounts as a dipping sauce.*

Crab Meat and Pork Toast

YIELD: 10 SERVINGS

Onion, chopped	4 oz	115 g
Garlic, minced	2 tsp	20 g
Pork, ground	6 oz	170 g
Sugar	2 tsp	10 g
Fish sauce	2 tsp	60 ml
Egg, large, beaten with 1 tbsp of water	1	1
Pepper, black, fine ground	1/2 tsp	1 g
Salt	pinch	pinch

Combine ingredients in the bowl of a food processor fitted with the steel blade. Process to a very smooth consistency. Place in a mixing bowl.

Crab meat, cooked	4 oz	115 g

Pick over crab meat to remove all cartilage. Incorporate the crab meat with the contents in the bowl, mixing by hand. Reserve in the refrigerator until needed.

TO PREPARE AN INDIVIDUAL SERVING

Sliced white bread	1 slice per serving	1 slice per serving
Reserved crab/pork mixture		
Oil, vegetable	as needed, 1/2-in. deep for frying	as needed, 1.5 cm deep for frying

Use sliced bread that is well chilled. Trim the crust and spread about 1/8-in. of the crab/pork mixture over one side of the slice. Cut the slice twice on the diagonal, (from corner to corner) to create 4 triangles. Fry pieces in 350°F (175°C) oil, mixture side down until lightly browned. Turn and fry the bread side for another 20–30 seconds. Drain on a clean towel and serve immediately.

Meat Patties with Bean Curd (Tofu)

YIELD: VARIABLE, DEPENDING ON SIZE OF PATTIES
[50–60 APPROXIMATELY 1 OZ (30 G) EACH]

Beef, ground twice	1 1/2 lb	680 g
Pork,* ground twice	1 1/2 lb	680 g
Bean curd, (tofu), mashed	12 oz	340 g
Oil, sesame	2 tbsp	30 ml
Sesame seeds, toasted	1 tbsp	6 g
Garlic, minced	1 tbsp or to taste	15 g or to taste
Scallion, white and green parts, minced	5–6	5–6
Salt	2 tsp or to taste	10 g or to taste
Pepper, black, fine ground	2 tsp or to taste	4 g or to taste

Combine ingredients thoroughly. Sauté a small spoonful of the mixture and taste. Adjust seasonings if necessary. Shape into small, round patties. Make a small depression in the center of each using your thumb and third finger. Place on a sheet pan in a single layer and reserve, refrigerated, until needed.

TO PREPARE AN INDIVIDUAL SERVING

Oil, sesame 50%	as needed	as needed
Oil, vegetable 50%	as needed	as needed
Meat patties	4–5 per serving	4–5 per serving
Flour	as needed	as needed
Egg, beaten	as needed	as needed

In a heavy skillet or wok combine oils to a depth of 1/4 in. (0.75 cm) over medium to high heat. Dredge patties first in flour, then in beaten egg. Fry, turning once, until browned on both sides.

*Ground chicken may be substituted for the pork. If grilling patties over coals or broiling, brush lightly with sesame oil. Eliminate the flour and egg coating.

Pickled Vegetables

YIELD: 4 LB (1.8 KG)

Cucumber, hothouse (seedless) or slicing	*2 lb*	*900 g*	*Peel and slice cucumbers 1/4-in. (0.75-cm) thick. If using slicing cucumbers, slice lengthwise and remove seeds with a spoon or small scoop.*
Carrots	*1 1/2 lb*	*680 g*	*Peel and slice 1/4-in. (0.75-cm) thick on the diagonal.*
Celery stalks	*1 lb*	*450 g*	*Remove strings with a vegetable peeler and slice 1/4-in. (0.75-cm) thick on the diagonal.*
Salt	*as needed*	*as needed*	*Place vegetables in a colander and salt lightly. Place a weighted plate on top and let stand at room temperature for 3 hours. This will remove excess liquid from the vegetables.*
Rice vinegar	*4 oz*	*120 ml*	*Combine the vinegar and sugar and mix until the sugar is completely dissolved. Place vegetables in a stainless steel or glass bowl and add the vinegar/sugar mixture. Toss to distribute the dressing evenly. Cover and refrigerate overnight before serving.*
Sugar	*4 oz*	*120 ml*	

Shrimp Balls

YIELD: VARIABLE

Shrimp, peeled and deveined	2 lb	900 g	*Place ingredients into the bowl of a food processor fitted with the steel blade. Process to a very fine puree.*
Water chestnuts, canned	10 oz	280 g	
Soy sauce, light	1 tbsp	15 ml	
Sesame oil	2 tsp	10 ml	
Sugar	1 tsp	5 g	
Oil, vegetable	as needed	as needed	*Heat oil for deep-frying over medium to high heat. Roll shrimp mixture into balls about the size of a walnut. Dip in beaten egg white and deep-fry at 350°F (175°C) until golden. Sprinkle with lemon juice just prior to serving.*
Egg white, beaten	as needed	as needed	
Lemon juice, fresh squeezed	as needed	as needed	

Shrimp, Stir-Fried Crisp

YIELD: 10 SERVINGS

MARINADE

Cornstarch	3 tbsp	30 g	*Combine ingredients and mix until the salt is completely dissolved.*
Egg whites	from 2 large eggs	from 2 large eggs	
Salt	2 tsp	10 g	
Shrimp, peeled, deveined and cut into 1/2-in. (1.5-cm) pieces; small whole shrimp may also be used	2 1/2 lb	1.15 kg	*Prepare shrimp and place in a stainless steel or glass bowl. Add the marinade and toss to coat shrimp. Cover and refrigerate overnight.*

TO PREPARE AN INDIVIDUAL SERVING

Cornstarch	pinch	pinch	*Combine ingredients and reserve.*
Sugar	pinch	pinch	
Chicken stock	2 tbsp	30 ml	
Oil, vegetable	for deep-frying	for deep-frying	*Deep-fry shrimp for 30 seconds in 350°F (175°C) oil. Remove from deep fryer and place in a very hot, lightly oiled wok or heavy skillet. Stir-fry briefly over high heat. Add a splash of sherry and stir. Add the cornstarch mixture and stir-fry for another 20–30 seconds. Add a pinch of sugar and salt to taste.*
Marinated shrimp	4 oz	115 g	
Sherry, medium dry	as needed	as needed	
Sugar	pinch	pinch	
Salt	to taste	to taste	

Spicy Roasted Spareribs

YIELD: 10 SERVINGS

SPICE RUB

Garlic, minced	3 tbsp	50 g
Soy sauce, light	4 oz	120 ml
Sesame oil	2 oz	60 ml
Honey	2 oz	60 ml
Salt	1 tbsp	15 g
Pepper, black, ground	1 tsp	2 g
Five-spice powder	1 tsp	2 g

Combine ingredients.

Spareribs	6 1/2 lb	3 kg
Water, boiling	8 oz	240 ml

Trim excess fat, then separate ribs between the bones. Spread the spice rub over all surfaces. Place ribs on a rack set over a roasting pan. Cover and allow to marinate for 1 hour. Roast in a 350°F (180°C) oven for 30 minutes. Turn ribs and add boiling water to the pan. Continue to roast, basting occasionally with the pan liquids. Serve with a dipping sauce such as plum sauce (available commercially) and prepared Chinese mustard.

Squid with Onion, Garlic, and Chili Sauce

YIELD: 10-12 SERVINGS

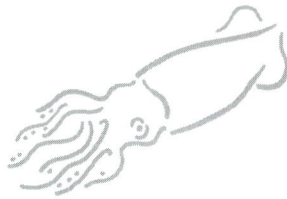

Squid*	2 lb, cleaned	900 g, cleaned
Lime juice, fresh squeezed	6 oz	180 ml

Pull out the head and tentacles. Cut off the tentacles just above the eyes. Squeeze out the beak at the base and discard. Reserve tentacles. Remove the transparent backbone and any other material from inside the body. Wash under running water, peeling off the purple skin. Place squid in a colander to drain. When drained, cut into 1/2-in. (1.5-cm) rings. Place in a stainless steel bowl and toss with the lime juice. Cover bowl and reserve in the refrigerator until needed.

SAUCE

Chili sauce**	6 oz	170 g
Shrimp paste	2 tsp or to taste	20 g or to taste
Garlic, minced	1 tbsp	15 g
Paprika	2 tsp	4 g
Sugar	2 tsp	10 g
Salt	to taste	to taste
Water	to make a medium-consistency paste	to make a medium-consistency paste

Combine ingredients and reserve.

*Available cleaned, fresh or frozen
**See Chili Sauce in glossary.

(Continued on next page)

To prepare an individual serving

Oil, vegetable	2 tsp	10 ml	*Heat oil in a heavy skillet or wok. Stir-fry the squid over medium heat until it is just cooked through. Remove from pan and reserve.*
Reserved squid	3 oz	85 g	
Onion, sliced thin	2 oz	60 g	*Using the same pan, raise the heat to high, add a little more oil if necessary, and stir-fry the onions until they begin to brown slightly. Add the chili/garlic sauce and mix well. Return the squid to the pan and heat through.*
Reserved chili/garlic sauce	1 tbsp	15 g	
Reserved squid	3 oz	85 g	
Lime juice, fresh squeezed	*as needed*	*as needed*	*Just prior to serving, top the dish with a squeeze of fresh lime juice.*

Steamed Stuffed Mushrooms

YIELD: APPROXIMATELY 40

Ingredient	US	Metric	Method
Mushrooms, white common, medium sized (1 1/4–1 1/2 in., 3–4.5 cm in diameter)	*2 lb or as needed*	*900 g or as needed*	*Clean mushrooms with a damp towel. Remove stems and reserve them for another purpose. Brush caps on both sides with a light coating of sesame oil.*
Sesame oil	*as needed*	*as needed*	
Pork, lean, ground twice	*2 lb*	*900 g*	*Combine ingredients thoroughly. Sauté a small spoonful and taste. Adjust seasonings if necessary.*
Water chestnuts, fresh if available, or canned	*4 oz*	*115 g*	
Gingerroot, peeled and minced	*1 tsp or to taste*	*4 g or to taste*	
Cornstarch	*2 tbsp*	*20 g*	
Soy sauce, light	*2 tbsp*	*30 ml*	
Salt	*1 tsp*	*5 g*	
Sugar	*1 tsp*	*5 g*	

TO SERVE

Ingredient	US	Metric	Method
Stuffed mushroom caps	*3–4 per appetizer portion 5–6 per entree portion*	*3–4 per appetizer portion 5–6 per entree portion*	*Stuff each cap with a generous spoonful of the meat mixture. Place the mushrooms, as needed, on a steamer tray. Cover and steam for about 20 minutes or until the pork is cooked through. May be prepared in quantity or to order.*

See color insert for photograph of recipe

Steamed Oysters

YIELD: 10-12 SERVINGS

Oysters	60	60
Pork, lean, or chicken breast meat ground twice	1 1/4 lb	570 g
Eggs, beaten	10	10
Scallions, minced	10	10
Sesame oil	3 oz	90 ml
Pine nuts	1 oz	30 g
Garlic, minced	2 tbsp	30 g
Sesame seeds, toasted	1 tbsp	6 g
Salt	to taste	to taste
Pepper, black, fine ground	to taste	to taste
Reserved shells		

TO PREPARE AN INDIVIDUAL SERVING

Stuffed oyster shells	6 per serving	6 per serving

Scrub oysters, then pry open the shells taking care to keep the shells hinged. Remove oysters, rinse if sandy, chop coarsely, and place in a mixing bowl. Rinse shells and reserve.

Lightly sauté the ground pork or chicken until almost cooked through but still moist. When cooled, add the meat or poultry to the oysters along with remaining ingredients. Mix thoroughly.

Keeping the shallow part of each shell on the top, place a heaping spoonful of the oyster mixture in the lower and deeper portion of each shell. Sprinkle several pine nuts on top of the filling and gently lower the upper shell until partially closed. Reserve refrigerated until needed.

Place stuffed shells in a steamer. If a steamer is not available, place on a rack in a pot with boiling water 1 in. (2.5 cm) below the shells. Cover with a tight-fitting lid and steam for 10–15 minutes.

Clams and Scallops Steamed on the Half Shell

YIELD: 10 SERVINGS

FLAVORING SAUCE:

Soy sauce, light	4 oz	120 ml	*Combine ingredients and reserve.*
Rice wine or dry sherry	2 oz	60 ml	
Vinegar, white, distilled	1 oz	30 ml	
Oil, sesame	1 oz	30 ml	
Sugar	1 tbsp	15 g	
Pepper, white, fine ground	1/2 tsp	1 g	
Scallops	large, as needed, sliced into 40 discs	large, as needed, sliced into 40 discs	*Clean scallops, then cut into 1/4-in. (0.75-cm) discs per scallop. The number of scallops you will need will be determined by their thickness. Use scallops that are no more that 1-1/2 in. (4 cm) in diameter. Place scallops in a stainless steel bowl and toss with the flavoring sauce. Cover, refrigerate, and let marinate for at least 1 hour before using.*
Clams, cherrystones on the half shell	40	40	*Scrub the clams. Open them and discard the top half of the shell. Detach the meat from the shell. Rinse if sandy. Cover and refrigerate. Reserve until needed.*

TO PREPARE AN INDIVIDUAL SERVING:

Clams, on the half shell	4 per serving	4 per serving	*Place clams on the half shell, in a small, individual, oven-proof serving dish. Top the clam meat with a teaspoon of fermented black beans and a scallop disc. Place in a steamer, along with a tablespoon (15 ml) of the flavoring sauce and steam for 3–4 minutes or until cooked as desired. Do not overcook; the seafood will become tough. Garnish with chopped scallion.*
Black beans, fermented	as needed	as needed	
Marinated scallop discs	4	4	
Flavoring sauce	1 tbsp	15 ml	
Scallion, minced	as needed	as needed	

Twice-Fried Steak Strips

YIELD: 10—12 SERVINGS

Flank steak, trimmed	2 lb	900 g	Cut steak across the grain into thin slices. Reserve.
Eggs, beaten	4	4	Mix the eggs and salt. Then add enough cornstarch to make a thick paste. Add water, as needed, to thin the mixture to a thin batter consistency. Add the garlic and scallions and mix well.
Salt	1 tsp or to taste	10 g or to taste	
Cornstarch	6 oz or as needed	170 g or as needed	
Water	as needed	as needed	
Garlic, minced	2 tbsp	30 g	
Scallions, white and green parts, minced	6	6	

TO PREPARE

| Oil, vegetable | for deep-frying | for deep-frying | Heat oil over high heat. Dip the steak strips, as needed, in batter. Deep-fry for 1 minute, then remove the strips and dip them in the batter again. Coat strips evenly on all surfaces. Return strips to the hot oil and deep-fry until they are browned and quite crisp. Drain on towels before serving. |
| Steak strips, dipped in batter | 2–3 oz per serving | 60–90 g per serving | |

Oysters Poached with Chili, Garlic, and Lemongrass

YIELD: 10 SERVINGS

Oysters, medium sized	60	60	*Shuck oysters and reserve. Strain and reserve the liquor separately. Wash and reserve the deeper halves of the shells.*
POACHING LIQUID			
Oil, vegetable	2 tbsp	30 ml	*Heat oil in a wok or saucepan over medium heat.*
Garlic, minced	2 tbsp	30 g	*Stir-fry the garlic, gingerroot, and lemongrass for*
Gingerroot, peeled and minced	1 tbsp	12 g	*1–2 minutes. Add the chili pepper and stir-fry for another 30 seconds.*
Lemongrass, lower white sections, chopped fine	1 tbsp	10 g	
Chili pepper, red, fresh, seeds and ribs removed	2 tsp or to taste	12 g or to taste	
Lime juice	8 oz	240 ml	*Add ingredients, mix well, and bring to a boil.*
Fish sauce	8 oz	240 ml	*Lower heat and simmer for 3–4 minutes. Taste and*
Reserved oyster liquor			*adjust seasonings if necessary. Let cool and reserve.*
Sugar	2 tbsp	30 g	
Salt	1 tsp	5 g	
Pepper, white	1 tsp	2 g	
TO PREPARE AN INDIVIDUAL SERVING			
Poaching liquid	as needed	as needed	*Place enough of the poaching liquid in a small*
Shucked oysters	6 per serving	6 per serving	*saucepan to just cover the oysters when they are*
Washed shells	6 per serving	6 per serving	*added. Heat to a low simmer. Add 6 oysters per*
Mint sprigs	as needed	as needed	*serving to the pan and poach gently for 20–30 seconds. When done, arrange the washed shells on a plate and place an oyster on each. Spoon a small amount of the poaching liquid over each of the oysters. Garnish with sprigs of fresh mint.*

Crisp Pork Ribs with Pepper-Salt

YIELD: 10 SERVINGS

MARINADE

Rice wine or dry sherry	6 oz	180 ml	*Combine ingredients and mix until the sugar has completely dissolved.*
Soy sauce, dark	3 oz	90 ml	
Vinegar, rice	3 oz	90 ml	
Garlic, minced	2 tbsp	30 g	
Sugar	1 tbsp	15 g	
Five spice powder	1 tbsp	7 g	
Salt	2 tsp	10 g	
Pepper, white	1 tsp	2 g	
Pork back ribs	5 lb	2.3 kg	*Trim fat, separate ribs, then cut the individual ribs into 3-in. (8-cm) long pieces. Place in a stainless steel pan and add the marinade. Toss well to coat pieces evenly. Cover pan and refrigerate for at least 4 hours before using.*

TO PREPARE AN INDIVIDUAL SERVING

Marinated ribs	6–8 oz per serving	170–226 g per serving	*Deep-fry in 375°F (190°C) oil until crisp and well browned. Serve with a small bowl of pepper-salt for dipping.*
Pepper-salt (see recipe)	as needed	as needed	

Satay

MARINADE NO. 1

Onion, diced	3/4 lb	340 g
Garlic, minced	2 tsp	10 g
Oil, vegetable	2 tbsp	30 ml
Fish sauce	2 tbsp	30 ml
Sugar, brown	2 tbsp	30 g
Tamarind pulp, dissolved in 2 oz (60 ml) of hot water/or tamarind concentrate: 1/2 tsp (10 ml) to 2 oz (60 ml) hot water	1 tsp	5 g

Place ingredients in the bowl of a food processor fitted with the steel blade. Process to a very smooth paste.

Lean beef, chicken or pork	2 lb	900 g
Thin bamboo skewers, 8 in. long, soaked in water	as needed	as needed

Cut the beef, chicken, or pork into very thin rectangular strips, approximately 4 in. (10 cm) long and 3/4 in. (2 cm) wide. Thread the strips on the skewers lengthwise, leaving a portion of the skewer bare to facilitate turning. Place the skewered meat in a shallow pan and cover with the marinade. Turn skewers to coat meat on all sides. Marinate for at least 2 hours, covered, in the refrigerator.

SWEET AND SOUR CUCUMBER SAUCE

Water	8 oz	240 ml
Sugar	4 oz	115 g
Salt	1 tsp	5 g
Vinegar, white	4 oz or to taste	120 g or to taste
Red pepper flakes	1 tsp	2 g or to taste

Combine ingredients in a small saucepan over low heat. When sugar and salt are completely dissolved, add the vinegar and red pepper flakes. Bring to a simmer, then remove from heat and reserve.

Cucumber	1 1/4 lb	680 g
Onion, red, sliced	8 oz	240 ml

Peel cucumbers, cut in half lengthwise, then slice thin into half rounds. Add the onions and the water/vinegar mixture, mix well and marinate, covered, in the refrigerator for 2–3 hours before serving.

(Continued on next page)

PEANUT SAUCE

Peanut butter	3/4 lb	340 g
Coconut milk, thick	12 oz	355 ml
Onion, minced	12 oz	340 g
Soy sauce, dark, sweet	2 oz	60 ml
Fish sauce	2 tbsp	30 ml
Sugar, brown	1 tbsp or to taste	15 g or to taste
Chili powder	1 tsp or to taste	2 g or to taste
Paprika	1 tsp	2 g

Combine ingredients in a small, heavy-bottomed sauce pan and bring to a boil over medium heat, stirring constantly. Lower heat and simmer for 3–5 minutes, stirring occasionally. Remove from heat and let cool. Serve at room temperature.

TO SERVE

Grill 2–4 skewers per serving 3–4 inches (8–10 cm) above hot coals for approximately 1 minute per side. A small dish of sweet and sour cucumbers and another containing the peanut sauce may be served on the side.

MARINADE NO. 2

Lemongrass, tender white section, minced	2 tbsp	25 g
Galangal or ginger-root, minced	1 tbsp	12 g
Coriander, ground	4 tsp	8 g
Sugar	4 tsp	8 g
Turmeric, ground	2 tsp	4 g
Cumin, ground	1 tsp	2 g
Salt	2 tsp	10 g
Pepper	1/2 tsp	1 g
Coconut milk	1 pt	0.5 L

Combine ingredients.

Add the coconut milk and blend. Proceed from step 2 of marinade 1.

Shrimp Toast

Ingredient	US	Metric	Method
Shrimp, peeled and deveined	2 lb after cleaning	900 g after cleaning	*Grind the shrimp, alternating with the pork fat, twice through a food grinder using the fine blade.*
Pork fat	8 oz	226 g	
Egg whites	3 large	3 large	*Mix the egg whites, ginger juice, and salt together. Add enough cornstarch to make a very thin paste. Add this to the ground shrimp and mix thoroughly. Place in a glass or stainless steel bowl, cover, and refrigerate for several hours.*
Ginger juice	2 tbsp	30 ml	
Cornstarch	as needed	as needed	
White sandwich bread	25 slices or as needed	25 slices or as needed	*Trim bread crusts, then brush with beaten egg yolk. Cover slices with a generous, uniform layer of the shrimp paste. Cut each slice in half on the diagonal. Brush with egg again, then sprinkle with sesame seeds. Deep-fry at 350°F (175°C) until crisp. Drain on towels and serve with sweet and sour sauce.*
Egg yolk, beaten	as needed	as needed	
Sesame seeds	as needed	as needed	

Fried Shrimp

YIELD: VARIABLE

COATING

Chili powder	1 part	1 part	Mix ingredients in equal parts. Reserve.
Turmeric	1 part	1 part	
Salt	1 part	1 part	

Shrimp, medium to large	4 per serving	4 per serving	Peel and devein shrimp leaving on the tail section of the peel. Skewer shrimp through the tail section then through the opposite end to create a half circle. Any number can be prepared and kept refrigerated until needed.
Skewers, bamboo			

TO SERVE

Skewered shrimp	as needed	as needed	Dip shrimp lightly into the coating mixture. Heat the oils in small skillet and fry the shrimp, turning once, until lightly browned.
Reserved coating	as needed	as needed	
Oil for shallow frying, 50% vegetable; 50% toasted sesame	as needed	as needed	

Mushrooms Stuffed with Ground Chicken

YIELD: 10 SERVINGS

PEANUT CURRY SAUCE

Coconut milk	1 qt	1 L	*Combine ingredients and blend thoroughly.*
Peanut butter	8 oz	230	
Red curry paste	4 oz	115 g	
Sugar	4 oz	115 g	
Tamarind juice	4 oz	120 ml	
Salt	to taste	to taste	

DIPPING SAUCE

Soy sauce, dark	10 oz	300 ml	*Combine ingredients and reserve.*
Vinegar, rice	5 oz	150 ml	
Mushrooms, medium (18–20 per lb)	2 lb	1 kg	*Remove stems and reserve for another recipe. Clean caps by wiping them with a damp towel. Reserve.*
Eggs, beaten	2 large	2 large	*Combine ingredients in a mixing bowl.*
Ginger juice (see recipe)	1 tbsp or to taste	15 ml or to taste	
Scallions, white and green parts, minced	4 oz	115 g	
Pepper, black, fine ground	1 tsp	2 g	

(Continued on next page)

Chicken, ground twice	2 lb	900 g	*Add chicken to the flavoring ingredients in the mixing bowl and blend well. (Sauté a teaspoon of the mixture in a small amount of vegetable oil, then taste. Adjust seasonings if necessary.) Stuff the mushroom caps with the chicken mixture. Level the tops slightly with a spatula. Place the stuffed mushrooms on a sheet pan lined with parchment paper, cover with plastic wrap, and refrigerate until needed.*
Reserved mushroom caps			

TO PREPARE AN INDIVIDUAL SERVING

Oil	1 tsp	5 ml	*Heat oil in a small sauté pan over medium heat. When just below the smoking point, place the mushroom in the pan, stuffing side down. Sauté for 2–3 minutes or until nicely browned and cooked through. Turn and continue to cook, covered, for another 2 minutes. Serve with several tablespoons (30 ml) of the reserved dipping sauce or a small amount of hot mustard served on the side.*
Stuffed mushrooms	3–4 per serving, depending on size	3–4 per serving, depending on size	
Reserved dipping sauce or hot mustard	as needed	as needed	

CHAPTER THREE

Soup

Spinach Soup with Rice

YIELD: 10-12 SERVINGS

Clarified butter	3 oz	90 ml
Onion, sliced thin	1 lb	450 g
Garlic	2 tsp	10 g
Cumin, ground	2 tsp	4 g
Nutmeg, ground	1/2 tsp or to taste	1 g or to taste
Cloves, ground	1/2 tsp or to taste	1 g or to taste
Pepper, black, fine ground	1/2 tsp or to taste	1 g or to taste

In a heavy skillet, heat the clarified butter over medium heat. Add the onions and sauté until they begin to color slightly. Add the garlic, cumin, nutmeg, cloves, and pepper and mix well. Continue to cook, stirring, for a half minute. Remove pan from heat and reserve.

Spinach, cleaned	3 lb	1.4 kg

Wash spinach in several changes of cold water. Remove and discard all tough stems. Place spinach in a pot with a tight-fitting lid adding no additional water. Cook briefly until just wilted. When done, immediately place spinach in iced water. When cooled, drain and chop spinach. Squeeze gently to remove excess liquid.

Rice, cooked	8 oz	225 g
Spinach, cooked		
Onion/spice mixture		
Milk	1 pt	470 ml
Chicken stock	2 qt	2 L

Using a food processor fitted with the steel blade, puree the rice and spinach. Add the onion/spice mixture along with a small amount of the milk to help liquify the mixture. When smooth, place the contents of the processor bowl in a soup pot and combine with the remaining milk and chicken stock. Bring soup to a simmer, stirring, over medium heat and adjust seasonings if necessary. Remove from heat and cool. Place in refrigerator until needed.

TO PREPARE AN INDIVIDUAL SERVING

Reserved soup	8 oz per serving	240 ml
Heavy cream	1 tbsp per serving	15 ml
Lemon juice, fresh squeezed	as needed	as needed
Lemon slices	as needed	as needed

Heat the soup as needed. When just below the boiling point, add the heavy cream and heat through. Pour into heated bowl and add a splash of fresh lemon juice. Float a thin slice of fresh lemon on top.

Hot and Sour Shrimp Soup No. 1

Ingredient	US	Metric	Method
Shrimp, medium	2 lb	900 g	Peel and devein the shrimp, reserving the shells. Place the shrimp in a stainless steel bowl and add the lemon juice. Toss to distribute the lemon juice, cover, and refrigerate until needed.
Lemon juice, fresh squeezed	2 oz	60 ml	
Chicken or fish stock	2 1/2 qt	2.4 L	Combine ingredients in a soup pot and bring to a boil. Lower heat and simmer, partially covered, for 30 minutes. When done, strain through a double layer of cheese cloth. Rinse the pot and return the strained stock.
Reserved shrimp shells			
Lemongrass stalks, fresh, white base sections washed and chopped	4	4	
Kaffir leaves, dried	5–6	5–6	
Lime juice, fresh squeezed	3 oz or to taste	90 ml or to taste	Add ingredients to the soup pot and taste. Adjust seasonings if necessary. Let soup cool, then cover and refrigerate until needed.
Fish sauce	1 1/2 oz or to taste	45 ml or to taste	
Chili paste	1 tsp or to taste	10 g or to taste	

TO PREPARE AN INDIVIDUAL SERVING

Ingredient	US	Metric	Method
Reserved soup	6–8 oz per serving	180–240 ml per serving	Bring soup to a boil. Add the mushrooms and shrimp and simmer until the shrimp turn pink. Do not overcook, or the shrimp will toughen. Pour soup into a heated bowl.
Mushrooms, white button, small, trimmed and quartered	1 oz	30 g	
Reserved shrimp	2–3 oz per serving	60–80 g per serving	
Chili pepper, fresh green, seeds and ribs removed and sliced very thin	as needed	as needed	Garnish soup to taste with the chilies and cilantro.
Cilantro leaves, fresh, chopped	as needed	as needed	

Hot and Sour Shrimp Soup No. 2

YIELD: 10–12 SERVINGS

Chicken stock	2 1/2 qt	2.4 L
Lemongrass, tender white parts cut into 1/4-in. (0.75-cm) pieces	6–8 stalks	6–8 stalks
Kaffir lime leaves	4	4
Mushrooms, white, small, sliced	6 oz	180 g
Chilies, small, hot, fresh, whole	4 or to taste	4 or to taste
Lime juice	1 1/2 tbsp or to taste	20 ml or to taste
Fish sauce	1 1/2 tbsp or to taste	20 ml or to taste

TO PREPARE AN INDIVIDUAL SERVING

Reserved soup stock	8 oz	240 ml
Shrimp, peeled, deveined, and butterflied, tail section of peel on	4 medium	4 medium
Mushrooms, small button, cut in halves	1 oz	30 g
Cilantro or basil leaves	as needed	as needed

In a soup pot, bring the chicken stock to a boil. Add the lemongrass, Kaffir lime leaves, and mushrooms. Lower heat and simmer for 10 minutes. Remove from heat.

Add ingredients and let stand covered, off the heat, for 8–10 minutes. Taste and adjust seasonings if necessary. Strain stock and reserve.

Reheat stock to a boil. Lower heat to a very slow simmer and add shrimp and mushrooms. Cook for 1–2 minutes or until the shrimp turn pink. Garnish with a few fresh cilantro or basil leaves.

Mussel Pineapple Soup

YIELD: 10-12 SERVINGS

Mussels, medium (8–11 per lb), in shell	4 lb	1.8 kg	Wash and debeard the mussels. Place in a soup pot with 2 inches of water. Cover and cook over high heat until the mussels open. When cool enough to handle, remove the mussel meat, rinse, and reserve. Discard the shells.

CHILI PASTE

Red chilies, small, hot, dried and soaked until soft; then drained	10	10	Place ingredients in a food processor or blender and puree into a smooth paste. Reserve.
Shallot, chopped	4 oz	115 g	
Garlic, chopped	2 oz	60 g	
Lemongrass, white tender parts sliced thin	1 tbsp	3 g	
Shrimp paste	1 tbsp	30 g	
Ginger root or Galangal, peeled and sliced thin	2 tsp or to taste	8 g or to taste	
Coriander stems, chopped	1 tbsp	3 g	
Salt	2 tsp or to taste	10 g or to taste	
Kaffir lime zest	1 tsp	3 g	

Coconut milk, thin	16 oz	470 ml	In a soup pot, heat the coconut milk over medium heat. Add the chili paste and blend. Simmer for 2–3 minutes.
Chili paste			

Coconut milk, thin	2 qt	2 L	Add ingredients and bring to a boil. Lower heat and simmer for 1–2 minutes.
Pineapple, fresh, cut in small dice	1 lb	450 g	
Reserved mussels			
Kaffir lime leaves, cut into small pieces	2	2	
Fish sauce	4 oz or to taste	120 ml or to taste	
Sugar, palm or brown sugar	1 tbsp or to taste	15 g or to taste	

Mulligatawany Soup

YIELD: 10-12 SERVINGS

Onion	1 lb	450 g
Potato	6 oz	170 g
Carrot	6 oz	170 g
Celery	4 oz	115 g
Parsnip	4 oz	115 g
Beef, lamb, or chicken stock	2 1/2 qt	2.5 L
Garlic, minced	1 tbsp	15 g
Gingerroot, peeled minced	2 tsp	10 g
Turmeric, ground	1 tsp	2 g
Cumin, ground	1 tsp	2 g
Cilantro leaves and stems, fresh, chopped	2–3 sprigs	2–3 sprigs
Pepper, cayenne	1/2 tsp or to taste	1 g or to taste
Pepper, black	to taste	to taste
Clarified butter	3 oz	90 ml
Onions, sliced thin	4 oz	115 g
Flour	3 tbsp	30 g

TO SERVE

Reserved soup	as needed	as needed
Heavy cream*	1 tbsp per serving	15 ml per serving
Cilantro leaves, chopped fine	1 tbsp per serving	3 g per serving

Yogurt may be substituted for the heavy cream. Add yogurt after removing reheated soup from heat.

Wash, peel, and chop vegetables. Place in a soup pot with the stock and bring to a boil. Skim surface of broth if necessary, then lower heat to a simmer.

Add ingredients to soup pot and simmer, partially covered, for 1 hour. When done, remove soup from heat and strain. Reserving the liquids, place the vegetables in the bowl of a food processor fitted with a steel blade and puree. Combine the pureed vegetables with the broth. Pass soup through a fine mesh china cap or strainer. Return soup to a simmer.

Heat the clarified butter in a skillet over medium to high heat. Add the onions and sauté until they are browned. Add the flour and blend thoroughly. Lower heat and cook, stirring, for 2–3 minutes. Add this mixture to the soup. Simmer until the soup thickens. Cool then reserve refrigerated until needed.

Bring soup to a simmer over medium heat. Add the cream and mix well. Pour into a heated bowl and garnish with chopped cilantro.

Fish Soup with Lettuce

YIELD: 10-12 SERVINGS

MARINADE

Rice wine or dry sherry	4 oz	120 ml
Ginger juice (see recipe)	3 oz	90 ml
Oil, sesame	1 tbsp	15 ml
Soy sauce, light	1 tbsp	15 ml
Cornstarch	2 tsp	7 g
Sugar	1 1/2 tsp	7 g
Pepper, white, fine ground	1/2 tsp	1 g

Combine ingredients and stir until the cornstarch and sugar are completely dissolved.

Fish fillet—flounder, fluke, scrod, or any other firm, white-fleshed fish	1 1/2 lb	680 g

Cut fillets into thin slices then cut into bite-sized pieces. Place fish in a stainless steel bowl along with the marinade. Toss to coat the pieces of fish evenly. Cover and refrigerate until needed.

TO PREPARE AN INDIVIDUAL SERVING

Fish stock	6–8 oz per serving	180–240 ml per serving
Ginger, shredded	1 tsp	4 g
Garlic, minced	1/4 tsp	2 g
Lettuce, shredded	3/4 cup	30 g
Reserved fish and 1 tbsp of the marinade	2–3 oz per serving	60–90 g per serving
Scallion, white and green parts chopped	as needed	as needed

Place the fish stock, ginger, and garlic in a small saucepan and bring to a boil. Add the lettuce and return the stock to the boil. Add the fish and the marinade and cook for 1–2 minutes or until the fish is firm. Remove from heat and pour into a heated bowl. Garnish with chopped scallion.

Egg Drop Soup with Chicken

YIELD: 10 SERVINGS

Chicken breast meat, skinned and boned	12 oz	340 g	*Cut the chicken into very small cubes. Place in a stainless steel mixing bowl and add the sake and*
Sake or dry, white wine	3 oz	90 ml	*salt. Mix well to coat the pieces evenly. Cover and*
Salt	1/2 tsp	3 g	*let marinate for 10–15 minutes.*
Carrot	10 uniform round slices	10 uniform round slices	*Blanch carrot slices in boiling water for 1–2 minutes. Plunge into iced water. When cold, drain and reserve.*
Dashi (see recipe)	2 qt	2 L	*In a small soup pot, bring the dashi to a rapid boil. Add the soy sauce and salt to taste. Add the chicken,*
Soy sauce, dark	1 tbsp or to taste	15 ml or to taste	*reduce heat, and simmer for 2–3 minutes or until*
Salt	to taste	to taste	*the chicken is cooked through.*
Marinated chicken			
Eggs, very lightly beaten, yolk and whites still slightly separated	4	4	*Increase heat to medium boil. Pour the eggs into the soup in a slow, steady stream, stirring constantly to create threads. When all of the egg has been incorporated, remove from heat. When serving, garnish*
Reserved carrot			*each bowl with a slice of carrot that has been heated briefly in the soup.*

Crab Asparagus Soup

YIELD: 10 SERVINGS

Asparagus	2 lb	900 g
Oil, vegetable	1 tbsp	15 ml
Crab meat, cooked	12 oz	340 g
Salt	1/2 tsp	3 g
Pepper, white	1/2 tsp	1 g
Chicken stock, Vietnam (see recipe)	2 1/2 qt	2.4 L
Cornstarch	1 tbsp	10 g
Water or cold chicken stock	2 oz	60 ml
Egg whites, lightly beaten	4	4
Scallion, green parts sliced in thin circles	as needed	as needed
Coriander, fresh, leaves only	as needed	as needed
Vinegar, rice	as needed	as needed
Pepper, black, crushed	as needed	as needed

Discard tough ends of stalks. Using a vegetable peeler, peel the lower sections of the stalks, then cut them into 1-in. (2.5-cm) pieces on the diagonal. Reserve.

In a small soup pot, heat the oil over high heat. Add the crab meat, salt and pepper, and cook, stirring, for 30–40 seconds.

Add the stock and bring to a boil. Add the asparagus pieces, lower heat, and simmer for 5 minutes or until the asparagus is just tender.

Mix the cornstarch with the water or stock until completely dissolved. Add to the soup and stir until the soup has thickened slightly.

Add the egg whites in a thin, slow stream, using a circular motion, to make thin, noodle-like threads. When serving, pour into heated bowls and garnish with scallion and a few coriander leaves. Serve with a cruet of vinegar and a small dish of crushed black pepper on the side.

See color insert for photograph of recipe

Fresh Corn and Chicken Soup

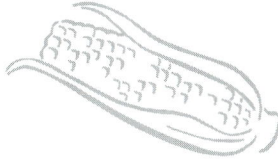

Corn kernels, fresh	1 1/2 lb	680 g
Soy sauce, light	1 tbsp	15 ml
Salt	2 tsp	10 g

Place ingredients into the bowl of a food processor fitted with a steel blade. Using the pulse action, process into a slightly coarse puree. Place puree into a small soup pot.

| Chicken stock | 2 qt | 2 lt |
| Chicken breast meat, finely chopped or ground | 8 oz | 220 g |

Add the chicken stock and chicken meat. Mix thoroughly, then bring to a boil over low to moderate heat, stirring occasionally. Lower heat and simmer for 4–5 minutes. Adjust seasonings if necessary.

Cornstarch	2 tbsp	20 g
Water, cold	2–3 oz	60–90 ml
Scallions, green parts, sliced thin	as needed	as needed

Combine the cornstarch and enough cold water to make a smooth paste, then add to the soup. Mix well and simmer until the soup thickens. When serving, garnish with sliced scallions.

Chicken Ginger Soup

YIELD: 10-12 SERVING

Chicken meat, dark, cubed	1 lb	450 g	*Place ingredients in a soup pot and bring to a boil over moderate heat.*
Coconut milk, thick	1 1/2 qt	1.4 L	
Chicken stock	1 qt	1 L	
Kaffir lime leaves	6	6	
Galangal, sliced thick	2 oz	60 g	
Red chilies, fresh, seeds and ribs removed, sliced very thin	3 or to taste	3 or to taste	*Add these ingredients, lower heat, and simmer for 6–8 minutes or until the chicken is tender. Remove and discard the chilies, Galangal, and Kaffir leaves. Adjust seasonings if necessary.*
Lime juice	2 oz or to taste	60 ml or to taste	
Fish sauce	2 oz or to taste	60 ml or to taste	
Coriander leaves, fresh, chopped	as needed	as needed	*Garnish with fresh, chopped, coriander leaves just prior to serving.*

Chicken Coconut Soup

YIELD: 10-12 SERVINGS

Ingredient	US	Metric
Coconut milk, thin	2 1/2 qt	2.4 L
Chicken meat, dark, cut into small cubes	1 1/2 lb	680 g
Lemongrass, tender white parts, cut into 1-in. (2.5-cm) lengths	5–6 stalks	5–6 stalks
Gingerroot, peeled, cut in 2–3 pieces	1 oz	30 g

Place ingredients in a small soup pot and bring to a boil slowly. Do not cover pot. Lower heat and simmer for 10 minutes.

Ingredient	US	Metric
Scallions, white and tender green parts chopped fine	6–7	6–7
Cilantro leaves, fresh, chopped fine	10 sprigs	10 sprigs
Chilies, serrano, seeds and ribs removed, chopped fine	4 or to taste	4 or to taste
Lime juice, fresh	2–3 oz or to taste	60–90 ml or to taste
Fish sauce	3 oz or to taste	90 ml or to taste

Add the scallions, cilantro, and chilies, lower heat to just below a boil, and simmer for another 2 minutes. Remove pot from heat and add the lime juice and fish sauce to taste.

Watercress Soup

YIELD: 10-12 SERVINGS

Chicken stock	2 1/2 qt	2.4 L	Bring chicken stock to a boil. Add the red dates and gingerroot slices. Lower heat and simmer for 20 minutes.
Chinese red dates (jujubes)	10–12	10–12	
Gingerroot, peeled and sliced very thin	10–12 very thin slices	10–12 very thin slices	
Watercress, washed and trimmed	1 3/4 lb	800 g	Add ingredients to the stock and simmer for 5 minutes or until the watercress is tender.
Rice wine or dry sherry	2 tbsp	30 ml	
Soy sauce, light	2 tbsp	30 ml	
Sugar	1 tbsp or to taste	15 g or to taste	
Salt	to taste	to taste	

Stock Made from Chicken, Pork, and Ham

YIELD: 3 QUARTS (3L)

Chicken parts	3 lb	1.4 kg	Place ingredients in a stock pot and bring to a boil. Lower heat, partially cover, and simmer for 3–3 1/2 hours, skimming as needed. Strain stock and discard solids. Meats can be reserved for another purpose. Reduce remaining liquid, if necessary, to measure approximately 3 qt (3 L). Strain through a fine sieve and cool long enough to congeal any fats. Discard fat before using.
Pork shoulder	3 lb	1.4 kg	
Ham, lightly smoked	3 lb	1.4 kg	
Water	5 qt	5 L	

Shrimp and Okra

Y I E L D :   1 0   S E R V I N G S

Shrimp	10–20, medium to large (1–2 shrimp per serving depending on size)	10–20, medium to large (1–2 shrimp per serving depending on size)	*Peel and devein the shrimp leaving the section of the shell closest to the tail on. Place the shrimp in simmering water for 1–2 minutes. Cooking time will depend on the size of the shrimp. When done, remove shrimp and cool in iced water. Drain and reserve.*
Water, lightly salted	*as needed*	*as needed*	
Okra	*as needed*	*as needed*	*Select small, tender okra. Wash okra and trim the stem ends. Cut into 1/4-in. (0.75-cm) round slices. You will need 5–6 slices per serving. Place okra in boiling water for 1–2 minutes. When done, remove okra and cool in iced water. Drain and reserve.*
Dashi (see recipe)	*2 1/2 qt*	*2.4 L*	*Combine ingredients and bring to a boil. Let cool and reserve.*
Soy sauce, dark	*1 tbsp or to taste*	*15 ml or to taste*	
Salt	*to taste*	*to taste*	

TO PREPARE AN INDIVIDUAL SERVING

Dashi mixture	*8 oz per serving*	*240 ml per serving*	*Bring the dashi mixture to a simmer. Add the shrimp and okra. Heat through quickly, then pour into heated bowl(s). Garnish with the lemon peel.*
Shrimp	*1–2*	*1–2*	
Okra	*5–6 slices*	*5–6 slices*	
Lemon peel, cut into very fine strips	*4–5 strips*	*4–5 strips*	

Savory Meatball Soup

YIELD: VARIABLE

Beef, top or bottom round	3 lb	1.4 kg	Trim meat of all fat and gristle then cut into cubes. Place meat into the bowl of a food processor fitted with a steel blade and puree. Add the remaining ingredients to the meat and, using the pulse action, blend thoroughly. Place meat in a clean mixing bowl and refrigerate for several hours or until well chilled.
Fish sauce	2 oz	60 ml	
Water	2 oz	60 ml	
Oil, vegetable	1 oz	30 ml	
Sugar	1 tbsp	15 g	
Baking powder	1 tbsp	10 g	
Cornstarch	1 tbsp	10 g	
Garlic, minced	1 tbsp	15 g	
Pepper, white	2 tsp	4 g	
Lime juice, fresh squeezed	1–2 oz. or to taste	30–60 ml or to taste	Using the processor again, blend the lime juice into the meat. Form into meatballs approximately 1 in. (2.5 cm) in diameter. Place on a tray, cover, and refrigerate until needed.

To prepare an individual serving

Beef Stock Vietnamese (see recipe)	7–8 oz per serving	200–230 ml per serving	Bring stock as needed to a boil, then add the meatballs. When the stock has returned to a boil, lower heat and simmer for 3–4 minutes or until the meatballs are cooked through. (Meatballs may also be cooked in advance and reheated in the hot stock as needed.)
Meatballs*	6–7 per serving	6–7 per serving	
Cilantro leaves, fresh	as needed	as needed	Garnish soup with fresh coriander or basil leaves. Serve with a side dish of bean sprouts and a small dish of Hoisin sauce laced with chili sauce as a dipping sauce for the meatballs.
Bean sprouts	as needed	as needed	
Hoisin sauce	as needed	as needed	
Chili sauce	as needed	as needed	

*Noodles and/or other vegetables may also be added. If so, reduce the number of meatballs per serving.

Pork Tenderloin and Cucumber Soup

CHINA

YIELD: 10 SERVINGS

Pork tenderloin	1 1/2 lb	680 g
Oil, sesame	1 1/2 tbsp	20 ml
Egg whites	from 3 medium eggs	from 3 medium eggs
Cornstarch	1 tbsp	10 g
Salt	1 tsp	5 g
Pepper, white	1/2 tsp	1 g

Cut the pork into very thin slices, then cut each slice into half-inch strips. Mix the oil, egg whites, cornstarch, salt and pepper into a smooth paste. Pour this mixture over the pork and toss to coat the pieces well. Cover and refrigerate for 1 hour.

Chicken stock	2 1/2 qt	2.5 L
Cilantro, fresh	6–8 sprigs	6–8 sprigs
Gingerroot, peeled and sliced thin	2-in. piece	5-cm piece
Salt	if needed	if needed
Pepper, white	if needed	if needed

Bring the stock to a boil in a small soup pot. Add the cilantro and ginger. Lower heat and simmer, partially covered, for 30 minutes. Strain the stock, and discard the cilantro and ginger. Adjust for salt and pepper. Let cool and reserve, refrigerated, until needed.

Reserved stock	8 oz	240 ml
Marinated pork		

Bring 8 oz (240 ml) of the reserved stock to a boil in a wok or large skillet. Add the pork, lower heat, cover, and cook for several minutes, stirring, until the pork is cooked through. Drain and reserve the pork, returning the stock to the soup pot.

TO PREPARE AN INDIVIDUAL SERVING

Reserved stock	8 oz per serving	240 ml per serving
Reserved pork	2 oz per serving (approximately)	60 g per serving (approximately)
Cucumber, peeled, sliced thin	1 oz per serving	30 g per serving
Cilantro leaves, fresh, chopped	as needed	as needed

Bring the stock to a boil. Add the pork and cucumber and cook briefly until these ingredients are just heated through. Pour into a heated bowl and garnish with cilantro leaves.

55.

Pork and Mustard Green Soup

YIELD: 10-12 SERVINGS

MARINADE

Rice wine or dry sherry	3 oz	90 ml
Soy sauce, light	2 oz	60 ml
Oil, peanut	1 tbsp	15 ml
Oil, sesame	1 tbsp	15 ml
Ginger juice	1 tbsp	15 ml
Cornstarch	2 tbsp	20 g
Sugar	2 tsp	10 g
Salt	1 tsp	5 g
Pepper, white	1 tsp	2 g

Combine ingredients and mix until the cornstarch and sugar are completely dissolved.

Pork, shoulder, trimmed	1 1/2 lb	680 g

Slice the pork into very thin slices, then cut each slice into 2 x 1/2 in. (5 x 1.5 cm) strips. Place in a stainless steel mixing bowl and add the marinade. Toss well to coat the pieces evenly. Cover, refrigerate and allow to marinate for 30–60 minutes. Reserve.

Chicken broth	2 1/2 qt	2.5 L
Mustard greens, sliced across the stem into very thin strips	2 lb	900 g
Reserved pork		

Place broth in a soup pot and bring to a boil. Add the mustard greens and pork and return stock to a boil. Lower heat and simmer until the pork is cooked through, about 4–5 minutes.

TO PREPARE AN INDIVIDUAL SERVING

Chicken stock	8 oz	240 ml
Marinated pork strips	2 oz	60 g
Mustard greens	2–3 oz	60–90 g

Bring stock to a boil, add the pork strips and mustard greens, and simmer until the pork is cooked through.

Lemon juice, fresh squeezed	as needed	as needed
Cilantro leaves, fresh, chopped	as needed	as needed

When serving, add a squeeze of fresh lemon juice and a heaping teaspoon full of chopped cilantro per serving.

Oyster Beef Soup

YIELD: 10-12 SERVINGS

Oysters	36	36	*Shuck oysters, retaining as much of the liquor as possible. Strain the liquor. Reserve the oysters and the liquor separately.*
Oil, sesame	3 tbsp	45 ml	*Heat oil in a soup pot over medium to high heat. Add the beef and stir-fry until browned. Add the remaining ingredients and stir-fry for another 30–40 seconds.*
Beef, top round, sliced thin, then cut into julienne 2 in. (5 cm) in length	1 lb	450 g	
Turnip, peeled and shredded	8 oz	230 g	
Scallions, white and green parts cut into 1-in. (2.5) pieces	5–6	5–6	
Garlic, minced	1 tbsp	15 g	
Soy sauce	1 tbsp or to taste	15 ml or to taste	
Stock, beef	2 1/2 qt	2.5 L	*Add the stock and bring to a boil. Skim, lower heat and simmer for 25 minutes, partially covered. Add the oyster liquor and simmer for another 5 minutes. Let cool and reserve.*
Reserved oyster liquor			

TO PREPARE AN INDIVIDUAL SERVING

Reserved beef soup	as needed	as needed	*Reheat beef soup as needed and bring to a boil. Add the shucked oysters, cover the pot, and remove from heat immediately. Let sit for 2–3 minutes before serving in a large, heated bowl.*
Reserved oysters	3–4 per serving	3–4 per serving	

Mussel and Tofu Soup

YIELD: 10-12 SERVINGS

Mussels	30–40, depending on size	30–40 depending on size	*Clean and debeard the mussels and reserve.*
Beef, top round	1 1/2 lb	680 g	*Cut beef into thin slices, then into very thin strips 2–3 in. long (5–8 cm). Heat oil in a soup pot over medium to high heat. Stir-fry the beef strips until browned.*
Oil, vegetable	2 tbsp	30 ml	
Scallions, white and green parts, sliced thin	5–6	5–6	*Add the scallions and garlic and continue to stir-fry for another 30 seconds.*
Garlic, sliced thin	1 tbsp	15 g	
Beef stock	2 1/5 qt	2.5 L	*Add the stock and tofu cubes and bring to a boil. Lower heat and simmer, partially covered, for 10 minutes. Let cool and reserve.*
Tofu, cut into 3/4-in. (1.5-cm) cubes	12 oz	340 g	

TO SERVE

Reserved beef soup	as needed	as needed	*Bring the soup, as needed, to a boil. Add 3–4 mussels per serving and cover the pot. Cook until the mussels open. Adjust seasoning for salt if necessary. Serve in large, heated bowl(s).*
Reserved mussels	3–4 per serving	3–4 per serving	
Salt	to taste	to taste	

Miso Soup with Shiitake Mushrooms and Tofu

YIELD: 10 SERVINGS

Tofu	12 oz	340 g
Fresh Shiitake Mushrooms*	10	10
Dashi (see recipe)	2 1/2 qt	2.5 L
Reserved tofu		
Reserved mushrooms		
Miso	7 oz	200 g

Cut tofu into very small cubes. Reserve. Remove the stems from the mushrooms and reserve for other purposes. Clean the caps, then cut into 1/4-in. (0.75 cm) slices. Reserve.

In a small soup pot bring the dashi to a simmer. Remove 3–4 ladles and place in a mixing bowl. Add the tofu and mushrooms to the soup pot. Return the soup to a simmer. Add the miso to the dashi in the bowl and stir to dissolve completely. Pour this mixture into the soup pot and return the soup to a simmer. When it starts to simmer, remove from heat immediately. If soup is made in advance, reheat to just below the boiling point before serving.

*If Shiitake mushrooms are not available, other fresh mushrooms may be substituted.

Miso Soup with Daikon and Green Beans

YIELD: 10 SERVINGS

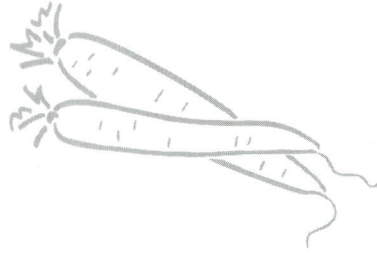

Daikon radish, peeled	12 oz	340 g
Green beans, ends trimmed	12 oz	340 g
Dashi (see recipe)	2 1/2 qt	2.5 L
Reserved daikon		
Reserved green beans		
Miso, red	7 oz	200 g

Cut the daikon into quarters lengthwise, then cut each quarter into thin slices to create pie-shaped pieces. Reserve. Cut the green beans into 1-in. (2.5 cm) lengths. Reserve.

In a small soup pot over medium heat, bring the dashi to a simmer. Remove 3–4 ladles and place in a mixing bowl. Add the daikon and green beans to the soup pot and reduce the heat to a simmer. Add the miso to the dashi in the bowl and whisk to dissolve completely. Pour this mixture into the soup pot and return the soup to a simmer. When it begins to simmer, remove from heat immediately. If soup is made in advance and reserved, reheat to just below the boiling point when serving.

Lobster and Beef Soup

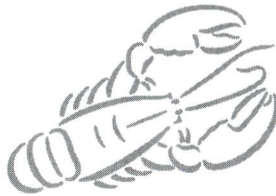

Ingredient		
Oil, sesame	2 tbsp	30 ml
Beef, top round, sliced thin then cut into 1-in. (2.5-cm) squares	1 lb	450 g
Whole lobsters, chopped into 2-in. (5-cm) pieces, claws and tails only (reserve lobster bodies for other purposes.)	*three, 1 1/4 lb each*	*three, 570 g each*
Scallions, white and green parts cut into 1-in. (2.5-cm) pieces	*12*	*12*
Garlic, minced	*1 tbsp or to taste*	*15 g or to taste*
Salt	*to taste*	*to taste*
Fish or other stock	*2 1/2 qt*	*2.5 L*
Soy sauce, dark	*3 oz*	*90 ml*

Heat oil in a soup pot over medium to high heat. Add ingredients and fry, stirring, until the meat begins to brown and the lobster shell has turned red.

Add the stock or water and the soy sauce and bring to a boil. Lower heat and simmer for 15–20 minutes. Skim as needed. Adjust seasonings if necessary.

Hot and Sour Soup

YIELD: 10-12 SERVINGS

Mushrooms, black, dried	4 oz	115 g	*Soak dried vegetables in warm water for 30 minutes. Remove, discard the stems from the mushrooms, and julienne the caps. Slice the cloud ears and cut the golden needles in half. Reserve.*
Cloud ears	2 oz	60 g	
Golden needles (Lily Bulb)	2 oz	60 g	
Cornstarch	1 tbsp	10 g	*Combine the cornstarch and rice wine in a mixing bowl. Add the pork strips and toss to coat the meat. Reserve.*
Rice wine or dry sherry	1 tbsp	15 ml	
Boneless pork, julienne	8 oz	230 g	
Bean curd	3/4 lb	340 g	*Cut the bean curd into small cubes. Reserve.*

FLAVORING MIXTURE

Rice wine vinegar	3 oz or to taste	90 ml or to taste	*Combine ingredients and reserve.*
Pepper, black, fine ground	2 tsp or to taste	4 g or to taste	
Chili oil	2 tsp or to taste	10 ml or to taste	
Sesame oil	2 tsp or taste	10 ml or to taste	

Chicken stock	2 1/2 qt	2.5 L	*In a soup pot, bring the chicken stock and sesame oil to a boil. Add the pork and cook for 1 minute. Add the soaked vegetables and cook until they are tender. Lower the heat to medium. Mix the cornstarch with enough water or stock to make a smooth, rather thick, paste. Add this, stirring, to the pot and mix well. When the soup begins to thicken, lower heat to a simmer and add the flavoring mixture. Taste, and adjust the seasonings, if necessary.*
Sesame oil	1 tbsp	15 ml	
Reserved pork			
Reserved soaked vegetables and bean curd			
Cornstarch	4 tbsp	40 g	
Water or cold stock	as needed	as needed	
Reserved flavoring mixture			
Eggs, beaten	2 large	2 large	*Pour the beaten eggs in a slow stream, stirring with a large tined fork, to form a soft thread. Garnish each bowl with a teaspoon of sliced scallion.*
Scallions, white and green parts, sliced thin	as needed	as needed	

Ginger-Flavored Soup with Pork and Mushrooms

YIELD: 10-12 SERVINGS

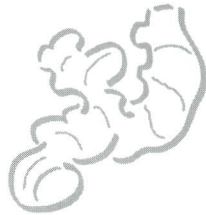

Dried mushrooms, Chinese black or wood ear fungus	2 oz	60 g	*Remove stems, if any, and rinse well. Place in bowl with enough boiling water to cover and soak until the mushrooms or fungus are tender and plump. If very large, cut into bite-sized pieces.*
Pork, lean	1 lb	450 g	*Slice pork into very thin strips, then slice again into bite-sized pieces. Reserve.*
Oil, peanut	2 oz	60 ml	*Heat wok or small soup pot over high heat. When very hot add the oil and distribute over surface of pot. Add the gingerroot and stir-fry for 10–15 seconds. Add the pork and stir-fry until the meat loses all color, about 1 minute.*
Gingerroot, peeled and cut into fine julienne	3 oz	90 g	
Reserved pork			
Reconstituted mushrooms, drained well.			
Stock, chicken	2 qt	2 L	*Add the remaining ingredients and bring to a boil. Lower heat, skim surface, then simmer for 15 minutes. Adjust seasonings if necessary.*
Shaohsing wine or dry sherry	2 oz	60 ml	*Serve in warm bowls and garnish with scallions.*
Soy sauce, light	2 oz	60 ml	
Salt	to taste	to taste	
Scallions, white and tender green parts, sliced thin	as needed	as needed	

Duck and Crab Soup

YIELD: 10-12 SERVINGS

Wonton wrappers	20–25	20–25	*Cut each wrapper in half diagonally, then fold each of the pieces in half again. Heat oil to 350°F (175°C) and deep-fry the wrappers a small batch at a time until they expand and begin to brown lightly. Remove from oil and drain. Reserve in an airtight container.*
Oil, peanut	*for deep-frying*	*for deep-frying*	
Stock (chicken, pork and ham—see recipe)	*2 1/2 qt*	*2.5 L*	*In a soup pot, bring the stock to a boil. Add the remaining ingredients and return to the boil. Lower heat to a very slow simmer.*
Crab meat, cooked and shredded	*12 oz*	*340 g*	
Duck meat, roasted and diced small	*10 oz*	*280 g*	
Straw mushrooms, canned	*8 oz*	*225 g*	
Chinese black mushrooms, soaked in hot water until plump, then sliced thin (discard tough stems)	*4 oz*	*115g*	
Bamboo shoots, sliced into fine julienne	*2–3 oz*	*60–90 g*	
Soy sauce, light	*2 tbsp or to taste*	*30 ml or to taste*	*Add ingredients and simmer for 5 minutes. Cool and reserve.*
Salt	*to taste*	*to taste*	
Pepper, black, fine ground	*to taste*	*to taste*	

(Continued on facing page)

Reserved soup	8–9 oz per serving	240–270 ml per serving
Reserved wonton wrappers	4–5 per serving	4–5 per serving
Scallions, white and green parts cut into thin circles	as needed	as needed

Bring soup, as needed, to a boil. Pour into warm bowl(s) and add the fried wonton wrappers. Garnish with sliced scallion.

J A P A N

Dashi (Soup Stock)

YIELD: APPROXIMATELY 3 1/2 QUARTS (3.5 L)

Cold water	3 1/4 qt	3 L
Konbu (dried kelp), cut into strips	4 oz	115 g
Hana-katsuo (dried bonito flakes)	4 oz	115 g
Water	as needed	as needed

Put the water and kelp into a soup pot. Heat over medium heat, uncovered, until the temperature is just under the boiling point. Remove a piece of the kelp. If it is soft, remove the remaining pieces. If not, return it to the pot, add 1/2 cup (120 ml) of cold water, and heat for another minute or two. Do not let the water reach the boiling point. When you have removed the kelp, bring the water to a full boil. Add another 1/2 cup (120 ml) of cold water to bring the temperature down and add the bonito flakes. When stock returns to a boil, immediately remove the pot from the heat. Let sit for 1 minute. Skim the surface if necessary, then strain the stock through a double layer of cheesecloth. When cool, refrigerate until needed. Will keep 3–4 days under refrigeration.

Soup Stock

YIELD: 4 QUARTS (4 L)

Water, cold	5 qt	5 L	Place water and bones in a soup pot and bring to a
Chicken bones, or beef or pork bones	5 lb	2.2 kg	boil. Partially cover the pot, reduce heat, and simmer for 1/2 hour. Skim surface as needed.
White radish (daikon), thick sliced	2 lb	1 kg	Add ingredients and continue to simmer for another 45–60 minutes. Remove from heat and strain.
Onion	1 lb	450 g	When cool, refrigerate. When thoroughly chilled,
Celery	1 lb	450 g	remove congealed fat.
Garlic cloves, peeled	2 oz	60 g	
Shallots, peeled	2 oz	60 g	
Ginger, ground	2 tsp	4 g	
Pepper, ground	1 tsp	2 g	

Chicken Stock

YIELD: APPROXIMATELY 4 QUARTS (4 L)

Chicken parts, backs, wings, necks	6 lb	2.7 kg	Place chicken parts and water in a soup pot and bring to a boil. Lower heat and simmer for 30 minutes, skimming as necessary.
Water	5 qt	5 L	
Peppercorns, white	1 tbsp	8 g	When the liquid is clear, add ingredients and continue to simmer for another 1 1/2 hours. When
Gingerroot, peeled and smashed flat	4 oz	115 g	done, strain stock, discard the solids, and let cool. Refrigerate overnight. When thoroughly chilled,
Salt	1–2 tbsp or to taste	15–30 g or to taste	remove congealed fat from surface.

Beef Stock

Ingredient	US	Metric
Lean beef, oxtail, shin or neck meat	5 lb	2.2 kg
Water	5 qt	5 L
Onion, cut in quarters or large pieces	2 lb	900 g
Gingerroot, peeled	4 oz	115 g
Star anise, whole	1/2 oz	15 g
Fennel seeds	1 tbsp	6 g
Cloves, whole	1 tsp	1 g
Cinnamon stick	4-in. piece	10-cm piece
Bay leaf	4–5	4–5
Sugar	1 tbsp	15 g
Salt	1 tbsp	15 g

Trim excess fat and place meat in a soup pot. Add water to cover and bring to a boil. Drain, discarding the water. Add 5 qt (5 L) of fresh cold water. Return to a boil then lower heat and simmer for 1 hour, skimming the surface as necessary.

Char ingredients under the broiler, in a hot oven, or directly over a low gas flame, then add them to the soup pot.

Wrap the anise, fennel seeds, cloves and bay leaf in cheesecloth and tie to form a small bag. Add this and the remaining ingredients to the pot. Cover partially and simmer, skimming as needed, for another 2 hours. When done, strain stock through a fine sieve and cool. Reserve the meat for other purposes and discard all other solids. Place strained stock in the refrigerator overnight. When thoroughly chilled, remove congealed fat from surface.

Beef Soup with White Radish

YIELD: 10-12 SERVINGS

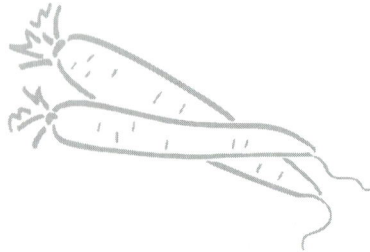

SEASONING MIXTURE

Soy sauce, dark	4 oz	120 ml	*Combine ingredients and reserve.*
Sesame oil	1 tbsp	15 ml	
Scallions, white and tender green parts sliced thin	3	3	
Garlic, minced	1 tbsp	15 g	
Pepper, black, ground	1 tsp	2 g	
Eggs, large	2	2	*Separate the whites from the yolks and place in separate mixing bowls. Add a pinch of salt to each, then beat each separately. In a lightly oiled, shallow frying pan, preferably a nonstick one, fry the yolks into a thin pancake. Remove from pan, roll, then cut into thin strips. Repeat this process with the beaten whites. Reserve.*
Salt	pinch	pinch	

(Continued on facing page)

Beef, short ribs	3 lb	1.4 kg
Beef stock	4 qt	4 L
White radish (daikon), peeled and cut in half lengthwise	1 lb	450 g
Reserved seasoning mixture		

Cut the ribs across the bone into 2-in. (5-cm) pieces. Trim any excess fat, then score each piece across the grain, almost to the bone, at 1/2-in. (1.5-cm) intervals. Place the ribs in a soup pot with 4 qt (4 L) of beef stock. Bring to a boil over high heat. Lower heat and simmer very slowly, uncovered, skimming the stock as necessary. When the meat has cooked for 1 1/2 hours, add the radish and cook for another 30 minutes. Remove the ribs, strip the meat from the bone, and reserve. Remove the radish and slice it into very thin slices. Put the meat and the radish into a mixing bowl, add the seasoning mixture, and let sit for 15–20 minutes. Degrease the stock, which should measure approximately 3 qt (3 L). Adjust volume by adding stock or reduction. Return the meat, radish, and seasoning mixture to the stock. Adjust seasonings if necessary.

TO SERVE

Beef rib soup	as needed	as needed
Egg strips	as needed	as needed
White, cooked rice	as needed	as needed

Reheat soup as needed. Place the liquid along with pieces of rib and slices of radish into deep, heated bowl(s). Garnish with strips of egg yolk and egg white pancake. Accompany with a small bowl of white rice served on the side.

Crab Soup

YIELD: 10-12 SERVINGS

Chicken or fish stock (see recipe)	*2 1/2 qt*	*2.4 L*
Soy sauce, light	*2 tbsp or to taste*	*30 ml or to taste*
Salt	*to taste*	*to taste*
Pepper, black, fine ground	*to taste*	*to taste*

Combine ingredients in a small soup pot and bring to a boil. Lower heat and simmer for 2–3 minutes. Adjust seasonings if necessary.

Crab meat	*1 1/2 lb*	*680 g*

Remove any shell or cartilage from the crab meat. Add to the soup pot and simmer for 2–3 minutes.

Cornstarch	*3 tbsp*	*30 g*
Cold stock	*as needed*	*as needed*

Mix cornstarch with cold stock or water to make a smooth paste. Add this to the soup, stirring until the soup begins to thicken.

Egg whites, from large eggs, beaten	6	6

Beat the egg whites until they just begin to foam. Pour them, stirring constantly, in a slow stream into the simmering soup.

VARIATION

Eliminate the cornstarch and egg whites. Instead, add 2 bunches of trimmed watercress and small cubes of bean curd. Cook briefly, until the watercress is just tender.

Chicken Stock

YIELD: 4 QUARTS (4 L)

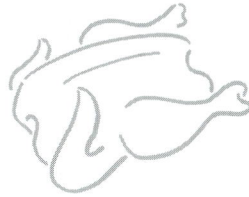

Chicken parts, backs, wings, etc.	8 lb, or more for a richer stock	3.5 kg, or more for a richer stock
Water, cold	5 qt	5 L
Ginger root, peeled and smashed	4 oz	115 g
Onion, quartered	2 lb	1 kg
Leek, white part only, cleaned thoroughly and sliced	4	4
Celery (optional)	3 ribs	3 ribs

Wash the chicken parts and place in a soup pot with water to cover. Bring to a boil over high heat and boil for 1 minute. Discard water and rinse chicken. Return the chicken parts to a clean soup pot, add 5 qt (5 L) of cold water, and bring to a boil once again. Lower heat and simmer, partially covered, for 30 minutes, skimming until no more scum rises to the surface and the liquid is clear. Add the vegetables and continue to simmer for another hour. When done, strain the stock, discarding all of the solids. Refrigerate overnight. When cold, remove any congealed fat from the top of the stock before using.

CHAPTER FOUR

Vegetables

Watercress Salad

YIELD: 10 SERVINGS

DRESSING

Soy sauce	*4 oz*	*120 ml*
Sesame oil	*2 oz*	*60 ml*
Sugar	*2 oz*	*60 g*
Sesame seeds, toasted	*2 tbsp*	*12 g*
Garlic, minced	*2 tsp*	*10 g*

Combine ingredients and mix well.

Watercress	*2 lb*	*900 g*

Trim the stem ends only if they are tough and/or discolored. Place the washed watercress in a steamer for 1–2 minutes. Remove when done and plunge immediately into iced water. Drain, pat dry, and chop coarsely. Add the dressing and toss to coat the watercress evenly. Chill before serving.

Apple and Grape Salad

Ingredient	US	Metric	Method
Apples, Granny Smith, Golden Delicious, or Macintosh	2 lb	900 g	*Peel, core, and dice apples. Reserve in lemon water to cover, until needed.*
Lemon juice, fresh squeezed	2 oz	60 ml	
Water	as needed	as needed	
Yogurt, plain	8 oz	220 g	*Combine ingredients in a small mixing bowl. Reserve.*
Lemon juice	2 oz	60 ml	
Almonds, blanched, crushed fine	3 oz	85 g	
Cardamom seeds, crushed fine	1/2 tsp	1 g	
Mint leaves, fresh, chopped	4 tbsp	30 g	
Grapes, seedless, red or white or in combination sliced in half	8 oz	220 g	*Prepare the grapes. Drain the apples well, then combine all ingredients. Chill for at least an hour before serving. When serving, garnish with fresh, whole mint leaves.*
Reserved diced apples			
Reserved yogurt sauce	as needed	as needed	
Mint leaves, fresh			

Bean Curd in Oyster Sauce

YIELD: 1 SERVING

Water	*8 oz*	*240 ml*	*In a small saucepan, bring water to a boil, then allow it to cool slightly. Place bean curd in water for 15 minutes. Drain well, then slice into 1/2-in. (1.5-cm) cubes.*
Bean curd	*approx.*	*approx.*	
	4 oz	*115 g*	
Oil, peanut	*2 tsp*	*10 ml*	*Heat wok or small skillet over high heat. Add the oil and distribute it over the surface of the pan. When the oil is just below the smoking point, add the scallions and stir-fry for 10–15 seconds. Add the bean curd and stir-fry for about 1 minute, gently turning the cubes until they are well coated with the oil and scallions.*
Scallion, white parts only, cut into thin 1/8-in. (0.5-cm) rings	*2*	*2*	
Bean curd cubes			
Oyster sauce	*1 tbsp*	*15 ml*	*Lower heat to medium and add ingredients. Continue to gently stir-fry for another minute.*
Soy sauce	*2 tsp*	*10 ml*	
Sherry, dry	*2 tsp*	*10 ml*	
Sugar	*pinch*	*pinch*	
Salt	*pinch*	*pinch*	
Scallion, green parts cut into 1/8-in. (0.5-cm) circles	*2*	*2*	*Add the scallion and incorporate with the other ingredients. Place on a heated serving plate.*

See color insert for photograph of recipe

Bean Curd (Tofu) with Tomato

YIELD: 10 SERVINGS

SAUCE

Chicken stock, cold	8 oz	240 ml	*Combine ingredients, stirring, until the cornstarch is completely dissolved. Reserve.*
Cornstarch	2 tbsp	20 g	
Oyster sauce	2 tbsp	30 ml	
Soy sauce, light	2 tsp	10 ml	
Soy sauce, dark	2 tsp	10 ml	
Sesame oil	2 tsp	10 ml	
Sugar	1 tsp	5 g	
Pepper, white	1/2 tsp	1 g	
Oil, vegetable	2 tbsp	30 ml	*Heat a wok or heavy skillet over high heat. Add the oil and heat to just below the smoking point. Add the ginger and salt. Stir-fry until the ginger becomes aromatic, then add the tomatoes. Stir-fry for about 1 minute, then add the sugar and bean curd. Lower heat to medium and continue to stir-fry for another minute or two. Add the scallions.*
Gingerroot, peeled and, minced	1 tbsp or to taste	12 g or to taste	
Salt	1 tsp	5 g	
Tomato, firm, peeled, seeded, and coarsely chopped	3 lb	1.4 kg	
Sugar	2 tsp	10 g	
Bean curd (tofu), drained, diced into 1-in. cubes	1 1/2 lb	680 g	
Scallions, white and green parts, cut on the diagonal into 1-in. (2.5-cm) pieces	6–7 *depending on size*	6–7 *depending on size*	
Reserved sauce			*Add the sauce and stir-fry until the sauce reaches a boil and begins to thicken.*

Bean Sprouts Stir-Fried with Ginger and Scallion

YIELD: 1-2 SERVINGS

Oil, peanut	2 tsp	10 ml
Scallion, white parts only, sliced thin	2	2
Gingerroot, peeled, sliced very thin, then cut julienne	2 slices	2 slices

Heat wok or skillet over high heat. When very hot, add the oil and distribute evenly over the surface of the pan. When oil is just below the smoking point, add the scallions and stir-fry for 10–15 seconds. Add the ginger and stir-fry for another 10 seconds.

Bean sprouts, trimmed	2–3 oz	60–90 g
Scallion, green parts, sliced thin	2	2
Salt	as needed	as needed
Oyster or soy sauce	as needed	as needed

Add the bean sprouts and stir-fry until they are hot but still crisp. Add the green sections of the scallion and a pinch of salt and continue to stir-fry for another 10–15 seconds. Place contents of pan on a heated serving plate and sprinkle lightly with oyster or soy sauce.

Bean Sprouts with Meat Sauce

YIELD: 10-12 SERVINGS

MEAT SAUCE

Sesame oil	1 tbsp	15 ml
Beef, ground twice	1 lb	450 g
Garlic, minced	2 tbsp	25 g

Heat a heavy-bottomed saucepan over medium to high heat. Add the sesame oil. When oil is just below the smoking point, add the ground meat and sauté, stirring frequently. When the meat has browned, add the garlic and sauté for another minute.

Stock, beef	12 oz	350 ml
Soy sauce	8 oz	235 ml
Sugar	1 tbsp or to taste	15 g or to taste
Salt	1 tsp or to taste	5 g or to taste

Add ingredients and bring to a boil. Lower heat and simmer uncovered, stirring occasionally, for 15–20 minutes. Let cool, then refrigerate overnight. Remove any congealed fat before using.

Bean sprouts	2 lb	900 g
Water, rapidly boiling	as needed	as needed

Trim ends of sprouts, then place in rapidly boiling water. Cook for 1–2 minutes or until done as desired. Drain sprouts and place them immediately in iced water. When cooled, drain and reserve until needed.

TO PREPARE AN INDIVIDUAL SERVING

Reserved sauce	as needed	as needed
Sesame oil	1 tsp	5 ml
Sugar	pinch	pinch
Salt	pinch	pinch
Cooked bean sprouts	2–3 oz per serving	60–90 g per serving

Place a portion of the reserved sauce, sesame oil, and a pinch each of sugar and salt per serving in a sauté pan and bring to a boil over high heat. Add the bean sprouts as needed and heat through, stirring constantly. This sauce can be made in quantity and stored in the refrigerator for use with other steamed or boiled vegetables.

Carrot, Coconut, and Radish Salad

YIELD: 10-12 SERVINGS

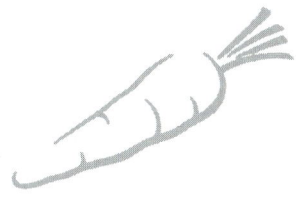

Carrots, peeled and trimmed	12 oz	340 g	Using the shredder blade on a food processor, shred these ingredients one at a time. Place them separately in clean kitchen towels, gather the corners together, and wring gently to remove excess liquid.
Coconut, fresh	12 oz	340 g	
Radish, red	12 oz	340 g	
Coriander leaves, fresh, chopped	3 oz	85 g	Place drained vegetables in a mixing bowl. Add ingredients and mix thoroughly. Reserve.
Salt	1 tsp or to taste	5 g or to taste	
Cayenne pepper	3/4 tsp or to taste	3 g or to taste	
Clarified butter	4 oz	120 ml	Heat butter over medium high heat in a small pan. When the oil is hot, but below the smoking point, add the seeds and fry, stirring, until they begin to darken slightly. Remove from heat, let cool, then add to the reserved vegetables. Stir well to distribute evenly. Chill well before serving.
Cumin seeds	1 tsp	2 g	
Celery seeds	1 tsp	2 g	
Fennel seeds	1 tsp	2 g	

Chickpeas in Ginger and Garlic Sauce

YIELD: 10 SERVINGS

Chickpeas, dried	1 lb	450 g	*Soak chickpeas for at least 4 hours. Drain and rinse in cold water. Place in a pot with enough water to cover by 3–4 inches (8–10 cm) and bring to a boil. Let boil for several minutes, then lower heat and simmer, partially covered, for 2–2 1/2 hours or until the chickpeas are tender. Cooking time will vary depending on the dehydration of the beans. When done, drain and reserve.*
Clarified butter or vegetable oil	2 oz	60 ml	*Heat oil over medium heat in a heavy-bottomed skillet. Add onions, lower heat, and cook, stirring occasionally, until the onions are lightly browned. Add the gingerroot and garlic and cook for another 2 minutes.*
Onion, small dice	1 lb	450 g	
Gingerroot, peeled and chopped fine	2 tbsp	25 g	
Garlic, chopped fine	1 tbsp	15 g	
Coriander, ground	2 tsp	4 g	*Add the spices to the onion mixture, stir well, and cook briefly until the spices become aromatic. Add the chopped tomatoes and vegetable stock and bring to a boil. Lower heat and simmer until the sauce has thickened slightly. Adjust salt and other spices to taste.*
Cardamom, ground	1 tsp	2 g	
Pepper, black	1 tsp	2 g	
Red pepper flakes	1/2 tsp	2 g	
Tomatoes, peeled and chopped	1 lb	450 g	
Vegetable stock	8 oz	240 ml	
Salt	to taste	to taste	
Reserved chickpeas			*Add the cooked chickpeas and bring the liquids to a boil. Lower heat and simmer, stirring occasionally, for 10–12 minutes. When serving, garnish portions with a squeeze of fresh lemon juice. Serve thinly sliced onions and jalapeño peppers on the side.*
Lemon juice, fresh squeezed	as needed	as needed	
Onion, sliced thin	as needed	as needed	
Jalapeño peppers, seeded, ribs removed and sliced thin	as needed	as needed	

Fresh Corn Fritters

YIELD: 10-12 SERVINGS

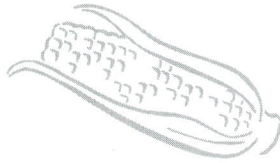

Corn on the cob	eight ears, yield approximately 2 lb	eight ears, yield approximately 900 g
Garlic	1 tbsp	15 g
Eggs, beaten	3 large	3 large
Flour	2–4 oz	60–115 g
Salt	2 tsp	10 g
Pepper, white	1 tsp	2 g
Oil, vegetable	as needed	as needed

Strip the kernels from the cobs and place them in a mixing bowl. Extract any remaining juices by running the back of the knife blade firmly down the length of the cobs. Add the remaining ingredients and knead, adding flour as needed, to make a stiff dough. The amount of flour will vary.

Make tablespoon-sized patties that resemble small irregular pancakes. Deep-fry at 350°F (175°C) until golden brown on both sides. Serve as an accompaniment with meat or poultry dishes, or as an appetizer. If served as an appetizer, accompany with a side dish of hot chili sauce for dipping.

See color insert for photograph of recipe

Cucumber Salad

Cucumber	2 lb	900 g
Onions, small size	1/2 lb	220 g

Peel cucumbers leaving thin strips of the green skin. If cucumbers are waxed, remove all of the peel. Slice each cucumber in half lengthwise. Using a small scoop or teaspoon, remove the seeds. Cut the cucumber into paper-thin slices. Peel onions, then cut in half, root to stem. Cut the onion halves into paper-thin slices.

Oil, vegetable	3 oz	90 ml
Lemon juice	2 oz	60 ml
Soy sauce, light	2 oz	60 ml
Scallions, white and tender green parts sliced very thin	3	3
Sugar	to taste	to taste
White pepper	to taste	to taste
Salt	to taste	to taste

Combine ingredients and mix until the sugar dissolves. Pour over the cucumber and onion slices and toss to distribute the dressing evenly. Cover and refrigerate for at least 1 hour before serving.

Cucumber in Hot Sauce

YIELD: 2-3 SERVINGS

Cucumber, seeded and peeled; sliced 1/8 in. (0.5 cm) thick	10 oz	280 g
Oil, peanut	2 tsp	10 ml
Oil, sesame	1 tsp	5 ml
Chinese brown peppercorns, cracked	1/2 tsp	1 g
Chili pepper, fresh, red, chopped fine	1 tsp or to taste	4 g or to taste
Scallion, white part, cut into fine julienne	2	2
Reserved cucumber	2 thin slices	2 thin slices
Gingerroot, peeled and minced		
Scallion, green part, cut into fine julienne	2	2
Garlic, minced	1/2 tsp or to taste	2–3 g or to taste
Soy sauce, light	2 oz	60 ml
Vinegar, white	1 oz	30 ml
Water	1 oz	30 ml
Cornstarch	1 tsp	4 g

Place cucumber in a bowl and lightly sprinkle with salt. Let rest under a weighted plate for 10–15 minutes. Rinse with cold water and pat dry.

Heat wok over medium heat. Add the oils and heat until moderately hot. Add the Chinese peppercorns and stir-fry briefly. Add the chili and scallion and stir-fry for another 10–15 seconds.

Add ingredients and stir-fry until the cucumber is heated through but still crisp.

Combine ingredients. Stir until the cornstarch has completely dissolved, then add to the pan. Bring liquids to a boil and cook briefly until slightly thickened.

Cucumber and Red Pepper Salad

YIELD: 10 SERVINGS

Cucumbers	2 lb	900 g	*Peel the cucumbers, leaving thin strips of green skin. If cucumbers are waxed, remove all of the skin. Cut cucumbers in half lengthwise. Using a small scoop or teaspoon, remove and discard the seeds. Slice into half moon shaped pieces 1/8 in. (0.5 cm) thick. To remove excess moisture from the cucumber pieces, lightly salt them, then toss to distribute the salt evenly. Put the cucumber pieces in a colander placed over a plate or shallow bowl. Place a heavy plate or other weight on top. Let stand for 1–2 hours.*
Salt	2 tsp	10 g	
Pepper, red bell	1 medium	1 medium	*Remove the core, seeds, and membranes. Julienne fine. When cucumber has drained, combine with the pepper and mix well.*
Vinegar, white distilled	4 oz	120 ml	*Combine ingredients and stir until the sugar is completely dissolved. Pour over the vegetables and toss to distribute the dressing evenly. Cover and refrigerate overnight before serving.*
Water	2 oz	60 ml	
Sesame oil	2 tbsp	30 ml	
Sugar	2 tbsp or to taste	30 g or to taste	

Eggplant with Minced Pork in Lime Sauce

YIELD: 10 SERVINGS

Eggplants, Oriental variety, 6–8 in. (15–20 cm) long	10 approximately 4 oz each	10 approximately 115 g each	*Wash eggplants. Do not trim cap. Prick each several times with the sharp tines of a fork or cut several small slits in each with a paring knife. Place the eggplant in a 350°F (180°C) oven for 15–20 minutes until soft. When cool enough to handle, remove skins and place in a shallow glass or stainless steel pan. Cover and refrigerate until needed.*
Oil, vegetable	2 tbsp	30 ml	*Heat the oil in a skillet over medium to high heat. Stir-fry the onion and garlic for 10–15 seconds. Add the pork, pepper, and salt. Stir-fry until the pork is lightly browned and cooked through. Add the scallion and stir-fry for another 10–15 seconds. Remove from heat, let cool, and reserve in the refrigerator.*
Onion, chopped fine	4 oz	115 g	
Garlic, minced	2 tsp or to taste	10 g or to taste	
Pork, ground fine	12 oz	340 g	
Pepper, black	1 tsp or to taste	2 g or to taste	
Salt	1 tsp	5 g	
Scallions, white and green parts sliced thin	2	2	

TO SERVE

Reserved eggplants	as needed (one per serving)	as needed (one per serving)	*Distribute pork mixture evenly over the eggplants. Garnish with a liberal sprinkling of fish sauce flavored with lime juice. Serve at room temperature.*
Fish sauce with lime juice (see recipe)	as needed	as needed	

Fried Sweet Potatoes

YIELD: 10 SERVINGS

Sweet potatoes	4 lb	1.8 kg	*Peel, then slice the potatoes on the diagonal to pro-duce oval-shaped slices 1/4 in. (0.75 cm) thick. Place potatoes into a pot with rapidly boiling water. Cook until the potatoes are cooked through but still firm. Place in iced water and reserve until needed.*
Water, boiling	as needed	as needed	

TO PREPARE AN INDIVIDUAL SERVING

Cooked potato	6 oz per serving	170 g per serving	*Drain cooked potatoes, and dredge individual slices in flour, then in beaten egg. Heat oil to a depth of 1/2 in. (1.5 cm) in a skillet over medium to high heat. Fry potatoes until browned, turning once. Serve with a small bowl of Chojang on the side. White boiling potatoes may also be prepared in the same manner.*
Flour	as needed	as needed	
Egg, beaten	as needed	as needed	
Oil, vegetable	as needed	as needed	
Chojang dipping sauce (see recipe)	as needed	as needed	

Green Beans with Soy Sauce/Sesame Dressing

YIELD: 10 SERVINGS

Ingredient	US	Metric
Green beans	2 lb	900 g
Water, lightly salted	as needed	as needed
Dashi (see recipe)	as needed	as needed

Wash, trim ends, then cut beans into 1 1/2-in. (4-cm) lengths. Place beans in rapidly boiling water to cover. Cook for 3–5 minutes or until the beans are cooked through but still quite crisp. When done, plunge beans immediately into iced water. When cooled, drain and place in a deep bowl with enough Dashi (stock) to cover. Reserve in refrigerator for at least 1 hour before using.

Ingredient	US	Metric
Sesame seeds	5 tbsp	30 g
Soy sauce, dark	3 oz	90 ml
Mirin (rice wine)	2 oz	60 ml
Dashi	2 oz	60 ml
Reserved green beans		

Toast the sesame seeds in a heavy-bottomed skillet over medium heat for 1–2 minutes. Place 4 tablespoons (24 g) of the toasted seeds in a blender or spice grinder and pulverize; reserving the remaining tablespoon (6 g) of seeds for garnish. Combine the ground seeds with the soy sauce, Mirin, and Dashi. Blend ingredients thoroughly. Drain the green beans, reserving the Dashi for other uses. Pour the dressing over the beans and toss to distribute evenly. Cover and refrigerate until needed. When serving, place the beans in the center of a salad plate or small bowl and sprinkle some of the whole, toasted sesame seeds on top.

Green Beans
and Water Chestnuts

YIELD: 10-12 SERVINGS

Ingredient	US	Metric	Instructions
Green beans, trimmed, cut into 1-in. lengths	2 lb	900 g	Place beans in a small amount of boiling water. Cover pot and cook until barely tender. Remove and place in iced water. When chilled, drain and reserve.
Mustard seeds, black	1 tbsp	6 g	In a large, heavy-bottomed frying pan, toast the mustard seeds over medium heat until they begin to pop. Add the clarified butter and mix.
Clarified butter	3 oz	90 ml	
Gingerroot, peeled and minced	1 tbsp	12 g	Add ingredients to the pan.
Coriander, ground	2 tsp	4 g	
Salt	1 tsp or to taste	5 g or to taste	
Cayenne pepper	1/2 tsp or to taste	1 g or to taste	
Reserved beans			Add the beans and chestnuts and heat through, stirring constantly.
Water chestnuts, canned, sliced	8 oz	230 g	
Lime juice, fresh squeezed	3 oz	90 ml	Garnish with fresh lime juice and a sprinkling of coarsely chopped fresh herbs.
Fresh green herbs: parsley, basil, mint, cilantro	as needed	as needed	

Kidney Beans and Tomato Curry

YIELD: 10-12 SERVINGS

Red kidney beans	2 lb	900 g
Water	as needed	as needed

Soak the beans for 10–12 hours. Change the water once. Wash well and remove debris, if any. Place in a pot large enough to hold the beans plus 2–3 in. (5–8 cm) of water above the level of the beans. Bring to a boil, lower heat, and simmer until the beans are tender, about 45 minutes. Drain and reserve.

Oil, vegetable	3 oz	90 ml
Tomatoes, chopped fine	2 lb	900 g
Onion, chopped	1 lb	450 g
Garlic, minced	2 tbsp	30 g
Gingerroot, peeled and minced	2 tbsp	30 g
Chili pepper, fresh, green, hot, minced	2 tbsp or to taste	30 g or to taste
Garam masala (see recipe)	1 tbsp	8 g
Coriander, ground	1 tbsp	6 g
Cumin seeds	2 tsp	4 g
Turmeric, ground	2 tsp	4 g
Cayenne pepper	1 tsp or to taste	2 g or to taste
Mustard seeds	1 tsp	2 g
Nigella seeds	1 tsp	2 g

Heat oil in a heavy-bottomed skillet over medium heat and sauté the onions until they are lightly browned. Add the remaining ingredients, lower heat, and sauté, stirring occasionally, for 5 minutes.

Water or vegetable stock	8 oz or as needed	240 ml or as needed
Yogurt	4 oz	115 g
Salt	to taste	to taste
Cilantro leaves, fresh, chopped	as needed	as needed

Add the water or vegetable stock, yogurt, and salt, mix well and simmer for 5 minutes. Adjust seasonings if necessary. Add the kidney beans and mix gently, taking care not to mash the beans. The consistency should be fairly thick. Adjust with additional stock if needed. Return contents of pan to a simmer and cook for another 5 minutes to heat through. Garnish with fresh, chopped cilantro leaves when serving. Serve with boiled white rice.

Long Beans, Stir-Fried

Y I E L D :   1 0   S E R V I N G S

Long beans (asparagus bean)	2 lb	900 g	*Wash beans, trim stem ends, and cut on the diagonal into 2-in. (5-cm) lengths. Blanch in boiling water, then place immediately in iced water. When cool, drain and reserve.*
Oil, peanut	2 tsp	10 ml	*Heat a wok or small skillet over high heat. Add the oil and distribute it over the surface of the pan. Add these ingredients and stir-fry briefly, until they become aromatic.*
Garlic, minced	1/2 tsp	3 g	
Gingerroot, minced	1/2 tsp	3 g	
Blanched long beans	3 oz per serving	90 g per serving	*Add the long beans and stir-fry for 1–2 minutes. Add the sesame oil and salt. Toss to mix, then place on a warmed serving plate.*
Sesame oil	dash	dash	
Salt	pinch	pinch	

Okra with Yogurt, Cumin, and Coriander

YIELD: 10 SERVINGS

Yogurt, plain	1 1/2 lb	680 g

Place yogurt in a colander lined with a square, double layer of cheesecloth. Tie the corners of the cheesecloth together to create a bag. Slip a wooden spoon handle or dowel through the knot and suspend the bag over a bowl or pot and refrigerate. Allow several hours for the yogurt to drain and thicken. Reserve.

Okra	2 lb	900 g
Garam masala (see recipe)	as needed	as needed
Salt	to taste	to taste
Coriander, powdered	to taste	to taste
Cayenne pepper	to taste	to taste

Select small, tender okra. Trim ends and cut each into 1/4-in. (0.75 cm) slices. Place okra into a fryer basket and deep-fry until lightly browned and slightly crisp. Drain on absorbent towels and sprinkle lightly with salt, coriander, and very small amount of cayenne pepper.

Reserved yogurt		
Cumin seeds, toasted and crushed	1 tbsp	6 g
Coriander leaves, fresh, coarsely chopped	2 sprigs	2 sprigs

Mix ingredients thoroughly. Add the yogurt mixture to the fried okra and mix gently to coat evenly. Chill well before serving.

Deep-Fried Potatoes and Carrots

YIELD 10-12 SERVINGS

Potatoes, Idaho	1 1/2 lb	680 g
Carrots	1 lb	450 g

Peel and wash the vegetables, then cut into fine, uniform julienne. Place potatoes and carrots into separate bowls of ice water for 45 minutes. Drain and spread on racks to air dry.

Clarified butter	as needed	as needed
Salt	to taste	to taste
Cayenne pepper	to taste	to taste
Lemon juice, fresh squeezed	to taste	to taste

When vegetables are thoroughly dry, deep-fry, separately, in clarified butter. When crisp, drain on towels and season to taste with salt, cayenne pepper, and fresh lemon juice. May be served combined as an appetizer or as a side dish for meat, poultry, or fish entrees.

Potatoes and Cauliflower in Yogurt Sauce

YIELD: 10-12 SERVINGS

Potatoes, Idaho	2 lb	900 g	*Peel, wash, and slice the potatoes into 1/4-in. (0.75-cm) round slices. Blanch until barely cooked. Drain and reserve.*
Cauliflower	2 lb	900 g	*Cut cauliflower into small florets and blanch until barely cooked. Drain and reserve.*
SAUCE			
Yogurt	1 lb	450 g	*Combine ingredients thoroughly and reserve.*
Salt	to taste	to taste	
Cumin seeds	1 tbsp	6 g	
Pepper, ground white	2 tsp	4 g	
Turmeric	1 tsp	2 g	
Cayenne pepper	to taste	to taste	
TO PREPARE AN INDIVIDUAL SERVING			
Oil or clarified butter	1 oz	30 ml	*Heat oil over medium to high heat. Fry the vegetables until lightly browned. Drain on a towel to remove excess oil. Place in a mixing bowl then immediately add enough sauce to coat thoroughly. If preparing for buffet service, vegetables may be fried in advance and held in a warm oven. Dress with yogurt sauce just before serving. Garnish with parsley or watercress sprigs.*
Blanched potatoes and blanched cauliflower	5–6 ounces mixed	140–170 g mixed	
Yogurt sauce at room temperature	as needed	as needed	
Parsley or watercress sprigs	as needed	as needed	

Potatoes in Yogurt Sauce

YIELD: 10-12 SERVINGS

Potatoes, small, red bliss	4 lb	1.8 kg	*Peel and wash the potatoes. Using the sharp tines of a fork, pierce each potato several times and place in cold water. Drain potatoes, pat dry, then sauté over medium-high heat, until they are lightly browned on all sides. Remove from pan and place in a baking pan in a single layer.*
Oil, vegetable or clarified butter	4 oz	120 ml	
Oil, vegetable or clarified butter	as needed	as needed	*Using the same sauté pan, lower heat and add a little oil, if necessary. Sauté the onions until they are browned.*
Onion, small diced	1 1/2 lb	680 g	
Gingerroot, minced	2 tbsp	24 g	*Add ingredients to the onions and, stirring, sauté for about a mimute.*
Coriander, ground	2 tbsp	14 g	
Cumin, ground	1 tbsp	7 g	
Turmeric	2 tsp	4 g	
Red pepper flakes	1 tsp or to taste	2 g or to taste	
Mughal garam masala (see recipe)	2 tsp to taste	4 g or to taste	
Tomato, peeled and chopped	2 lb	900 g	*Add ingredients to the pan and gradually bring to a boil. Stir to blend ingredients thoroughly. Adjust seasonings if necessary. Pour mixture over potatoes. Cover pan and place in a 350°F (175°C) oven for 30 minutes or until the potatoes are tender. Add heavy cream to adjust consistency of sauce if it is too thick, and return to oven, uncovered, for another 5 minutes.*
Yogurt	12 oz	340 g	
Salt	2 tsp or to taste	10 g or to taste	
Heavy cream	as needed	as needed	

Potato Cakes with Mint

YIELD: 10-12 SERVINGS

Potatoes, Idaho or Russet	4 lb	1.8 kg	*Place potatoes in boiling water with the skins on. When water returns to the boil, lower heat to medium and cook until the potatoes are tender. Drain. When potatoes are cool enough to handle, peel and discard the skins.*
Clarified butter	3 oz	90 ml	*Place the peeled potatoes in the bowl of an electric mixer and combine with ingredients at low speed. Add hot milk gradually until a smooth, thick consistency has been reached. Taste and adjust seasonings, if necessary, to obtain a distinct lemony, slightly salty flavor. Shape into oval or round cakes and serve warm or at room temperature. Garnish each cake with fresh mint leaves.*
Lemon juice, fresh squeezed	3 oz or to taste	90 ml or to taste	
Salt	1 1/2 tsp or to taste	8 g or to taste	
Mint leaves, fresh, chopped fine	3 tbsp	10 g	
Scallion, white and tender green sections, chopped fine	3 tbsp	10 g	
Milk, hot	as needed	as needed	
Mint leaves, whole	as needed	as needed	

Potatoes with Chili and Ginger

YIELD: 10-12 SERVINGS

Potatoes, all-purpose	4 lb	1.8 kg

Boil the potatoes with the skins on. When they are barely fork tender place them in iced water and let cool. When cooled through, peel and cut into 1-in. (2.5-cm) cubes. Reserve.

Oil, vegetable, clarified butter or a 50/50 mixture of oil and clarified butter	4 oz	120 ml
Mustard seeds, black	1 tbsp	6 g
Split peas, yellow	1tbsp	6 g

Heat oil in a large, heavy-bottomed pan over medium-high heat. Add the mustard seeds and cook, stirring, for a minute or so until they begin to turn gray. Add the split peas and continue to cook, stirring, until they brown lightly.

Gingerroot, coarsely chopped	4 tbsp	50 g
Chilies, jalapeño, seeded and sliced thin	2–3 or to taste	2–3 or to taste
Coriander, ground	2 tbsp	15 g
Turmeric	2 tsp	4 g
Paprika	2 tsp	4 g

Lower heat, add the gingerroot and chilies, and cook, stirring, until the chilies begin to brown lightly. Add the remaining spices and cook, stirring, for 4–5 minutes until they are throoughly blended and become very aromatic.

Reserved potatoes		
Onions, chopped	2 lb	900 g
Vegetable stock or water	12 oz	350 ml
Salt	2 tsp or to taste	10 g or to taste

Add the potatoes and onions. Mix gently to coat the potatoes with the spice mixture and sauté over low to medium heat for 5–6 minutes. Add the stock and bring to a boil. Lower heat immediately and simmer for about 5 minutes or until the potatoes are very tender. Adjust salt if necessary.

Cilantro leaves, fresh, chopped	as needed	as needed
Lemon juice, fresh squeezed	as needed	as needed
Red pepper flakes	optional	optional

When serving, garnish each portion with a small amount of chopped cilantro and a squeeze of fresh lemon juice. Red pepper flakes may be served on the side.

Potatoes with Yogurt and Chilies

YIELD: 10-12 SERVINGS

Yogurt, plain	2 lb	900 g	*Place yogurt in a colander lined with a square, double layer of cheesecloth. Tie the corners of the cheesecloth together to create a bag. Slip a wooden spoon handle or dowel through the knot and suspend the bag over a bowl or pot and refrigerate. Allow several hours for the yogurt to drain and thicken.*
Potatoes, all-purpose	4 lb	1.8 kg	*Steam, boil, or bake potatoes, skins on, until just fork tender. Cool, peel, and cut into 1-in. (2.5-cm) cubes. Reserve.*
Clarified butter	4 tbsp	60 ml	*Heat clarified butter in a small sauté pan over medium high heat. When just below the smoking point, add the chilies and mustard seeds. Fry, stirring, until the mustard seeds begin to pop. Allow to cool, then add this mixture to the yogurt. Add the chopped coriander leaves and mix well. Add salt to taste.*
Chilies, jalapeño, minced, seeds and ribs discarded	3 or to taste	3 or to taste	
Mustard seeds, black	1 tbsp	6 g	
Reserved thickened yogurt			
Coriander leaves, fresh, chopped	2 oz	60 g	
Salt	to taste	to taste	
Reserved potatoes			*Pour the yogurt mixture over the potatoes and mix gently to coat them evenly. Serve cold or at room temperature. Garnish individual servings with a dash of paprika.*
Paprika	as needed	as needed	

Roasted Eggplant Curry

Ingredient	US	Metric	Method
Eggplant, washed	4 lb	1.8 kg	*Prick each eggplant 4–5 times with a fork. Place on a baking sheet and bake at 400°F (200°C) until they become very soft and the skins begin to char. When cool enough to handle, remove the pulp, chop coarsely, and place in a colander. Cover with a heavy dinner plate and weight down to extract the juices. Reserve.*
Oil, vegetable	2 oz	60 ml	*Heat the oil in a heavy skillet over low to medium heat and sauté ingredients, stirring constantly.*
Garlic, sliced thin	4 medium cloves	4 medium cloves	
Gingerroot, peeled and sliced thin	2-in. piece	5-cm piece	
Cumin seeds	2 tsp	4 g	
Onions, chopped fine	1 lb	450 g	*Add ingredients and cook for another 5 minutes.*
Tomato, chopped fine	1 lb	450 g	
Chili pepper, green, hot, minced	1 tbsp or to taste	6 g or to taste	
Coriander, ground	1 tbsp	7 g	*Add seasonings and mix well. Adjust amounts to taste. Add the reserved eggplant and combine thoroughly. Partially cover the pan and simmer mixture for 5–6 minutes. When done, remove from heat and add lemon juice to taste. When serving, garnish portions with chopped fresh cilantro or mint leaves. May be served warm or at room temperature.*
Garam masala (see recipe)	2 tsp	4 g	
Cayenne pepper	1/2 tsp or to taste	1 g or to taste	
Salt	to taste	to taste	
Lemon juice, fresh squeezed	to taste	to taste	
Cilantro leaves or mint leaves, fresh, chopped	as needed	as needed	

Roasted Tomato Onion Relish

YIELD: VARIABLE

Onion, sweet, Spanish	3 lb	1.4 kg
Salt	as needed	as needed

Peel onions and slice in half from the stem to the root end. Trim the ends, then cut each half into thin, half-moon slices. Sprinkle lightly with salt. Place onion slices in a colander with a weighted plate on top for 1 hour to express some of the juices. Rinse onions under running cold water. Drain, then place in a clean towel and squeeze gently to eliminate excess liquid. Reserve.

Tomatoes, medium sized, red, fully ripe	6 lb	2.7 kg
Reserved onions		
Salt	to taste	to taste

Wash and lightly oil the tomatoes. Using a small baking pan, place them in a 500°F (260°C) oven for 10–15 minutes or until the tomatoes are cooked through. When sufficiently cooked, the tomato skins will have cracked and become slightly charred. Remove tomatoes from oven and allow to cool until they are just cool enough to handle comfortably. Peel the skins, then place tomatoes in a mixing bowl and mash to a lumpy consistency. Add the reserved onions, mix thoroughly. Add salt to taste. Serve chilled or at room temperature.

Shredded Radish with Chili

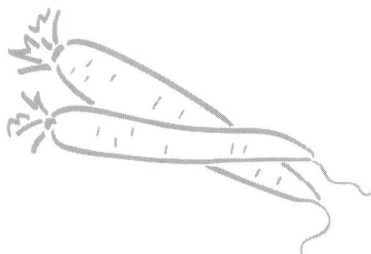

Daikon radish	1 1/2 lb	680 g	*Peel, then finely shred the daikon. Place in a mixing bowl and sprinkle generously with salt. Let sit for 10 minutes. Knead the daikon until it becomes soft. Wash off the salt under running cold water and place the daikon in a colander to drain.*
Salt	as needed	as needed	
Chili peppers, red, fresh, New Mexican or Anaheim for a milder taste	3–4 or to taste	3–4 or to taste	*Slice the chilies in half lengthwise and remove the seeds and membranes. Cut the halves into long, very thin, shoestring strips. Place in a mixing bowl along with the drained daikon.*

DRESSING

Vinegar, Japanese rice	6 oz	180 ml	*Combine ingredients and stir until the sugar is completely dissolved. Taste and adjust seasonings if necessary. Pour over the daikon and chilies. Toss to distribute the dressing evenly, then cover and refrigerate for 1 hour before serving.*
Sesame oil	1 oz	30 ml	
Sugar	2 tsp	10 g	
Salt (optional)	1/2 tsp	3 g	

Spicy Cucumber Salad

YIELD: 10-12 SERVINGS

Cucumber	2 lb	900 g
Salt	as needed	as needed

Peel cucumbers and slice in half lengthwise. Remove the seeds with a small scoop or teaspoon. Cut into thin, half-moon slices and sprinkle with salt. Let sit for 15 minutes to express some of the liquid, then rinse and pat dry. Reserve.

Scallions, white and green parts, chopped fine	5–6, depending on size	5–6, depending on size

Prepare and reserve.

Oil, sesame	3 tbsp	45 ml
Soy sauce, light	4 tbsp	60 ml
Sugar	1 tbsp	15 g
Chili powder	1 tsp or to taste	2 g or to tast
Sesame seeds, toasted and ground	as needed	as needed

Heat a wok or skillet over medium to high heat. Add the sesame oil. When hot, stir-fry the cucumbers and scallions until slightly soft. Mix the soy sauce, chili powder, and sugar. Stir to dissolve the sugar completely, then add this mixture to the pan. Stir to coat the cucumbers well, then remove from heat. May be served warm or cold. Garnish with ground, toasted sesame seeds.

Spicy Vegetable Curry

YIELD: 10-12 SERVINGS

Potatoes, boiling, cut into 1-in. (2.5-cm) cubes	2 lb	900 g
Cauliflower, florets	12 oz	340 g
Oil, vegetable	3 oz	90 ml
Onion, sliced thin	1 lb	450 g
Garlic, minced	1 tbsp	15 g
Gingerroot, peeled and minced	1 tbsp	12 g
Cumin seeds	2 tsp	4 g
Chili peppers, fresh, red, hot, seeds and ribs removed, then minced	2 tbsp or to taste	12 g or to taste
Coriander seeds	1 tbsp	7 g
Turmeric, ground	2 tsp	4 g
Garam masala (see recipe)	2 tsp	4 g
Water or vegetable stock	8 oz or as needed	240 ml or as needed
Salt	to taste	to taste
Reserved vegetables		
Peas, fresh or frozen	12 oz	340 g
Lemon juice, fresh squeezed	as needed	as needed
Cumin seeds	a sprinkling	a sprinkling

Blanch the potatoes in boiling water for 2–3 minutes or until they are barely fork tender. Remove from water and plunge immediately into iced water. Repeat this process with the cauliflower. Drain and reserve.

Heat the oil in a large, heavy skillet over low heat. Add the onions and sauté until they begin to brown. Add the remaining ingredients and sauté, stirring, for another 2–3 minutes.

Add the chili peppers, coriander, turmeric, and garam masala, and mix well to incorporate thoroughly. Continue to cook, stirring for another minute. Add the water or vegetable stock and bring to a boil. Lower heat and simmer for 10 minutes. Add salt to taste and adjust seasonings if necessary.

Add the blanched vegetables and peas to the pan and combine gently with the onion/spice mixture. Cover and simmer over very low heat for 5–6 minutes. Add a splash of lemon juice when serving. Garnish with powdered, roasted cumin seeds. To prepare this garnish, place seeds in a dry, heavy skillet over medium to high heat. Shake pan or stir seeds over heat until they have toasted to a deep brown color. Grind them to powder using a spice grinder, coffee mill, or mortar and pestle. If made in advance, store this garnish in a tightly sealed jar.

Deep-Fried Tofu Served with Dashi Sauce

YIELD: 10-12 SERVINGS

| Tofu | 2 lb | 900 g | *Cut tofu into even squares and place in a colander for 30 minutes to drain.* |

DASHI SAUCE

Dashi (see recipe)	24 oz	710 ml	*In a small saucepan, heat the dashi over medium heat until it just reaches the boiling point. Lower heat, then add the remaining ingredients and simmer for 1 minute. Remove from heat and reserve.*
Soy sauce, dark	6 oz	180 ml	
Sake	6 oz	180 ml	
Sugar	4 tsp	20 g	

Egg, beaten	as needed	as needed	*Dip the tofu squares into the beaten egg, then into the cornstarch. Shake pieces to remove excess cornstarch. Deep-fry at 350°F (175°C), turning once, until all sides are lightly browned. Drain on wire rack. To serve an individual portion, place several pieces (3 oz/85 g) of the tofu in a shallow bowl and pour 3–4 oz (90–120 ml) of the warmed Dashi broth on top. Garnish with scallion and several gingerroot slices.*
Cornstarch	as needed	as needed	
Oil, vegetable	to deep-fry	to deep-fry	
Scallion, white and tender green parts, thinly sliced	as needed	as needed	
Gingerroot, peeled and sliced paper thin	as needed	as needed	

Fresh Tomato Chutney

YIELD: VARIABLE

Cumin seeds	2 tbsp	12 g
Coriander seeds	2 tbsp	12 g

Place cumin and coriander seeds in a small heavy-bottomed fry pan over low heat. Toast the seeds, stirring, until lightly browned. Remove from heat and grind in a spice mill or with a mortar and pestle. Reserve.

Tomatoes, ripe, vine-ripened if available, seeded, peeled, and diced	6 lb	2.7 kg
Chilies, fresh, jalapeño, seeds and ribs removed, then minced	3–4 or to taste	3–4 or to taste
Gingerroot, peeled and minced	2 tbsp or to taste	24 g or to taste
Oil, toasted sesame	1 oz	30 ml
Currants, dried	1 oz	30 g
Lime juice, fresh squeezed	2 tbsp	30 ml
Salt	to taste	to taste
Reserved cumin and coriander seeds		

Combine ingredients and refrigerate for 1–2 hours.

Coriander leaves, fresh, chopped	1 oz	30 g

Before serving, add the coriander leaves to the tomato mixture. Serve chutney at room temperature.

Tomato Ginger Chutney

YIELD: VARIABLE

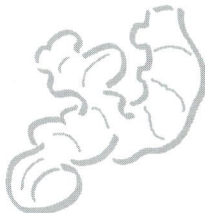

TOMATO PUREE

Tomatoes, ripe, cut into quarters	6 lb	2.7 kg
Onion, diced	1 lb	450 g
Garlic, peeled and chopped	1 tbsp	15 g

Place ingredients in a heavy-bottomed stainless steel saucepan and bring to a boil over medium heat. Lower heat and simmer until most of the liquid has evaporated and the tomatoes are soft. Stir frequently to prevent sticking. When done, puree, using a food mill. Discard the skins and seeds.

Tomato puree		
Sugar, granulated	10 oz	280 g
Vinegar, cider	5 oz	150 ml
Gingerroot, minced	1 tbsp or to taste	12 g or to taste
Salt	2 tsp or to taste	10 g or to taste
Clove, ground	1/2 tsp	1 g
Pepper, cayenne	1/4 tsp	0.5 g

Return the tomato puree to the pot and add ingredients. Mix well to thoroughly blend. Simmer over very low heat, stirring frequently, for 15 minutes. Taste and adjust seasonings if necessary. Continue to simmer for another 10–15 minutes or until the sauce has become very thick. Allow to cool, then place in covered glass jars and refrigerate until needed.

Zucchini with Sesame

YIELD: 10 SERVINGS

Zucchini	2 lb	900 g	Wash and trim the zucchini. Cut each lengthwise down the middle, then cut into 1/4-in. (0.75-cm) thick, half-moon slices. To remove excess liquid, sprinkle lightly with salt and place in a colander under a weighted plate. Let stand for at least 1 hour.
Salt	as needed	as needed	

TO PREPARE AN INDIVIDUAL SERVING

Reserved zucchini	3 oz per serving	90 g	When ready to prepare, rinse zucchini, as needed, under running water. Pat dry with a clean towel. Heat wok or heavy skillet over high heat. Add the oil and heat to just below the smoking point. Add the garlic and stir-fry until it begins to become aromatic, then add the zucchini. Stir-fry for 1–2 minutes or until the zucchini are cooked through, but still crisp.
Oil, peanut	2 tsp	10 ml	
Garlic, finely chopped	1/2 tsp	3 g	

Sesame seeds, toasted	1 tsp	2 g	Add ingredients and stir-fry to mix thoroughly and heat through. Serve as an accompaniment with grilled or roasted meats. May be served hot or at room temperature.
Scallions, sliced into thin circles, white and green parts	1 small	1 small	
Sesame oil	1/2 tsp	5 ml	
Salt	pinch	pinch	

See color insert for photograph of recipe

Bean Sprouts with Scallions

Bean sprouts	1 1/2 lb	680 g
Scallions, white and tender green parts, sliced into 1-in. (2.5-cm) pieces	10	10
Gingerroot, peeled and chopped fine	3 tbsp	30 g

Wash the bean sprouts and trim ends, if necessary. Place in boiling water for 20–30 seconds. Drain in a colander, then plunge them immediately into iced water. When cold, drain, pat dry with towels and reserve. Prepare the scallions and reserve. Prepare the gingerroot and reserve.

TO PREPARE AN INDIVIDUAL SERVING

Oil, peanut	2 tsp	10 ml
Gingerroot	1 tsp	4 g
Salt	pinch	pinch
Scallions	1	1
Bean sprouts	2–2 1/2 oz	60–70 g

In a wok or heavy skillet, heat the oil until it just reaches the smoking point. Add the gingerroot and salt. Stir-fry for 20–30 seconds, then add the scallions and stir-fry for another 30 seconds. Add the bean sprouts and continue to stir-fry for another minute or until they are heated through.

Black-Eyed Pea, Tomato, and Spinach Salad

YIELD: 10-12 SERVINGS

SALAD INGREDIENTS

Black-eyed peas, dried	1 1/2 lb	680 g
Water	as needed	as needed

Soak the peas for 10–12 hours. Change the water once. Wash well and remove debris, if any. Place in pot large enough to hold the peas plus 2–3 inches (5–8 cm) of water above the level of the peas. Bring to a boil, lower heat, and simmer until the peas are tender. Drain and reserve.

Spinach, fresh	2 lb	900 g

Wash spinach in several changes of cold water to remove any debris. Remove and discard any tough stems. Place spinach in a covered pan with no additional water. Cook over medium heat until wilted. Remove from heat, drain, then place in clean towel or a double layer of cheese cloth. Gently squeeze out excess liquid. Chop fine.

Tomato, peeled and chopped	8 oz	230 g
Onion, chopped fine	6 oz	170 g
Green chili, fresh, seeds and ribs removed, chopped fine	1–2 or to taste	1–2 or to taste

Combine ingredients with the black-eyed peas and spinach and mix gently so as not to mash the peas.

SALAD DRESSING

Oil, vegetable	4 oz	120 ml
Lemon juice, fresh	2 oz	60 ml
Coriander leaves, fresh, chopped	5–6 sprigs	5–6 sprigs
Mint leaves, fresh, chopped	2–3 sprigs	2–3 sprigs
Sugar	2 tsp or to taste	10 g or to taste
Salt	2 tsp or to taste	10 g or to taste

Mix ingredients until the sugar and salt are dissolved completely. Taste and adjust the seasonings if necessary. Pour over the salad ingredients and toss gently. Let stand, refrigerated, for an hour or two before serving.

Cold Marinated Cauliflower

YIELD: 10-12 SERVINGS

DRESSING

Vinegar, white distilled	6 oz	180 ml
Sesame oil	3 tbsp	45 ml
Sugar	2 tbsp or to taste	30 g or to taste
Salt	2 tsp or to taste	10 g or to taste
Pepper, white	2 tsp or to taste	4 g or to taste
Chili pepper, fresh, red, hot, seeds and ribs removed, then minced	2 tsp or to taste	4 g or to taste
Cauliflower	2 1/2 lb	1.1 kg
Water	8 oz	240 ml
Ginger, peeled and sliced	2 oz	60 g
Garlic cloves, whole	3–4	3–4
Reserved dressing		
Cooked cauliflower		

Combine ingredients and let sit for 30 minutes before using. Reserve.

Trim cauliflower, then separate into florets. Reserve.

Combine ingredients in a small soup pot and bring to a boil. Lower heat and simmer, uncovered, for 10–15 minutes. Add the cauliflower, cover pot, and raise the heat to high. Boil/steam for 2–3 minutes or until the cauliflower begins to soften. Do not allow the cauliflower to overcook. When done, drain, then plunge the cauliflower immediately into iced water and let cool. When cool, discard the garlic cloves and ginger slices. Place the cauliflower in a colander and drain well.

Combine the cooked cauliflower and the reserved dressing in a stainless steel mixing bowl. Toss to cover the florets evenly. Cover and refrigerate for at least 4 hours before serving.

Eggplant, Shrimp, and Pork Salad

YIELD: 10 SERVINGS

Eggplant, preferably long thin Japanese variety	1 1/2 lb	680 g

Wash the eggplant, then pierce each one in several places with the tines of a fork. Place on a sheet pan and roast at 350°F (175°C) for 15–20 minutes or until soft. Roasting time will vary depending on thickness of eggplant. When done, let cool a little, then peel and discard the skin. Cut the eggplant into bite-sized pieces and place in a mixing bowl.

Oil, vegetable	2 tbsp	30 ml
Pork, ground fine	6 oz	170 g

Heat the oil in a wok or skillet over high heat and stir-fry the pork until done, about 5–6 minutes. Add pork to the eggplant.

Dried shrimp	4 oz	110 g
Chili peppers, fresh green, chopped	2 tsp or to taste	4 g or to taste
Shallot or onion, sliced thin	4 oz	110 g

Place the shrimp in a strainer and immerse in very hot water for a few seconds or until they become soft. Drain well. Add the shrimp, chili peppers, shallot or onion to the eggplant.

Lime juice, fresh	4 oz	120 ml
Fish sauce	2 tsp or to taste	10 ml or to taste
Sugar	1/2 tsp or to taste	3 g or to taste

Combine the lime juice, fish sauce, and sugar. Mix until the sugar is dissolved. Taste dressing and adjust seasonings if necessary. Pour dressing on top and toss to coat all of the ingredients uniformly. Serve with a side dish of white rice.

Lentil Cakes

Lentils, yellow	1 lb	450 g	Wash lentils and remove any debris. Place the lentils in a bowl with enough water to cover to a depth of 2 inches (5cm). Soak overnight. Drain well, then place into the bowl of a food processor fitted with a steel blade. Process the lentils to a smooth puree.
Water	as needed	as needed	
Scallions, white and green parts, minced	6–8	6–8	Add ingredients to the processor bowl and, using the pulse action, blend thoroughly.
Cilantro leaves, fresh, chopped	3 tbsp	10 g	
Chili, fresh, red, seeds and ribs removed, minced	1 tbsp or to taste	6 g or to taste	
Garlic, minced	2 tsp	4 g	
Turmeric, ground	1 tsp or to taste	5 g or to taste	
Salt			
Oil, vegetable	for deep-frying	for deep-frying	Test a spoonful of the lentil mixture by deep-frying it until well browned. Adjust seasonings if necessary. Shape the remaining mixture into small, slightly flattened balls. Reserve refrigerated. Deep-fry as needed. May be served as an appetizer or as an accompaniment for meat, poultry, or fish entrees.

Fish and Seafood

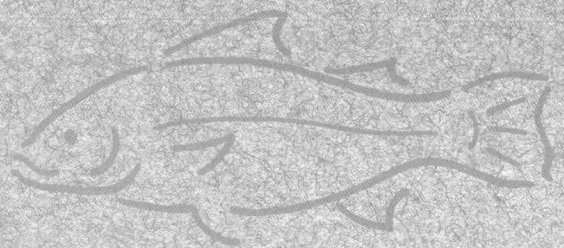

Sushi is probably the most well known culinary concept associated with the cuisine of Japan. Made familiar around the world by chefs who specialize in creating this dish, suchi combines the subtle flavor of lightly vinegared rice with the mild tastes and textures of the freshest possible raw fish and shellfish. With the notable exception of oysters, practically all creatures of the sea are used to create a wide variety of these formed, bite-sized morsels. Other flavorings that contribute to the complex flavors of sushi are *wasabi,* a fiery substance derived from the root of the *Wasabia japonica* plant, pickled giner, shredded vegetables, and soy sauce. Combined with the subtle flavors of the sea provided by the fish, these other ingredients contribute their individual flavors to the complex and distinctive taste of sushi.

The two most familiar types of sushi are maki-sushi and nigiri-sushi. Maki-sushi, a rolled sushi, is made by placing strips of seafood, crisp vegetables or pickles on a thin bed of vinegared rice which has itself been placed over a sheet of lightly tasted nori seaweed. The seaweed is then rolled, compressing the rice and other ingredients, and sliced into discs for serving. Wrappings other then seaweed, such as sweet omelet or bean curd, are also used, contributing variety not only to the flavor but to the texture as well. In nigiri-sushi, the other highly popular form of sushi, individual pieces are formed by hand and display an oblong slice of fresh fish which has been pressed on top of a similarly sized finger of rice. In principle, sushi is a simple preparation. In practice, however, sushi is quite exacting, requiring skills involving the correct preparation of the rice, the proper forming and assembly of the pieces, and the esthetic placement of the other ingredients. Most important, sushi requires an in-depth knowledge of how to buy and handle the very special cuts of fish and other seafood products necessary for its preparation.

Nigiri Sushi

THE FISH

Tuna,* snapper, salmon, or other suitable fish, fillet, skin removed	2 lb	1 kg

Choose only the freshest fish in season. Do not use frozen fish or other seafood products which have been frozen. Cut fillets into thin slices about 1/8–1/4 in. (0.5–0.75 cm) thick. If fillets are very thin, cut diagonally to make larger slices. Cover and refrigerate until needed.

Sushi rice, cooked	4 cups	4 cups

Prepare recipe on page 307.

Wasabi horseradish	1 tbsp	20 g

If the fresh root is available, scrape clean and remove knobs. Using a very fine grater, prepare just the amount needed. Wasabi can more commonly be found in dry, powdered form which must be mixed with water to produce a very thick paste. It also can be purchased in tubes, ready to use in paste form.

VINEGAR WATER

Water	3 parts	3 parts
Rice vinegar	1 part	1 part

Prepare 3–4 oz (90–120 g) total or as needed. Used to moisten fingers when assembling sushi.

TO ASSEMBLE

Sushi rice, cooked	as needed	as needed
Sliced fish	as needed	as needed
Wasabe horseradish	as needed	as needed

Nigiri sushi are hand-formed to order. Moisten fingers and hands lightly with the vinegar water to prevent the rice from sticking. Place approximately 1 tbsp of cooked rice across the first and middle joints of the fingers of one hand. Close the hand. Using the index and middle fingers of the other hand press the rice gently into a finger shaped form. Rice should be compressed just enough to hold together. Keep the formed rice in the palm of the hand, and, using the index finger of the same hand, smear a small dab of wasabi on a slice of fish cut just large enough to cover the rice. Press the fish, wasabi side down, to cover the rice and form a firm unit. Several different varieties of fish with different colors and textures can be used. Serve on a board or platter with small mounds of wasabi and pickled ginger slices. A small dish of soy sauce for dipping is served on the side.

* Shrimp that has been deveined and butterflied or squid may also be used. Cook these ingredients first.

Nori-Maki Sushi

UTENSILS
Bamboo mat

Maki-sushi (rolled sushi) can vary in diameter. The number of ingredients used for the center filling and the amount of rice will determine the diameter. Small mats, about 10 in. (25 cm) square made with thick or thin strips of bamboo are used to form and press the cylindrical rolls. Use mats with the thinner strips of bamboo when making smaller diameter sushi (Kappa-maki).

Asakusa Nori (laver)

A commercially grown seaweed available fresh, but more commonly found in thin dried sheets approximately 6 x 8 in. (17 x 20 cm). One side of the sheet has a glossy surface; the other a more textured appearance. Place the rice and other ingredients on the textured, nonglossy side.

TO ASSEMBLE
Bamboo mat
Nori, seaweed
Sushi rice (see recipe)
Filling ingredients*
Vinegar/water (see nigiri-sushi)

Briefly toast the shiny side of the Nori sheet over an open flame. The color will become a dark green. Place a sheet of nori over the mat and spread a 1/8-in. (0.5-cm) layer of rice over three-fourths of the mat, leaving the farthest quarter of the mat uncovered. Keeping your hands slightly moist with the rice/vinegar water, pat the rice in place lining up the edges of the rice evenly with the edges of the seaweed sheet. Place the filling ingredients in a line across the center of the rice (not the mat).

*Filling ingredients may include: raw fish such as tuna or any other firm-fleshed white fish, wasabi horseradish, bean curd, mushrooms, cucumber julienne, pickled vegetables, omelet pancake cut into thin strips, cooked shrimp. These ingredients may be used singly or in combination.

(Continued on facing page)

Keeping the filling ingredients firmly in place with your third, fourth, and fifth fingers, lift the edge of the mat with your thumbs and index fingers and bring that edge over until it reaches the opposite side of the sheet. Press the bamboo mat to compress the ingredients into a firm cylinder. The line of filling ingredients should be approximately in the center of the roll. Compress firmly before removing the mat.

TO SERVE

Cut roll in half, then cut each half into three or four cylindrical pieces. Serve with pickled, sliced ginger and soy sauce for dipping.

OTHER VARIATIONS

If making rolled sushi that is small in diameter, cut the seaweed in half lenghtwise, then fill and roll. For another variation, cover half sheets of the seaweed with the rice, then turn them over so that the rice is on the bottom. Smear a thin line of wasabi down the length of the seaweed, then add strips of whatever filling you choose. Roll up as per instructions. The seaweed will then be part of the core and the rice will be on the outside. A tight wrapping of plastic wrap may be placed over the bamboo mat to prevent the rice from sticking after being rolled. To facilitate slicing, moisten the knife first with the vinegar/water solution.

Fish with Ginger and Chili, Steamed on a Plate

YIELD: 1 SERVING

Mushrooms, Chinese dried, black	2 large	2 large
Water, boiling	as needed	as needed

Place mushrooms in a small bowl and add just enough boiling water to cover. Soak for 20–30 minutes, drain, then remove and discard the tough stems. Slice the mushroom caps into strips 1/4 in. (1 cm) wide. Reserve.

Whole fish (sea bass, porgy, croaker, perch) or any firm, white fish	1, 3/4–1 lb	1, 340–450 g
fillet	6–8 oz	170–225 g
Salt	as needed	as needed
Cornstarch	as needed	as needed

Clean and gut fish. Wash fish under running water to remove any remaining scales. If using whole fish, slash diagonally 2–3 times on each side. Dry fish with a towel, then rub salt lightly on both sides. Dredge in cornstarch and shake off any excess. Place the fish on an oval, individual serving, heat-proof plate.

Scallions, white parts cut into thin strips lengthwise (reserve the tender green parts)	2	2
Chili pepper, fresh, red (New Mexican for hot flavor or Anaheim for a milder taste); seeds and ribs removed, sliced into very thin strips lengthwise	1 or to taste	1 or to taste
Gingerroot, peeled and shredded	1 tbsp	12 g
Reserved mushrooms		

Place the white parts of the scallions into the cavity of the fish. Arrange the chili strips and the shredded ginger in an attractive pattern over the fish. Place the sliced mushrooms around the edges of the plate.

Rice wine	1 tbsp	15 ml
Soy sauce	1 tsp	5 ml
Oil, peanut	1 tsp	5 ml
Scallion, reserved tender green parts cut into 1/2-in. (1.5-cm) rings		
Cilantro leaves, fresh, chopped	1 sprig	1 sprig

Combine ingredients thoroughly and pour over fish. Steam fish until done as desired. Cooking time will vary depending on thickness of fish. When done, top the fish with raw scallion rings and chopped cilantro. When serving, place a liner under the plate used in the cooking process.

Shrimp Poached in Coconut Milk

INDIA

YIELD: 10 SERVINGS

COCONUT POACHING BROTH

Clarified butter	2 tbsp	30 ml
Onion, minced	2 lb	900 g
Gingerroot, peeled and minced	1 1/2 tbsp	20 g
Garlic, minced	1 tbsp	15 g
Chili pepper, fresh, red	2–4 or to taste	2–4 or to taste
Turmeric	2 tsp	5 g
Bay leaf	4–5	4–5
Coconut milk, thin	1 1/2 qt	1 1/2 L
Salt	to taste	to taste

TO PREPARE AN INDIVIDUAL SERVING

Reserved coconut broth	4–5 oz per serving	120–150 ml per serving
Shrimp, peeled and deveined	6 oz per serving	170 g per serving

Heat clarified butter over low to medium heat in a heavy-bottomed saucepan. Sauté the onion, gingerroot, and garlic until the onion becomes soft.

Slit the chilies and remove the seeds and ribs. Add the chilies, turmeric, and bay leaf and mix well, and cook, stirring, for another minute.

Add the coconut milk and bring to a slow simmer, stirring constantly. Add salt to taste, lower heat, and continue to simmer, uncovered, for 10–15 minutes. Adjust seasonings if necessary. Strain the broth and discard the solids. Let cool and reserve.

Place the coconut broth in a small saucepan or sauté pan over medium heat and reheat to just below the boiling point. Add the shrimp, lower heat, cover and cook for 3–4 minutes or until the shrimp turn pink and are cooked through. To serve, place the shrimp and the liquid in which they were poached in a small, heated bowl. Serve with lemon wedges on the side.

Clams with Chili and Basil

Chicken stock	4 oz	120 ml	*Combine these ingredients and reserve.*
Soy sauce, light	2 tsp	10 ml	
Chili paste, hot	1 tsp or to taste	5 g or to taste	
Oil	1 oz	30 ml	*Heat a wok or skillet over high heat. When hot, add the oil and reheat to just below the smoking point. Distribute the oil over the surface of the pan. Add the clams, garlic, and chilies. Cook, stirring, until the clams begin to open.*
Clams, small, in the shell, well scrubbed	10–12 depending on size	10–12 depending on size	
Garlic, minced	1 tsp	5 g	
Chili peppers, red, fresh, split lengthwise	2	2	
Reserved chicken stock mixture			*Add the chicken stock mixture, stir well, cover pan, and cook over low to medium heat for another 2 minutes. Add the basil leaves and stir to mix. Place entire contents of pan in a warm, deep bowl. Accompany with white rice served in a separate bowl.*
Basil leaves, fresh	8–10	8–10	

See color insert for photograph of recipe

Shrimp Poached in Dashi

YIELD: 10 SERVINGS

DRESSING

Rice vinegar	4 oz	120 ml
Dashi (see recipe)	4 oz	120 ml
Soy sauce, dark	2 oz or to taste	60 ml or to taste
Sugar	1 tbsp or to taste	15 g or to taste
Sesame oil	1 tsp	5 ml

Combine ingredients in a stainless steel mixing bowl large enough to hold the shrimp and reserve.

Shrimp, peeled, deveined	2 1/2 lb	1.15 kg
Dashi (see recipe)	enough to cover shrimp	enough to cover shrimp
Reserved dressing	as needed	as needed

Prepare shrimp. If using small shrimp, leave them whole; if large, cut into halves or thirds. In a sauce pan, heat the Dashi to just below the boiling point. Add the shrimp, cover, and return the Dashi to a simmer. Remove from heat and let sit, uncovered, until cool. Drain the shrimp and reserve the Dashi for other purposes. Add the shrimp to the reserved dressing and toss well to distribute the dressing evenly. Cover and reserve in the refrigerator.

Cucumber, peeled	2 lb	900 g
Salt	as needed	as needed

If skins are unwaxed and tender, do not peel. Cut into thin, round slices. Place in a stainless steel mixing bowl and sprinkle lightly with salt. Let sit at room temperature for 1 hour. Place the cucumbers in a clean kitchen towel and gently squeeze to remove liquid. Reserve in the refrigerator until needed.

TO PREPARE AN INDIVIDUAL SERVING

Reserved cucumbers	3 oz per serving	90 g per serving
Reserved shrimp	4 oz per serving	115 g per serving

Pat the cucumber slices dry. In a small mixing bowl, combine the cucumbers, shrimp, and a small amount of the dressing and toss well. Place, in a mound, on a chilled salad plate or small bowl.

Shrimp with Sesame Seeds

Shrimp, large	*4 oz per serving*	*115 g per serving*	*Remove all of the shell except for the section nearest the tail. Butterfly, devein, then press lightly to flatten the shrimp.*
Sesame seeds, toasted	*as needed*	*as needed*	*Lightly sprinkle the shrimp with sesame seeds, salt and pepper, then dust with flour.*
Salt	*as needed*	*as needed*	
Pepper, black, fine ground	*as needed*	*as needed*	
Flour	*as needed*	*as needed*	
Oil, sesame	*2 tsp*	*10 ml*	*Heat oil in a sauté pan over medium to high heat. Dip the floured shrimp into the beaten eggs and sauté until golden on both sides. Serve with a dipping sauce made of soy sauce and rice vinegar to taste.*
Eggs, beaten	*as needed*	*as needed*	

Shrimp with Chili and Lime

YIELD: 10-12 SERVINGS

FLAVORING MIXTURE

Chili peppers, dried, red, hot	2–3 or to taste	2–3 or to taste
Water	10 oz	300 ml
Nuts, cashews	6 oz	170 g

Slit peppers. Remove the seeds and ribs, then chop the chili peppers into small flakes. Prepare 1–2 tbsp (15–30 g) more or less, according to taste. Place peppers in the water along with the nuts and soak for 45–60 minutes. Remove the nuts with a slotted spoon and place them in a food processor fitted with a steel blade. Chop the nuts as fine as possible; then, with the motor still running, add the soaked chili pepper flakes. When chopped as fine as possible, add the water in which the nuts and pepper flakes have soaked.

Onion, chopped	1 lb	450 g
Anchovy paste	2 tsp or to taste	15 g or to taste
Water	if needed	if needed

Add ingredients to the processor bowl and process into a smooth paste. Add more water, if needed, to make a batterlike consistency. Reserve.

TO PREPARE AN INDIVIDUAL SERVING

Oil, vegetable	2 tsp	10 ml
Reserved flavoring mixture	2–3 oz	60–90 g
Sugar	1/2 tsp	3 g
Salt	pinch	pinch
Shrimp, peeled and deveined, tail section of shell left on	4–5 oz per serving	115–140 g per serving
Lime juice, fresh squeezed	as needed	as needed
Cilantro leaves, fresh, chopped	as needed	as needed

Heat oil in a wok over high heat. Add the flavoring mixture and stir-fry briefly until it becomes aromatic. Lower heat and continue to stir-fry for another minute. Add the sugar and salt. Raise the heat to high and add the shrimp. Stir-fry until the shrimp are cooked through. Cooking time will vary depending on the size of the shrimp used. Place shrimp and other pan contents on a warmed plate and sprinkle with lime juice. Garnish with fresh, chopped, cilantro leaves.

Shrimp and Scallops with Straw Mushrooms

YIELD: 1 SERVING

Egg white, beaten	1 medium	1 medium	*Mix the egg white, rice wine, and salt. Add just*
Rice wine or dry sherry	1 tbsp	15 ml	*enough cornstarch to make a very thin paste.*
Cornstarch	as needed	as needed	
Salt	pinch	pinch	
Shrimp, medium, peeled and deveined	3 oz	85 g	*Place shrimp and scallops in a small mixing bowl. Add the egg white mixture and toss to coat evenly.*
Scallops, if large, cut each into 1–2 discs	3 oz	85 g	*Allow to marinate for 10–15 minutes.*
Carrot, fine julienne	1 oz	30 g	*Assemble ingredients and reserve.*
Bamboo shoot, cut into thin slices	1 oz	30 g	
Straw mushrooms	1/2 oz	15 g	
Chicken stock	2 oz	60 ml	*Mix ingredients and reserve.*
Rice wine or dry sherry	1 oz	30 ml	
Sesame oil	dash	dash	
Salt	pinch	pinch	
Cornstarch	large pinch	large pinch	

TO PREPARE

Oil, peanut	1 tbsp	15 ml	*Heat a wok or skillet over medium to high heat.*
All of the above ingredients			*Add the oil and distribute evenly over the pan. Stir-fry the carrots, bamboo shoots, and mushrooms for 1 minute. Add the shrimp and scallops and stir-fry until the shrimp turn pink. Add the chicken stock mixture and continue to stir-fry for another minute. Serve with white rice or noodles.*

Seafood and Pork in a Sweet and Sour Sauce

YIELD: 10-12 SERVINGS

Pork, tenderloin	*2 lb*	*900 g*
Shrimp, jumbo	*2 lb*	*900 g*
Clams, small	*40*	*40*
Mushrooms, white, small	*1/2 lb*	*225 g*
Scallions, white and green parts	*4*	*4*
Carrot	*4 oz*	*115 g*
Garlic	*1 tbsp*	*15 g*
Cornstarch	*4 oz*	*115 g*
Water, cold	*as needed*	*as needed*
Eggs, lightly beaten	*4, large*	*4, large*
Oil, vegetable	*as needed for deep-frying*	*as needed for deep-frying*

TO PREPARE AN INDIVIDUAL SERVING

Soy sauce, dark	*2 oz*	*60 ml*
Vinegar, rice	*1 oz*	*30 ml*
Sugar	*2 tsp*	*10 g*
Salt	*to taste*	*to taste*
Pepper	*to taste*	*to taste*
Reserved deep-fried product	*1 portion (7–9 oz)*	*1 portion (200–250 g)*
Cornstarch	*1 tsp*	*3 g*
Water, cold	*as needed to make a thin, smooth paste*	*as needed to make a thin, smooth paste*

Cut the pork into thin, bite-sized slices. Peel and devein the shrimp, leaving on the section of shell nearest the tail. Then, cut the shrimp into pieces about the same size as the pork. Open the clams and rinse them. Discard the shells. Place these ingredients in a large mixing bowl.

Cut the mushrooms, caps and stems, into quarters. Slice the scallions into 1-in. (2.5-cm) pieces. Julienne the carrots and slice the garlic. Add these vegetables to the pork, shrimp, and clams.

Mix the cornstarch and water to make a thin, smooth paste. Add the eggs and mix well. Pour this mixture over the ingredients in the mixing bowl and toss until all the pieces are well coated.

Heat oil over medium to high heat. Deep-fry the meat, seafood, and vegetables in 350°F (175°C) oil until they begin to brown lightly. When done, drain on clean towel, divide these products into 10 equal portions and reserve.

Over medium to high heat, combine the soy sauce, vinegar, sugar, salt and pepper in a small saucepan or wok and bring to a boil. Add a precooked portion of the reserved deep-fried products. When the liquids return to a boil, add the cornstarch mixture and cook, gently stirring, until the sauce thickens.

Salmon Teriyaki

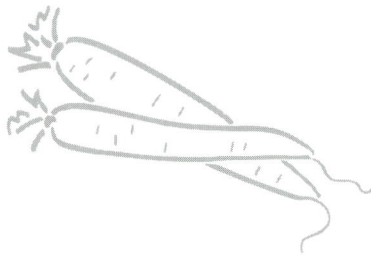

Salmon steak or fillet, skin on	6 oz	170 g
Teriyaki sauce (see recipe)	2 oz	60 ml
Oil, vegetable	1 tsp	5 ml
Daikon, peeled and grated	as needed	as needed
Lemon slices	as needed	as needed

If using the fillet rather than the salmon steaks, cut the fillets into 1 1/2-in. (4-cm) strips. Place fish in a shallow, stainless steel tray or glass bowl. Pour the teriyaki sauce on top and toss well to coat the fish evenly. Marinate for 10–15 minutes. Heat oil in a sauté pan over moderate heat and sauté the salmon on both sides until done as desired. Place fish on a warm plate and pour the pan juices on top. Serve with lemon slices and a small mound of fresh grated daikon placed next to the fish.

TO BROIL

Marinate fish, then place 4–5 in. under broiler flame. Broil until lightly browned on one side. Turn fish and brush with marinade. Broil until done as desired.

Grilled Fish Kebabs with Onion/Chili Relish

ONION/CHILI RELISH

Onion, thin sliced	3 lb	1.4 kg
Vinegar, white distilled	4 oz	120 ml
Lemon juice, fresh squeezed	4 oz	120 ml
Salt	1 tbsp or to taste	15 g or to taste
Chili peppers, Jalapeno, fresh, hot, green, seeds and ribs removed and sliced very thin	2 or to taste	2 or to taste

Combine ingredients and reserve. When serving, use a slotted spoon to drain the liquids.

MARINADE

Yogurt	1 lb	450 g
Garlic, minced	2 tbsp	30 g
Garam masala (see recipe)	2 tbsp	30 g
Coriander, ground	1 tbsp	7 g
Salt	1 tsp or to taste	5 g or to taste

Combine ingredients.

(Continued on next page)

Fish, white, firm-fleshed (cod, haddock, flounder)	*4 lb*	*1.8 kg*	*Cut the fish into 1 1/2-in. (4-cm) cubes. A single portion size is 6 oz (170 g) which may be presented on 2 3-oz (85-g) skewers or 1 6-oz (170-g) skewer. Thread the fish onto the skewers and place in a stainless steel pan. Cover all surfaces of the fish with the marinade. Cover and refrigerate for 3–4 hours before using.*
Skewers, stainless steel or bamboo	*as needed*	*as needed*	

TO PREPARE AN INDIVIDUAL SERVING

Marinated fish	*1 or 2 skewers containing a total of 6 oz of fish*	*1 or 2 skewers containing a total of 170 g of fish*	*Grill over coals or under a broiler flame until done as desired. Serve with a portion of the onion/chili pepper relish scattered on top of the fish. Garnish with lemon wedges and whole cilantro leaves arranged around the fish.*
Reserved onion/chili relish	*as needed*	*as needed*	
Lemon wedges	*as needed*	*as needed*	
Cilantro leaves, whole, fresh	*as needed*	*as needed*	

Whole Flounder Poached in a Savory Broth

YIELD: 10 SERVINGS

POACHING LIQUID

Dashi (see recipe)	*1 qt*	*1 L*
Mirin	*1 pt*	*480 ml*
Sake	*1 pt*	*480 ml*
Soy sauce, dark	*12 oz*	*360 ml*
Soy sauce, light	*6 oz*	*180 ml*
Sugar	*2 tsp or to taste*	*10 g or to taste*

Combine ingredients in a heavy-bottomed saucepan and bring to a boil. Lower heat and simmer for 10 minutes. Remove from heat and reserve.

Flounder, or other whole, firm, white-fleshed fish	*10, 3/4 lb each*	*10, 340 g each*
Salt	*as needed*	*as needed*

Gut, scale, and wash fish thoroughly. Make 2–3 diagonal cuts on each side of the fish perpendicular to the spine. Salt fish lightly, inside and out. Reserve refrigerated until needed.

TO PREPARE AN INDIVIDUAL SERVING

Poaching liquid	*8 oz*	*250 ml*
Reserved flounder	*1*	*1*
Lemon slices	*as needed*	*as needed*
Watercress sprigs	*as needed*	*as needed*
Parsley sprigs	*as needed*	*as needed*

Place poaching liquid in saucepan just large enough to hold the fish and the liquid. Bring the liquid to a boil then add the fish—if flounder, the dark skin side up. Partially cover the pan and return the liquid to a boil. Lower heat and simmer gently for 5–6 minutes or until the fish is done as desired. Carefully remove the fish and place it on a heated plate topped with 3–4 (45–60 ml) tbsp of the poaching liquid. Garnish with lemon slices, watercress or parsley sprigs. Poaching liquid may be reversed.

Shrimp and Cucumber Salad

YIELD: 10-12 SERVINGS

Cucumbers, Kirby or other small variety, unwaxed	1 1/2 lb	680 g	*Peel cucumbers if skins are thick. Cut into thin slices. If using large cucumbers, peel, then slice in two lengthwise. Cut into very thin slices. Lightly salt the cucumbers and let stand for 45 minutes. Squeeze gently to remove as much liquid as possible. Reserve, refrigerated.*
Shrimp, small, peeled and deveined. If large shrimp are used, slice each in half, lengthwise	1 1/2 lb	680 g	*Place shrimp in boiling water until they just begin to turn pink. Drain and let cool.*
Water	as needed	as needed	

DRESSING

Japanese rice vinegar (or 4 oz [120 ml] distilled vinegar and 2 oz [60 ml] water)	6 oz	180 ml	*Combine ingredients and mix until the sugar is completely dissolved.*
Soy sauce, dark	2 oz or to taste	60 ml or to taste	
Chicken stock, unsalted	2 tbsp	30 ml	
Sesame oil	2 tsp	10 ml	
Sugar	1/2 oz	15 g	

Cooked shrimp			*Combine ingredients and mix well. Refrigerate until needed. Serve in chilled individual bowls. Garnish with fresh, seasonal, garden vegetables.*
Reserved cucumbers			
Dressing			

Trout with Black Bean Garlic Sauce

YIELD: 2 SERVINGS

Trout or other white, firm-fleshed fish	1, 1–1 1/4 lb	1, 450 – 570 g
Salt	as needed	as needed
Gingerroot, peeled and sliced thin	3–4 slices	3–4 slices

Clean fish inside and out, removing all scales and fins. Leave head on. Sprinkle lightly with salt. Place the gingerroot along the entire cavity of the fish.

Fermented black beans*	1 1/2 tbsp	20 g
Sugar	pinch	pinch
Sherry, dry	1 tbsp	15 ml
Garlic, minced	1 tsp	5 g

Rinse beans, then combine them with the remaining ingredients and mash lightly, leaving some of the beans intact. Distribute the mixture over the surface of one side of the fish. Put the fish on a heat-proof plate bean mixture side up, and place in a steamer for 5–8 minutes or until done as desired. Cooking time will vary depending on the thickness of the fish.

Oil, peanut	2 tbsp	30 ml
Scallions, white and green sections cut into thin circles	2 medium-sized	2 medium-sized
Soy sauce	1–2 tbsp	15–30 ml

Heat oil in a small pan over high heat. Remove fish from steamer. Distribute the scallions over the surface of the fish, then pour the hot oil over the scallions. Sprinkle soy sauce over the fish and serve.

*Available packed in bottles, cans, or plastic bags.

Steamed Shrimp with Soy/Chili Dipping Sauce

YIELD: 10 SERVINGS

DIPPING SAUCE

Soy sauce, dark	12 oz	350 ml
Oil, vegetable	8 oz	240 ml
Chili, red, fresh, sliced very thin, seeds and ribs discarded*	1 oz or to taste	30 g or to taste
Sugar	1 1/2 tbsp or to taste	25 g or to taste

Combine ingredients and stir until the sugar is completely dissolved. Reserve.

Shrimp, shell on	8 oz per serving	225 g per serving
Oil, vegetable	as needed	as needed
Water, lightly salted	as needed	as needed

Wash shrimp and place in an individual ovenproof serving dish. Sprinkle shrimp with oil then add 2 oz (60 ml) of lightly salted water. Steam over rapidly salted water until done, 4–5 minutes, depending on size of shrimp. Drain and serve immediately with 2 oz (60 ml) of the dipping sauce served on the side.

*Thinly sliced scallions mixed with finely shredded, fresh gingerroot can be substituted.

Steamed Fish with Spicy Ginger Sauce

YIELD: 10 SERVINGS

Whole fish (porgy, trout, croaker, bass)	10, 3/4 lb each	10, 340 g each

Wash fish inside and out, removing all traces of scales and gills. Cut off fins. Make 2–3 diagonal cuts on each side of the fish perpendicular to the spine.

MARINADE

Soy sauce, dark	12 oz	360 ml
Rice wine or dry sherry	8 oz	240 ml
Peanut oil	3 oz	90 ml
Gingerroot, peeled and minced	3 oz	85 g
Scallion, chopped, white and green parts	8–10	8–10

Combine ingredients. Place fish in a single layer in a stainless steel pan. Pour this mixture over all surfaces of the fish, inside and out. Cover and refrigerate for several hours before using. When ready to cook, place fish as needed (1 per serving) in steamer and cook for 10–15 minutes or until the fish flakes easily. Cooking time will vary depending on thickness of fish. When done, reserve in a warm place.

TO PREPARE SAUCE FOR A SINGLE SERVING

Oil, peanut	1 tbsp	15 ml
Scallions, white and green parts cut into 1-in. (2.5-cm) lengths	2	2
Gingerroot, peeled and cut fine julienne	1-in. piece	2–3-cm piece

In a wok or skillet, heat oil over high heat and stir-fry the scallions and ginger for 20–30 seconds.

Fish stock	2 oz	60 ml
Vinegar, white distilled	1 oz	60 ml
Sugar	1 tsp or to taste	5 g or to taste

Add ingredients and bring to a boil.

Soy sauce, dark	1 tbsp	15 ml
Rice wine or dry sherry	1 tbsp	15 ml
Cornstarch	1 tsp	3 g

Mix ingredients thoroughly to obtain a very smooth consistency, lower heat, then add to pan, stirring constantly, until the sauce thickens. Pour sauce over fish.

Cilantro, fresh, leaves, chopped	as needed	as needed

Garnish with a sprinkling of fresh, chopped cilantro leaves.

Steamed Fish with Lemon and Chili Sauce

YIELD: 1 SERVING

Whole fish (sea bass, porgy, croaker, perch)	1, 3/4–1 lb	1, 340–450 g	*Clean and gut fish. Wash fish under running water to remove any scales or other debris. Slash fish diagonally 2–3 times on each side. Place the fish in a steamer and cook for 8–10 minutes depending on thickness of fish.*
SAUCE			
Lime or lemon juice, fresh squeezed	2 oz	60 ml	*Combine ingredients. When fish is done, carefully remove it from the steamer and place it on a heated plate. Pour sauce on top.*
Fish sauce	1 tsp	5 ml	
Garlic, minced	1 tsp	5 g	
Chili, green, fresh, chopped fine	1 tsp or to taste	5 g or to taste	
Salt	to taste	to taste	
Sugar	to taste	to taste	
Cilantro leaves and tender stems, fresh, chopped	as needed	as needed	*Garnish with chopped cilantro and slices of fresh lemon or lime.*

Shrimp with Tomato and Scallion

YIELD: 1 SERVING

Ingredient	U.S.	Metric	Method
Shrimp, peeled and deveined, tail section of shell left on	5–6 oz	150–170 g	*Place shrimp in a bowl and sprinkle very lightly with salt. Reserve for 10–15 minutes.*
Salt	as needed	as needed	
Tomato, peeled and cut into large dice	6 oz	170 g	*Prepare tomato and reserve.*
Oil, peanut	1 tbsp	15 ml	*Heat wok or heavy skillet over high heat. When hot, add the oil and distribute evenly over surface of pan. Add white scallion sections and garlic. Stir-fry for 10–15 seconds. Add the shrimp and stir-fry until they just begin to turn pink. Do not overcook. Remove contents of pan to a warm plate.*
Scallions, white parts only, sliced thin into rounds (tender green parts prepared in the same way and reserved)	2 medium	2 medium	
Garlic, minced	1 tsp	5 g	
Reserved shrimp			
Reserved tomatoes			*Place these ingredients in the pan, lower heat, cover, and cook for 2–3 minutes. Adjust seasonings if necessary.*
Soy sauce	1–2 tsp or to taste	5–10 ml or to taste	
Sugar	pinch	pinch	
Salt	to taste	to taste	
Cornstarch	1 tbsp	10 g	*Add the dissolved cornstarch to the tomatoes and combine thoroughly.*
Water	1 tbsp	15 ml	
Reserved shrimp			*Return the shrimp to the pan along with the green parts of the scallions. Raise heat to medium high and stir-fry to heat through. Place on a heated dish and serve immediately.*
Reserved scallion, green sections			

Spicy Catfish Salad

YIELD: 10 SERVINGS

Catfish fillets	3 lb	1.4 kg	*Steam fillets for 10 minutes until well done. Cooking time will vary depending on thickness of fish. When done, chop fish into very small pieces.*
Oil, peanut	as needed for deep-frying	as needed for deep-frying	*Sprinkle the chopped fish pieces into 350°F (175°C) oil and deep-fry until the fish is browned and crisp. Remove from oil with a fine skimmer or slotted spoon and place on a towel to drain.*
Mangos, unripe, cut fine julienne	3	3	*Combine the fried fish with these ingredients and mix well. Refrigerate until needed.*
Peanuts, roasted, unsalted, crushed	4 oz	115 g	
Chili peppers, fresh, green, seeds and ribs removed, chopped fine	1 tbsp or to taste	15 g or to taste	
Scallions, white parts, sliced thin	4–5	4–5	
Fish sauce	2 oz	60 ml	

TO PREPARE AN INDIVIDUAL SERVING

Lettuce, Boston or other tender green leaf	as needed	as needed	*Place a bed of lettuce on a chilled platter and top with a 6-oz (170-g) mound of the fish mixture. Garnish with chopped, fresh cilantro, cucumber slices, and tomato wedges. Serve with white rice. This dish may be served in smaller portions as an appetizer or without the garnishes, as a snack with drinks.*
Reserved fish mixture	as needed	as needed	
Cilantro, leaves and tender stems coarsely chopped	as needed	as needed	

Shrimp Sausage and Bean Sprouts

YIELD: 10 SERVINGS

SHRIMP SAUSAGE

Shrimp, peeled and deveined	2 lb	900 g
Egg whites	from 4 medium eggs	from 4 medium eggs
Cornstarch	4 tbsp	40 g
Oil, vegetable	4 oz	120 ml
Pepper, white	1 tsp or to taste	2 g or to taste

Place ingredients into the bowl of a food processor fitted with a steel blade and process into a smooth paste. Place contents of bowl into a pastry bag containing a tip with a 1/2–3/4-in. (1.5–2-cm) opening. Size can vary.

Water, lightly salted, simmering	6 qt	6 L

Pipe the mixture into simmering water in a continuous stream. When the entire contents of the pastry bag have been piped into the water, cook for 1–2 minutes. When done, drain pot and fill with cold water to stop the cooking process. When cool, cut into 2–3 in.-pieces and reserve.

SAUCE

Chicken stock, cold	16 oz	475 L
Rice wine or dry sherry	4 oz	120 ml
Cornstarch	2 1/2 tbsp	25 g
Sesame oil	2 tbsp	30 ml
Sugar	1 tsp	5 g
Salt	1 tsp	5 g
Pepper, white	1 tsp	2 g

Combine ingredients and stir until the cornstarch is completely dissolved. Reserve.

(Continued on next page)

TO PREPARE AN INDIVIDUAL SERVING

Oil, vegetable or rendered chicken fat	1 tbsp	15 ml	Heat wok or heavy skillet over high heat. Add the oil. When the oil is just below the smoking point, stir-fry the scallions and gingerroot for 20–30 seconds. Add the bean sprouts and continue to stir-fry until the bean sprouts begin to soften. Remove contents of pan and reserve in a warm place.
Scallion, white and green parts, cut julienne	1	1	
Gingerroot, shredded	2 tsp	10 g	
Bean sprouts	3 oz	85 g	
Shrimp sausage	3 oz	90 g	Using the same pan, sauté the shrimp sausage for 1–2 minutes or until they begin to color lightly. Add the reserved sauce and the stir-fried vegetables. Cook, stirring, until the sauce has thickened.
Reserved sauce	2 oz	60 ml	
Stir-fried vegetables			

Shrimp with Garlic and Chili Peppers

YIELD: 1 SERVING

Scallion, sliced into 1/2-in. (1.5-cm) pieces, white and tender green parts	1	1	*Combine ingredients and reserve.*
Garlic, sliced thin	*2–3 medium cloves*	*2–3 medium cloves*	
Red chili pepper, fresh, seeds removed, sliced very thin	*2 tsp or to taste*	*8 g or to taste*	
Shrimp, medium	*4–5 oz*	*115–140 g*	*Peel and devein the shrimp leaving the tail section of the shell on. Rinse under cold water, then pat dry. Heat wok or heavy skillet over high heat, then add the oil. When the oil has been reheated to just below the smoking point, stir-fry the shrimp briefly until they just begin to turn pink. Remove from pan and reserve in a warm place.*
Oil, vegetable	*1 tbsp*	*15 ml*	
Reserved vegetables			
Rice wine or dry sherry	*2 tbsp*	*30 ml*	*Using the same pan, stir-fry the reserved scallion, pepper, and garlic for a minute or less. Add the rice wine and deglaze the pan. Return the shrimp, continuing to stir-fry until they are heated through. Remove from heat and place on a serving plate with a sprinkle of salt and pepper.*
Reserved shrimp			
Salt	*pinch*	*pinch*	
Pepper, black	*pinch*	*pinch*	

Shrimp Cooked in Coconut Milk

YIELD: 1 SERVING

Coconut milk	4 oz	120 ml	*Combine ingredients in a small sauce or sauté pan. Bring to a boil over medium heat then lower heat, and simmer, uncovered, for 5 minutes.*
Garlic, minced	1/2 tsp	3 g	
Gingerroot, peeled and minced	1/2 tsp	3 g	
Salt	pinch	pinch	
Pepper, black, ground	pinch	pinch	
Shrimp, medium, peeled and deveined vein	5 oz	140 g	*Add shrimp, cover pan, and cook briefly until the shrimp turn pink. Serve on a bed of hot, white rice.*

See color insert for photograph of recipe

Shrimp and Bok Choy Stir-Fry

YIELD: 10 SERVINGS

Shrimp, medium, peeled, deveined, tail section of peel left on	2 1/2 lb (after removing shells)	1.15 kg (after removing shells)	*Prepare shrimp and reserve.*

SAUCE

Chicken stock	20 oz	600 ml	*Combine ingredients and stir until the cornstarch is completely dissolved. Reserve.*
Rice wine or dry sherry	8 oz	240 ml	
Soy sauce, light	4 oz	120 ml	
Cornstarch	3 tbsp	30 g	
Sugar	1 1/2 tbsp	25 g	
Oil, sesame	2 tsp	10 ml	
Salt	1 tsp	5 g	
Pepper, white	to taste	to taste	
Bok choy or choy sum,* washed and trimmed	3 lb	1.4 kg	*Select young plants with medium-sized stems. If plants with thicker stems are used, peel backs of stems with a vegetable peeler before using. Slice stems and leaves into 1-1/2 in. (4-cm) square pieces and blanch in boiling water for 1–2 minutes. Cooking time will vary depending on maturity and thickness of stems. Drain and plunge into iced water. When cool, drain again and reserve.*

TO PREPARE AN INDIVIDUAL SERVING

Oil, peanut	1 oz	30 ml	*Heat wok or heavy skillet over high heat, then add oil. When oil is just below the smoking point, add the ginger and stir-fry for 30 seconds. Add the shrimp and stir-fry until they become pink. Remove shrimp from pan and reserve in a warm place. Using the same pan, add the bok choy or choy sum and stir-fry for 1–2 minutes or until the vegetable begins to soften a little. Add the sauce and bring to a boil. Return the shrimp to the pan and heat through, stirring constantly.*
Gingerroot, peeled	3 thin slices	3 thin slices	
Reserved shrimp	4 oz	120 g	
Reserved sauce	3 oz	90 ml	
Reserved bok choy or choy sum	4 oz	120 g	

*Broccoli florets may be substituted. Follow the same procedure.

Crisp Shrimp

YIELD: 10 SERVINGS

MARINADE

Cornstarch	3 heaping tbsp	40 g	Combine ingredients and mix until the salt is completely dissolved.
Egg whites	from 3 large eggs	from 3 large eggs	
Salt	2 tsp	10 g	
Shrimp, peeled, deveined and cut into 1/2-in. (1.5-cm) pieces; small whole shrimp may also be used	3 lb	1.4 kg	Prepare shrimp and place in a stainless steel or glass bowl. Add the marinade and toss to coat shrimp evenly. Cover and refrigerate for 3–4 hours.

TO PREPARE AN INDIVIDUAL SERVING

Cornstarch	1/2 tsp	5 g	Combine ingredients and reserve.
Sugar	pinch	pinch	
Chicken stock	2 tbsp	30 ml	
Oil, vegetable	for deep-frying	for deep-frying	Deep-fry shrimp for 30 seconds in 350°F (175°C) oil. Remove from deep fryer and place directly in a very hot, lightly oiled wok or heavy skillet. Stir-fry briefly over high heat. Add the rice wine or sherry and stir. Add the cornstarch mixture and stir-fry until the pan liquids begin to thicken. Place on a heated serving plate and sprinkle with salt to taste.
Marinated shrimp	4–5 oz	115 g	
Rice wine or sherry, medium dry	2 oz	60 ml	
Sugar	pinch	pinch	
Salt	to taste	to taste	

Shrimp in Coconut Milk and Lemon

YIELD: 1 SERVING

Shrimp, medium to large	4 oz	115 g	*Peel, devein, and butterfly the shrimp. In a small skillet, bring the coconut milk to a boil. Add the shrimp and cook, partially covered, until they turn pink. When done, place the shrimp on a warm plate, reserving the coconut milk in the pan.*
Coconut milk, thin	2 oz	60 ml	
Lemon juice, fresh squeezed	2 tsp	10 ml	*Add ingredients to the pan and simmer for 1 minute. Pour this sauce over the shrimp.*
Fish sauce	dash	dash	
Sugar	to taste	to taste	
Salt	to taste	to taste	
Shallots, sliced very thin	1 tsp	10 g	*Sprinkle the shallots and chili peppers on top. Serve with white, boiled rice.*
Chili peppers, fresh, green, seeds and ribs removed, sliced very thin	1 tsp or to taste	10 g or to taste	

Scallops Grilled with Red and Green Peppers

YIELD: 10-12

MARINADE

Soy sauce	8 oz	240 ml	*Combine ingredients thoroughly and reserve.*
Sesame oil	2 oz	60 ml	
Vinegar, rice	2 oz	60 ml	
Sesame seeds, toasted	2 tbsp	12 g	
Gingerroot, peeled and minced	2-in. piece	5-cm piece	
Garlic, minced	1 tsp	5 g	
Red pepper powder	1–2 tsp or to taste	1–2 g or to taste	
Pepper, black, fine ground	to taste	to taste	
Scallops, cleaned	4 lb	1.8 kg	*If scallops are large, slice in half or thirds so that you have 2 or 3 thinner disk-shaped pieces per scallop. Lightly score the edges to prevent curling. Reserve.*
Bell pepper, red	as needed	as needed	*Peel and core the peppers, then cut them into 1-in. (2.5-cm) square pieces. Reserve.*
Bell pepper, green	as needed	as needed	
Skewers, bamboo	as needed	as needed	*Thread scallops and pepper squares alternating scallops —6 oz (170 g) per serving—and green and red pepper squares. Place in a glass or stainless steel pan. Distribute the marinade over the skewers. Cover and refrigerate for at least 1 hour before using. Turn skewers several times to marinate evenly.*

TO PREPARE AN INDIVIDUAL SERVING

Skewered scallops and peppers	2 skewers	2 skewers	*Grill over coals under broiler flame until lightly browned, 2–3 minutes per side. Take care not to overcook. Serve on a bed of white rice.*

Scallops Hunan Style

YIELD: 1 SERVING

Ingredient	US	Metric	Method
Mushrooms, Chinese, black, dried	2	2	*Soak the mushrooms in tepid water for 20–30 minutes. Remove and discard stems. Julienne the caps. Reserve.*
Scallops	4–5 oz	115–140 g	*Clean scallops. If scallops are large, slice in half or thirds so that you have 2–3 thinner disc-shaped slices per scallop. Mix the cornstarch and egg white in a small bowl. Add the scallops and toss well to coat each piece evenly. Reserve.*
Cornstarch	1 tsp	5 g	
Egg white	1 oz	30 ml	
Bamboo shoot, shredded	1 oz	30 g	*Prepare these vegetables and reserve.*
Chili pepper, fresh, red, seeds and membrane removed, sliced thin	1 or to taste	1 or to taste	
Water chestnuts,* canned, sliced thin	2–3	2–3	

FLAVORING MIXTURE

Ingredient	US	Metric	Method
Soy sauce, dark	2 tsp	10 ml	*Combine ingredients and reserve.*
Rice wine vinegar	1 tsp	5 ml	
Sugar, light brown	1 tsp	5 g	
Salt	to taste	to taste	

TO PREPARE

Ingredient	US	Metric	Method
Oil, peanut	1 tbsp	15 ml	*Heat wok or skillet over high heat. Add oil and heat to just below the smoking point. Add the scallops and gently stir-fry until they become opaque and slightly firm. Remove the scallops to a warm place. Add the vegetables including the mushrooms and stir-fry for another minute. Add the flavoring mixture, stir well, then return the scallops to the pan. Stir-fry briefly to heat through.*
Reserved scallops			
Reserved vegetables			
Reserved flavoring mixture			

*Available canned or fresh in season.

Scallops with Garlic and Ginger

YIELD: 1 SERVING

Scallops	5–6 oz	140–170 g
Butter, clarified	2 oz	60 ml
Lime juice, fresh squeezed	2 oz	60 ml
Cilantro leaves, chopped fine	1 tbsp	8 g
Gingerroot, peeled and minced	1 tsp	5 g
Shallot, minced	1 tsp	5 g
Garlic, minced	1 tsp or to taste	5 g or to taste
Salt	to taste	to taste
Pepper, white, fine ground	to taste	to taste

Clean scallops. If scallops are large, slice in half or thirds so that you have 2 or 3 thinner disc-shaped pieces per scallop. Mix the scallops with these ingredients. Place in a single-serving, heatproof dish. Cover, then bake in a 350°F (180°C) oven for 5–6 minutes or until the scallops become opaque and slightly firm. Use smaller portion size if served as an appetizer.

Scallops with Two Hot Peppers, Bamboo Shoots, and Basil

YIELD: 1 SERVING

Scallops	4 oz	115 g	*Clean scallops. If large, cut each into two or three discs depending on thickness. Place in a strainer or colander and submerge in boiling water for 3–4 seconds. Remove and drain. Reserve.*
Boiling water	as needed	as needed	
Oil	1 tbsp	15 ml	*Heat oil in wok or skillet over high heat. Add the garlic and cayenne pepper and stir-fry briefly until the garlic begins to color. Do not let the garlic brown.*
Garlic, chopped	1/2 tsp	3 g	
Cayenne pepper, dried, soaked in water until soft, then cut into several pieces. (Other dried, hot peppers may be substituted for a milder taste.)	1	1	
Reserved scallops			*Add ingredients and stir-fry for 20–30 seconds.*
Bamboo shoot, cut into 3–4 wedge-shaped pieces	2 oz	60 g	
Jalapeño pepper, seeded, ribs out, cut julienne	1 or to taste	1 or to taste	
Pepper, white	pinch	pinch	
Scallion, white and green parts cut into 2-in. (5-cm) pieces	1	1	*Add ingredients and stir-fry for another minute.*
Oyster sauce	1 tbsp	15 ml	
Sugar	pinch	pinch	
Fresh basil or mint leaves	5–6 depending on size	5–6 depending on size	*Add either of these herbs and stir-fry until they have wilted slightly. Serve with white rice and garnish with orange slices.*

Salmon with Mirin, Soy, and Vinegar Sauce

YIELD: 1 SERVING

Oil, vegetable	2 tsp	10 ml
Salmon steak or fillet with skin on	6 oz	170 g
Butter, whole	1 oz	30 g

Heat oil in a small sauté pan over high heat and sear the fish on both sides. Cook for a minute or two on each side until done as desired. Cooking time will vary depending on thickness of fish. Discard any oil remaining in the pan, then add the butter. When melted, turn fish several times to coat it well. Remove the fish and place it on a heated plate.

Mirin*	2 tbsp	15 ml
Rice vinegar	1 tbsp	15 ml
Soy sauce	1 tsp	5 ml
Scallion, white and tender green parts, sliced thin	1 small	1 small
Lemon wedges	2 small	2 small

Add the Mirin, rice vinegar, and soy sauce and cook, stirring, over high heat for approximately 30–45 seconds. Add the scallion and mix well. Pour this sauce over the fish. Garnish the plate with lemon wedges.

*A sweetened wine from Japan which adds a distinctive sweet flavor and a glaze to fried and grilled foods.

Deep-Fried
Batter-Dipped Oysters

YIELD: VARIABLE

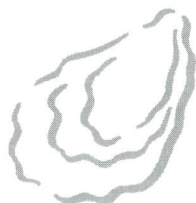

BATTER

Cornstarch	6 oz	170 g
Flour	4 oz	120 g
Baking powder	3 tbsp	30 g
Oil, vegetable	2 oz	60 ml
Salt	2 tsp	10 g
Pepper, white	1 tsp	2 g
Water, cold	as needed	as needed

Combine ingredients with enough cold water to make a moderately thick batter. Using a wire whisk, beat for 1–2 minutes. Allow the batter to rest for 5–10 minutes before using.

Oysters, fresh, shucked	4–6 medium size per serving	4–6 medium size per serving
Pepper-salt (see recipe)	as needed	as needed
Lettuce, shredded	as needed	as needed

Rinse oysters in lightly salted water, then sprinkle on all sides with the pepper-salt seasoning. Coat oysters with a heavy layer of the batter. Deep-fry at 375°F (190°C) until golden brown. When done, remove oysters and drain on absorbent paper or a clean kitchen towel. Arrange the fried oysters on a bed of finely shredded lettuce and accompany with a small dish of the pepper-salt mixture or other dipping sauce.

Mussels Steamed in a Spicy Broth

YIELD: 1 SERVING

Mussels, medium size	1 lb	450 g	Scrub and debeard mussels.
Clarified butter	1 tbsp	15 ml	In a saucepan large enough to hold the mussels, heat clarified butter over medium heat. Add ingredients and sauté until the onions are lightly browned.
Onion, chopped fine	4 oz	115 g	
Gingerroot, peeled and chopped	2 tsp	10 g	
Garlic, minced	2 tsp	10 g	
Chili pepper, red, fresh, minced	1 tsp or to taste	5 g or to taste	Add ingredients and continue to sauté until they are incorporated with the onion mixture.
Coriander, ground	1 1/2 tsp	3 g	
Turmeric, ground	pinch	pinch	
Water	4 oz	120 ml	Add the water and bring to a boil. Cover pan, lower heat, and simmer for 10 minutes.
Salt	pinch	pinch	
Reserved mussels			Add mussels, turn heat to high, cover pan and cook until the mussels have opened. Serve mussels and all pan liquids in a deep, heated bowl. Serve boiled rice on the side.

Mackerel Simmered in Sake

YIELD: 10 SERVINGS

POACHING LIQUID

Dashi (see recipe)	1 qt	1 L	*Combine ingredients and reserve.*
Sake	20 oz	600 ml	
Mirin	16 oz	480 ml	

TO PREPARE AN INDIVIDUAL SERVING

Mackerel fillet	6 oz per serving	170 g per serving	*Place fish in a pan of boiling water for 1/2 minute. Remove and place immediately in iced water. When cooled through, drain. Heat the poaching liquid to just below the boiling point. Add the Kombu and the fish fillet. Cover partially and cook on the lowest possible heat for 3–4 minutes. Cooking time will vary depending on the thickness of the fish fillet. When done as desired, place the fish on a heated plate and cut into strips, keeping the original shape of the fillet. Reserve in a warm place. Discard the Kombu.*
Water, boiling	as needed	as needed	
Kombu seaweed	1x2 inch piece	2.5 x 5 cm piece	
Reserved poaching liquid	6 oz	200 ml	
Bean curd	2–3-oz piece	60–85-g piece	*Add the bean curd to the simmering liquid and heat through, about 1–2 minutes. When done, remove the bean curd with a slotted spoon and place it next to the fish. Spoon a small amount of the cooking liquid over the fish. Garnish with a small mound of thinly sliced pickled ginger. Accompany with a dipping sauce served in a separate small bowl, made of a mixture of dark soy sauce and sugar to taste.*
Ginger, pickled*	1–2 tsp	10–15 g	
Soy sauce, dark	as needed	as needed	
Sugar	as needed	as needed	

*Pickled ginger or Beni Shoga is available commercially.

Grilled Marinated Mackerel

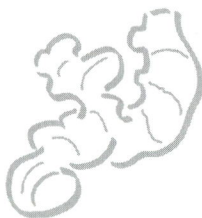

Mackerel, or other whole fish of choice	10, 3/4–1 lb each	10, 340–450 g each	Clean fish thoroughly. Make a series of diagonal cuts 1 in. (2.5 cm) apart and perpendicular to the back bone, on both sides of the fish. Place the fish in a single layer on a shallow stainless steel tray.
MARINADE			
Soy sauce, dark	8 oz	240 ml	Combine ingredients and mix until the sugar has dissolved. Pour the marinade over the fish, distributing it evenly. Cover and reserve in the refrigerator for several hours before using.
Garlic, minced	3 tbsp	40 g	
Sugar	2 tbsp	30 g	
Gingerroot, peeled and minced	2 tbsp	30 g	
Chili pepper, fresh, sliced thin	2 tbsp or to taste	25 g or to taste	
Sesame seeds	1 tbsp	6 g	
Sesame oil	1 tbsp	15 ml	
Salt	1 tsp	5 g	
Black pepper	1 tsp	2 g	
TO PREPARE AN INDIVIDUAL SERVING			
Oil, vegetable	as needed	as needed	Place mackerel on a well oiled grill and cook for 3–4 minutes on each side. Brush each side with the marinade 2–3 times during cooking period.* When done as desired, place the fish on a bed of finely shredded lettuce and garnish with lemon slices.
Mackerel	1	1	
Lettuce	as needed	as needed	
Lemon, sliced	as needed	as needed	

*Fish may also be butterflied and grilled skin side down. Cover with foil for several minutes toward end of cooking period. If done this way it is not necessary to turn fish.

Crab Asparagus Soup, page 48

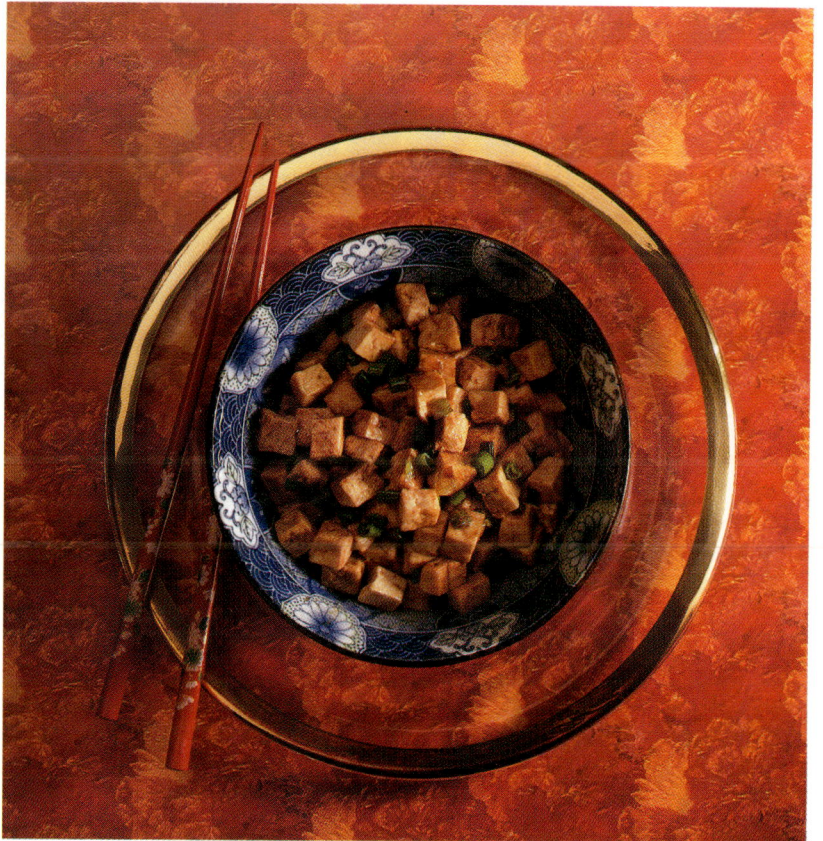

Bean Curd in Oyster Sauce, page 77

Fresh Corn Fritters, page 83

Zucchini with Sesame, page 108

Clams with Chili and Basil, page 122

Shrimp Cooked in Coconut Milk, page 142

Fish Balls, Barbecued on Skewers, page 171

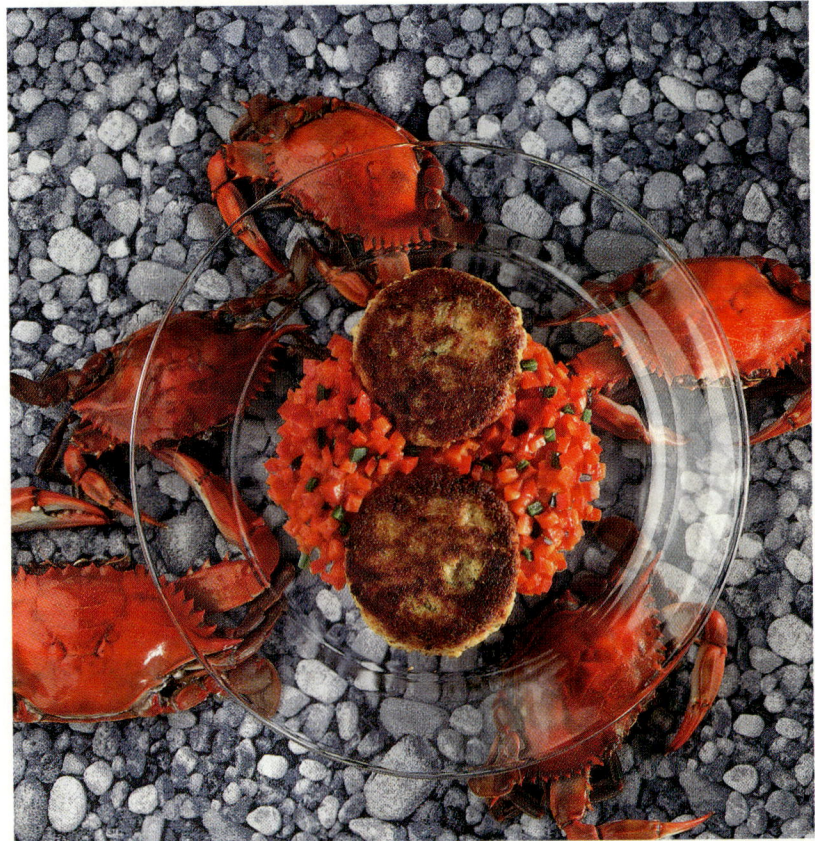

Crab Cakes with Sweet and Hot Peppers, page 173

Skewered Chicken with Peanut Sauce, page 177

Duck Braised in Wine, Ginger, and Five-Star Anise, page 190

Cornish Hens in Apricot Ginger Sauce, page 194

Tea-Smoked Duck, page 221

Mackerel with Gingerroot Threads and Scallions

CHINA

YIELD: 10 SERVINGS

Mackerel, gutted, head left on	10, 3/4–1 lb each	10, 340–450 g each	Clean fish, inside and out, under running water. Remove fins. Drain and rub all surfaces, including the cavity, lightly with salt. Place in stainless steel or glass pan in a single layer. Cover and refrigerate until needed.
Salt	as needed	as needed	
SAUCE			
Soy sauce, light	10 oz	300 ml	Combine ingredients and mix until the sugar is completely dissolved. Reserve.
Soy sauce, thick	10 oz	300 ml	
Shaohsing wine or dry sherry	5 oz	150 ml	
Sugar	2 tbsp	30 g	
TO PREPARE AN INDIVIDUAL SERVING			
Oil, peanut	2 tbsp	30 ml	Heat a wok or skillet over high heat. When hot, add the oil. When oil is just below the smoking point, add the ginger slices and sauté briefly until lightly browned. Discard the ginger slices.
Gingerroot, peeled and sliced thin	1-in. piece	2.5-cm piece	
Reserved fish	1	1	Sauté fish on one side until the skin is browned. Add a little oil and turn fish to other side and continue cooking until the fish is almost cooked through. Add the sauce and gingerroot and cook for another 2 minutes over medium heat. Or, after browning one side, the fish may be placed in a 400°F (200°C) oven until almost cooked through, then finished with the sauce on top of the stove.
Oil, peanut	as needed	as needed	
Reserved sauce	2 1/2 oz	75 ml	
Gingerroot, peeled and cut into very fine julienne	1-in. piece	2.5-cm piece	
Scallions, white and green parts cut into thin slices	as needed	as needed	Place fish on a warm serving plate. Pour the pan juices on top and garnish with scallions.

155

FISH AND SEAFOOD

Flounder Fillets Stuffed with Oysters

YIELD: 10 SERVINGS

MARINADE

Rice wine or dry sherry	6 oz	180 ml	*Combine ingredients and reserve.*
Soy sauce, light	6 oz	180 ml	
Oil, vegetable	1 tbsp	15 ml	
Oil, sesame	1 tbsp	15 ml	
Vinegar, white distilled	1 tbsp	15 ml	
Scallions, white and green parts, minced	6	6	
Black beans, fermented, rinsed	4 oz	115 g	
Garlic, minced	1 tbsp	15 g	
Sugar	1 tbsp	15 g	
Salt	1 tsp	5 g	
Pepper, white, ground	1 tsp	2 g	
Cilantro leaves, fresh, chopped fine	5–6 sprigs	5–6 sprigs	
Flounder	20, 3-oz fillets	20, 85-g fillets	*Place an oyster and a small amount of the scallion across the broad end of the fillet. Roll up the fish toward the tail end. Place the rolled fish, seam side down, in a stainless steel pan. Distribute the marinade evenly over the rolled fillets. Cover and marinate in the refrigerator for at least 1 hour before cooking.*
Oysters, shucked, medium size	20	20	
Scallions, julienne into 2–3-in. (5–8-cm) lengths, white and green parts	as needed	as needed	
Reserved marinade			

TO PREPARE AN INDIVIDUAL SERVING

Rolled fillets	2 per serving	2 per serving	*Place the rolled fillets along with a small amount of the marinade in an individual serving, ovenproof, serving dish. Steam fish for 5–6 minutes or until done as desired. Baste once with the pan juices just prior to serving.*

Flounder in Black Bean Sauce

YIELD: 10 SERVINGS

THE MARINADE

Rice wine or dry sherry	6 oz	180 ml
Egg whites, lightly beaten	3	3
Cornstarch	3 tbsp	30 g
Sesame oil	2 tbsp	30 ml
Salt	1 tsp	5 g
Pepper, black, finely ground	1 tsp	2 g

Combine ingredients and mix until the cornstarch is completely dissolved. Reserve.

Flounder or other flat, white fish, fillets	3 1/2 lb	1.5 kg

Remove all bones and bits of skin. Cut each fillet in half lengthwise, then cut crosswise, into 2-in. (5-cm) strips. Place fish into a glass or stainless steel mixing bowl and add the marinade. Mix to distribute the marinade evenly. Cover bowl and reserve, refrigerated, for 3–4 hours.

TO PREPARE AN INDIVIDUAL SERVING

Salted black beans, rinsed and chopped	1 tbsp	20 g
Garlic, minced	1 tsp	12 g
Gingerroot, minced	1 tsp	5 g

Combine ingredients and reserve.

(Continued on next page)

Chicken or fish stock	3 oz	90 ml	*Combine ingredients and stir until the cornstarch is completely dissolved. Reserve.*
Rice wine or dry sherry	1 tbsp	15 ml	
Cornstarch	1 tsp.	5 g	
Marinated fish	5–6 oz	150 g	*Using a wok or small skillet, bring enough water to a boil to barely cover the fish. Lower heat to simmer and gently poach the fish until the flesh turns white and becomes slightly firm. Gently remove the fish with a slotted spatula and reserve in a warm place. Discard water and wipe pan dry.*
Water	as needed	as needed	
Oil, peanut	2 tsp	10 ml	*Reheat the pan over high heat. Add the oil and heat to just below the smoking point. Add the black bean mixture and the chilies and stir-fry very briefly, 5–6 seconds, then remove pan from heat and add the chicken stock mixture. Mix well and place the pan over medium to low heat. Stir, cooking, until mixture begins to thicken. Return the fish to the pan and spoon the sauce over the fish. When heated through, place contents of pan on a warm serving dish and garnish with scallions.*
Reserved black bean mixture			
Small dried red chilies	1–2 or to taste (optional)	1–2 or to taste (optional)	
Reserved chicken stock mixture			
Reserved poached fish	5–6 oz	150–160 g	
Scallions, white and green sections, sliced thin into rounds	1	1	

Whole Fish with Vegetables in Hot Sauce

YIELD: 1-2 SERVINGS

SAUCE

Stock, fish or chicken	3–4 oz	90–120 ml	*Combine ingredients and stir until the cornstarch has completely dissolved. Reserve.*
Vinegar, white, distilled	2 oz	60 ml	
Soy sauce	1 tbsp	15 ml	
Tomato paste	1 tsp	5 g	
Cornstarch	1 1/2 tsp	5 g	
Sugar	1 tbsp or to taste	15 g	
Chili oil	1 tbsp or to taste	15 ml or to taste	

VEGETABLES

Bamboo shoots small dice	1 oz	30 g	*Prepare vegetables and reserve.*
Chili pepper, fresh, green, seed and ribs removed, fine julienne	1/2 oz or to taste	15 g or to taste	
Mushrooms, Chinese, black, soaked, stems removed and discarded, caps cut into 1/4-in. (0.75-cm) strips	2–3	2–3	
Whole fish—bass, porgy, croaker, snapper, perch	1, 3–4 1/2 lb	1, 340–680 g	*Clean fish taking care to remove any loose scales and fins. Leave head on.*

(Continued on next page)

POACHING LIQUID

Scallion, white and green parts, cut julienne	*1*	*1*
Gingerroot, peeled and cut julienne	*3 slices*	*3 slices*
Oil, vegetable	*1 tsp*	*15 ml*
Salt	*1 1/2 tsp*	*3 g*
Water or fish stock	*8 oz*	*240 ml*
Cleaned fish		

Place ingredients in a wok or other pan large enough to hold the fish. Add 8 oz (240 ml) of water or fish stock and bring to a boil. Cover pan, lower heat and simmer for 10 minutes. Add cleaned fish and more water or stock if needed, to barely cover the fish. Return poaching liquid to a boil, lower heat to simmer and cover pan. Poach gently for 6–8 minutes, depending on thickness of fish. When done, remove fish and place on a heated plate. Arrange the scallions and ginger on top. Reserve in a warm place on a serving plate.

Oil, vegetable	*2 oz*	*60 ml*
Reserved vegetables		
Reserved sauce		
Pepper, black, fine ground	*as needed*	*as needed*

Discard or reserve the poaching liquid for another purpose and wipe the pan dry. Add the oil and increase the heat to high. When oil has reached the smoking point, pour half over the fish. Stir-fry the reserved vegetables in the remaining oil for 1 minute. Add the reserved sauce and bring to a boil. Lower heat and simmer for 1–2 minutes. Pour contents of pan over fish, then sprinkle lightly with pepper.

Crisp Fried Fish in a Sweet and Sour Sauce

YIELD: 10 SERVINGS

SWEET AND SOUR SAUCE

Carrot, sliced thin (use carrots no more than 1 in. (2.5-cm) across	4 oz	115 g
Peas, fresh or frozen	4 oz	115 g

Blanch carrots and peas in boiling water. Place in iced water. When cool drain and reserve.

Water	1 pt	470 ml
Tomato sauce or catsup	4 oz	120 ml
Vinegar, white, distilled	4 oz	120 ml
Soy sauce	3 oz	90 ml
Rice wine or dry sherry	3 oz	90 ml
Sugar	3 oz	90 g

Combine ingredients and stir until the sugar is completely dissolved. Reserve.

Cornstarch	3 tbsp	30 g
Water	as needed	as needed

Mix the cornstarch with enough water to make a thin paste. Reserve.

Oil, vegetable	2 oz	60 ml
Garlic, minced	1 tbsp	15 g
Ginger root, peeled and minced	2 tsp	8 g
Onion, sliced root to stem to make thin wedges	2 small	2 small

Heat wok or saucepan. Add the oil and distribute it over the bottom of the pan. When the oil is just below the smoking point, stir-fry the garlic, ginger-root, and onion until the aroma of the garlic and ginger is released.

Reserved carrots and peas		
Reserved sweet and sour mixture		

Add ingredients to the pan and bring to a boil.

(Continued on next page)

Cornstarch mixture

Add the cornstarch mixture and cook, stirring, until the sauce thickens. Remove from heat and reserve in a warm place until needed.

TO PREPARE AN INDIVIDUAL SERVING

Fish, whole—snapper, bass, porgy, trout or any other firm-fleshed fish	3/4– 1 lb each	340–450 g each
Salt	2 parts	2 parts
Five-spice powder	1 part	1 part

Remove all scales and fins, leaving on the head and tail. Wash fish thoroughly and dry it with absorbent towels. Slash fish on the diagonal 2–3 times on each side. Rub all surfaces of the fish, including the inner cavity, with a 2 part to 1 part mixture of salt and five-spice powder.

Egg, beaten	as needed	as needed
Cornstarch	as needed	as needed
Oil, vegetable	for deep-frying	for deep-frying

Dip fish in beaten egg, then cornstarch. Cover all surfaces. Shake off any excess. Deep-fry in hot oil until the fish is cooked through and very crisp on the outside. When done, drain on absorbent towel, then place on a warm serving dish.

Reserved sweet and sour sauce	approximately 3 oz per serving	approximately 90 ml per serving
Scallions, white and tender green sections, sliced thin	as needed	as needed

Spoon sauce on top and garnish with a sprinkling of sliced scallions.

Flounder Fillet Deep-Fried in a Chickpea Batter

YIELD: 10 SERVINGS

Flounder fillet or other firm-fleshed, white fish fillet	10 fillets, 6 oz each	10 fillets, 170 g each	Trim fillets and sprinkle lightly with lemon juice. Place on a stainless steel tray, cover and refrigerate until needed.
Lemon juice, fresh squeezed	as needed	as needed	
Flour, chickpea,* sifted	12 oz	340 g	Combine ingredients and stir until smooth. The exact amount of water will vary and should be added slowly toward the end of the process. Batter should have the consistency of heavy cream. If a heavier coating is desired, use less water.
Water, iced	20–24 oz	600–700 ml	
Butter, clarified	2 oz	60 ml	Add ingredients to the batter and mix until thoroughly blended. Cover and let rest 10–15 minutes before using.
Garlic, puree	1 tbsp	15 g	
Cumin, ground	1 tbsp	7 g	
Salt	2 tsp	10 g	
Turmeric	1 tsp	2 g	
Pepper, black	1 tsp	2 g	

TO PREPARE AN INDIVIDUAL SERVING

Reserved fish cut lengthwise into 2 pieces	1 fillet, 6 oz	1 fillet, 170 g	Pat fish dry and dip into batter. Drain excess batter and deep-fry in vegetable oil at 375°F (190°C) until golden. Remove from oil and drain on towel prior to serving. Serve with rice pilaf and tomato/ginger chutney (see recipe).
Reserved batter	as needed	as needed	
Oil, vegetable	to deep-fry	to deep-fry	

*Also known as gram flour, the chickpea flour used for Indian recipes is made from chickpeas that have been roasted before being ground into flour. If this flour is not available, spread a thin layer of unroasted chickpea flour in a pan and place in a moderate oven until lightly toasted.

Fish Braised in a Spicy Sauce

Whole firm-fleshed fish—sea bass, porgy, trout	10, 3/4–1 lb each	10, 340–450 g each
Salt	as needed	as needed

TO PREPARE AN INDIVIDUAL SERVING

Oil, peanut	2 tbsp	30 ml
Reserved fish		

Clean fish thoroughly. Remove all scales, gills, and fins, leaving the head on. Rub a small amount of salt over the entire surface including the cavity. Place in stainless steel or glass pan in a single layer, cover, and refrigerate until needed.

Heat a wok or skillet over high heat. When very hot add the oil and distribute evenly over the surface of the pan. Lower to medium heat and sauté the fish briefly on one side until the skin has browned and is crisp. Using a large spatula, gently turn the fish to the other side and cook until crisp. Remove the partially cooked fish and reserve in a warm place.

Oil, vegetable	as needed	as needed
Gingerroot, peeled and chopped	1/2-in. piece	1.5-cm piece
Garlic, peeled and chopped	1 tsp	5 g
Szechwan chili paste (see recipe) or other hot soybean paste	2 tbsp or to taste	20 g or to taste
Dry sherry or Shaohsing wine	1 tbsp	15 ml
Sugar	1/2 tsp	2–3 g
Stock, chicken	4 oz	120 ml

Using the same pan, add a little more oil if needed, and raise heat to high. Stir-fry the ginger and garlic until they begin to color lightly. Add the chili paste, wine, and sugar and stir-fry for another 10–15 seconds. Add the stock and bring to a boil.

Partially cooked fish		

Return the fish to the pan and baste with the pan liquids. Lower the heat, cover, and simmer for 4–5 minutes depending on the thickness of the fish. When done, remove fish to a warm serving plate.

Chili oil (see recipe)	to taste	to taste
Scallions, green parts cut into very thin circles	as needed	as needed

Raise heat to high. Add a small amount of chili oil, then reduce sauce to a slightly syrupy consistency. Pour over fish and garnish with scallion.

Steamed Soft Shell Crabs with Ginger sauce

YIELD: 10 SERVINGS

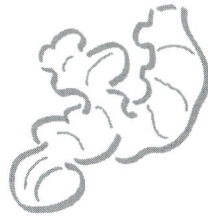

GINGER SAUCE

Rice vinegar	16 oz	480 ml
Sesame oil	4 oz	120 ml
Gingerroot, peeled and minced	2–3 tbsp	20–30 g
Sugar	2 tbsp	30 g

Combine ingredients and stir until the sugar is completely dissolved. Reserve.

Crabs, soft shell, cleaned*	*Serving size varies with season. Serve 2–4 per serving depending on size*	*Serving size varies with season. Serve 2–4 per serving depending on size*
Scallions, white and green parts, fine julienne	*1 per serving*	*1 per serving*
Gingerroot, fine julienne	*4 thin slices*	*4 thin slices*
Rice wine or dry sherry	*as needed*	*as needed*

Place crabs on an ovenproof plate and distribute the scallion, gingerroot, and rice wine or dry sherry over the tops. Steam over rapidly boiling water for 8–12 minutes. Cooking time will vary depending on the size of the crabs. When done serve immediately with 2 oz (60 ml) of the ginger dipping sauce served on the side in a small deep dish.

*Soft shell crabs are best when obtained fresh in season.

Crab Cakes

YIELD: VARIABLE DEPENDING ON SIZE OF PATTIES

Crab meat, cooked	2 lb	900 g	
Onion, grated	8 oz	230 g	
Egg, whole, beaten with 2 tsp water	3 large	3 large	
Red bell pepper, minced fine	2 oz	60g	
Pepper, white	2 tsp	4 g	
Salt	1 tsp	5 g	

Pick over crab meat to remove all cartilage. Place in a mixing bowl and combine with the remaining ingredients. Shape into 1-in. (2.5-cm) patties and refrigerate on a lined pan. Chill 1 hour before using.

TO PREPARE AN INDIVIDUAL SERVING

Butter, whole, and oil, vegetable, 50/50 mixture	as needed to sauté	as needed to sauté
Spicy red bell pepper sauce (see recipe)		

Heat the butter/oil mixture over medium to high heat in a small skillet. Sauté crab cakes on both sides until golden brown. Drain on clean paper or kitchen towel. Serve on a pool of spicy red bell pepper sauce.

Marinated Steamed Bass

YIELD: 2 SERVINGS

Sea bass, whole	1 1/2 lb	700 g
Salt	as needed	as needed

Clean fish taking care to remove all internal membranes, gills, and exterior fins. Wash fish under cold, running water. Make 2–3 diagonal cuts perpendicular to the backbone, on each side of the fish. Pat dry, lightly salt inside and out, then place in an ovenproof baking pan approximately the same size as the fish.

MARINADE

Rice wine or dry sherry	2 oz	60 ml
Soy sauce, light	1 oz	30 ml
Sesame oil	1 oz	30 ml
Vinegar, white, distilled	1 oz	30 ml
Pepper, white, fine ground	pinch	pinch
Scallion, white and green parts, sliced thin	2	2

Combine ingredients, mix well, then distribute evenly over fish. Cover and refrigerate for at least 1 hour before cooking. Any number of fish can be prepared in this manner in advance.

TO PREPARE

Marinated fish		
Cilantro leaves, fresh, chopped coarsely	as needed	as needed

Using the same dish in which the fish was marinated, place the fish in a steamer and cook for 10–15 minutes or until done as desired. Fish is done when flesh turns white and is firm to the touch. To serve, sprinkle fish with the chopped cilantro. Place cooking dish on a cool plate. Serve fish in the dish in which it was cooked.

Scallops Teriyaki

YIELD: 1 SERVING

Scallops	6 oz	170 g	*If scallops are large, slice in half or thirds so that you have 2 or 3 thinner discs per scallop. Place scallops and the teriyaki sauce in a small mixing bowl. Toss to thoroughly coat the scallops. Let marinate for 10 minutes.*
Teriyaki sauce (see recipe)	2 oz	60 ml	
Oil, vegetable	2 tsp	10 ml	*Heat oil in a skillet or wok over medium to high heat. Remove scallops from the marinade with a slotted spoon reserving the remaining marinade in the mixing bowl. Stir-fry the scallops briefly until lightly browned on all sides. Cooking time will vary depending on thickness of scallops. Reduce heat to low and add the reserved marinade. Bring the pan liquids to a boil tossing the scallops in the hot marinade until well coated. Do not over cook. Serve with steamed asparagus and rice.*

Red Cooked Fish

YIELD: 1-2 SERVINGS

Whole fish (porgy, croaker, trout or sea bass)	*3/4–1 lb for single serving; 1 1 1/2–1 3/4 lb for two servings*	*340–450 g for single serving; 680–800 g for two servings*	*Wash fish thoroughly, then pat dry. Slash each side diagonally 2 or 3 times, depending on length of fish. Rub a light layer of salt on all surfaces including the cavity. Reserve.*
Salt	*as needed*	*as needed*	

FLAVORING MIXTURE

Chicken stock	*6 oz*	*180 ml*	*Combine ingredients and stir until the sugar dissolves. Reserve.*
Soy sauce, dark	*2 oz*	*60 ml*	
Rice wine or dry sherry	*1 oz*	*30 ml*	
Sugar, brown	*2 tbsp*	*30 g*	
Scallions, white and green parts sliced into 1-in. (2.5-cm) pieces	*6*	*6*	
Gingerroot, peeled and sliced thin	*3–4 slices*	*3–4 slices*	
Bamboo shoots, sliced thin	*2 oz*	*60 g*	

TO PREPARE

Oil, peanut	*2–3 oz*	*60–90 ml*	*Heat wok or skillet over high heat. Add the oil and heat to just under the smoking point. Fry fish 2–3 minutes on each side, turning once, or until the skin is crisp. Pour off all but 1 tbsp (15 ml) of the oil. Add the flavoring mixture and bring to a boil. Lower heat, cover, and simmer for 3–4 minutes depending on the thickness of the fish. When done place the fish on a heated platter. Raise heat to high and reduce the cooking liquids by half. When done, pour the reduced sauce over the fish and serve.*
Reserved fish			
Reserved flavoring mixture			

Poached Sweet and Sour Trout

YIELD: 1 SERVING

Water or fish stock	8 oz	240 ml
Gingerroot, peeled and sliced thin	2 slices	2 slices
Scallions, white and green parts cut into 1-in. (2.5-cm) pieces	2	2
Trout or other firm-fleshed white fish	1, 3/4 lb	1, 340 g

SAUCE

Vinegar, wine	2 oz	60 ml
Oil, peanut	1 tbsp	15 ml
Soy sauce, dark		
Gingerroot, peeled and grated fine	2 tsp	8 g
Sugar, brown	2 tsp	10 g
Garlic, minced	1/2 tsp or to taste	3 g or to taste
Pepper, black	pinch	pinch
Cornstarch	2 tsp	8 g
Cold water	as needed	as needed

Place the water or stock in a skillet large enough to hold the fish after it has been split and spread open. Add the gingerroot and the scallions and bring to a boil. Lower heat and simmer for 2–3 minutes. Clean and debone the fish. First, split the head down the middle, then cut along the spine from the inside of the fish taking care not to pierce the skin. Spread open the fish so that the skin side faces upwards. Place fish in stock, cover, and poach for 2–3 minutes. Remove pan from heat and set aside for 4–5 minutes in a warm place.

Place fish on a heated plate. Add ingredients to the cooking liquid. Bring to a boil over high heat and reduce liquid by half.

Mix cornstarch with enough water to make a smooth paste. Add this to the sauce, stirring. When slightly thickened, pour over fish.

Fish Balls, Barbecued on Skewers

CAMBODIA

YIELD: 10 SERVINGS

Ingredient	US	Metric
Cod, fillet, cut into 1 1/2-in. (4-cm) pieces	3 lb	1.4kg
Scallion, minced	6 oz	170 g
Gingerroot, peeled and minced	2 tbsp	20 g
Lemon grass, tender inner stalk	1 tbsp or to taste	10 g or to taste
Chili pepper, fresh, green, seeds and ribs removed, minced	2 tsp or to taste	8 g or to taste
Salt	1 tbsp or to taste	15 g or to taste
Anise seed	2 tsp	4 g
Pepper, white	2 tsp	2 g
Water	6–8 oz or as needed	180–240 ml or as needed
Water, lightly salted	8–10 qt	8–9 L

Place ingredients into the bowl of a food processor fitted with a steel blade. Process into a smooth puree.

Add ingredients and process until smooth. The fish paste should have a consistency suitable for forming into balls for poaching. Add the water in small increments as needed, to achieve the proper consistency. Form the fish paste into 1–1 1/2-in. (2.5–4-cm) balls.

Bring water to a boil. Lower heat to medium and gently poach the fish balls. When they rise to the surface, cook for another minute or so, then remove with a slotted spoon and reserve.

TO PREPARE AN INDIVIDUAL SERVING

Ingredient	US	Metric
Reserved fish balls	4–5 oz per serving	115–140 g per serving
Oil, vegetable, and oil, sesame, 50/50 mixture	as needed	as needed
Lemon juice, fresh squeezed	as needed	as needed
Fish sauce	as needed	as needed

Thread fish balls onto oiled bamboo or stainless steel skewers. Brush the fish balls with the 50/50 oil mixture and grill over coals or under the broiler flame until heated through and lightly browned. Prior to serving, sprinkle lightly with fresh lemon juice and fish sauce.

See color insert for photograph of recipe

171

FISH AND SEAFOOD

Fish Coated with Peanuts or Sesame Seeds

YIELD: 10 SERVINGS

DIPPING SAUCE

Worcestershire sauce	6 oz	180 ml	Combine ingredients thoroughly. Reserve until needed. (Yield: 1 pint {475 ml}.)
Ketchup	6 oz	170 g	
Soy sauce dark	2 oz	60 ml	
Lemon juice, fresh squeezed	2 oz	60 ml	
Japanese mustard, powder	sparingly, to taste	sparingly, to taste	
Fish—fresh sardines or small smelt, gutted and cleaned	40, fish weighing approximately 4 lb after cleaning	40, fish weighing approximately 2 kg after cleaning	Remove heads and fins. Slice belly up to and through the tail. Spread open the fish and remove the spines. Lightly salt the fish on both sides. Place the spread fish on a stainless steel tray and let sit, refrigerated for 15 minutes.
Salted fish			Keeping the fish spread, dredge on both sides in flour. Shake to remove any excess flour. Dip the fish next into the beaten egg then into the crushed peanuts or sesame seeds, pressing to ensure that the fish are evenly coated. Refrigerate until needed.
Flour	as needed	as needed	
Egg beaten	as needed	as needed	
Peanuts, roasted, crushed fine, or white or black sesame seeds	as needed	as needed	

TO PREPARE AN INDIVIDUAL SERVING

Oil, vegetable	for deep-frying	for deep-frying	Deep-fry fish in 350°F (175°C) oil for 2–3 minutes or until the coating is nicely browned and crisp. Gently remove the fish from the oil with a slotted spoon or tongs. Drain on clean towel. Serve with lemon wedges and a small side dish of the dipping sauce.
Reserved fish	4 per serving	4 per serving	
Lemon wedges	2 per serving	2 per serving	

Crab Cakes with Sweet and Hot Peppers

YIELD: VARIABLE

CRAB CAKES

Crab meat, steamed	2 lb	900 g
Eggs, whole	4	4
Onion, grated	1 1/4 lb	560 g
Pepper, black, fine ground	2 tsp or to taste	4 g or to taste
Salt	1 tsp or to taste	5 g or to taste
Vegetable oil	6 oz	180 ml
Butter	2 oz	60 g
Red bell pepper, seeded and cut into small dice	1 1/2 lb	700 g
Green chili, fresh, seeds and ribs removed, minced	3–4 or to taste	3–4 or to taste
Salt	to taste	to taste

Combine ingredients, then form into small, flattened cakes. Size will depend on planned usage.* Place cakes on a tray covered with plastic wrap, cover and refrigerate for 1 hour.

Heat oil and butter over low to medium heat. Add the peppers and sauté until cooked through. Sprinkle with salt to taste. Reserve.

TO PREPARE AN INDIVIDUAL SERVING

Oil/butter, 50/50 mixture	as needed	as needed
Crab cakes	as needed	as needed
Reserved sweet and hot peppers	as needed	as needed
Butter, melted	as needed	as needed
Lemon juice, fresh squeezed	as needed	as needed
Hot sauce	as needed	as needed

Heat oil/butter mixture in a heavy skillet over medium to high heat. Sauté crab cakes until well browned on both sides. When done, remove to a warm place and discard oil from pan.

Reheat peppers as needed. Place a small mound of the peppers on a plate and arrange crab cakes on top. Top with a small amount of melted butter, a squeeze of lemon juice, and a few dashes of hot sauce.

See color insert for photograph of recipe

*Number of crab cakes served will be determined by size: smaller if served as an appetizer; larger if served as an entree.

CHAPTER SIX

Poultry

Skewered Chicken with Peanut Sauce

YIELD: 10 SERVINGS

MARINADE

Soy sauce, light	6 oz	180 ml
Lime juice, fresh squeezed	4 oz	120 ml
Onion, minced	4 oz	115 g
Gingerroot, peeled and minced	2-in. piece	5 cm-piece
Garlic, minced	1 tbsp	15 g
Coriander, ground	1 tbsp	7 g
Sugar	2 tsp	10 g
Pepper, cayenne	1/2 tsp or to taste	1 g or to taste

Combine ingredients and stir until the sugar is completely dissolved.

Chicken meat, leg and thighs or breast meat	4 lb	1.8 kg
Stainless steel skewers	as needed	as needed
Peanut sauce (see recipe)	as needed	as needed

Cut chicken into uniform cubes, about 1 in. (2.5 cm) square. Thread approximately 6 oz (170 g) of chicken on each skewer. Place skewers in a stainless steel pan and pour the marinade on top. Turn the skewers several times to distribute the marinade evenly. Cover pan and refrigerate overnight. Grill as needed over coals or under a broiler flame. Baste with the marinade once or twice during the cooking process. Serve with a small amount of warm peanut sauce for dipping.

See color insert for photograph of recipe

Chicken with Mango, Scallions, and Peppers

YIELD: 10 SERVINGS

MARINADE

Oyster sauce	3 oz	90 ml
Rice wine	2 oz	60 ml
Soy sauce, light	2 oz	60 ml
Oil, sesame	1 oz	30 ml
Ginger juice	1 oz	30 ml
Sugar	1 tbsp	15 g
Cornstarch	2 tsp	7 g
Salt	1 tsp	5 g
Pepper, white, fine ground	1/2 tsp	1 g

Combine ingredients and stir until the sugar and cornstarch are thoroughly dissolved. Reserve.

Chicken breast meat, trimmed, boned and skinned	2 1/2 lb	1.15 kg

Flatten the chicken breasts to a uniform thickness of about 1/4 in. (0.75 cm). Slice into 2 x 1/2 in. (5 x 1.5 cm) pieces. Place in a stainless steel bowl and add the marinade. Toss well to coat the pieces evenly. Cover and refrigerate. Allow to marinate for at least 30 minutes before using.

VEGETABLES

Pepper, green bell	1 lb	450 g
Mango	1 lb	450 g
Scallions	15	15
Water chestnuts	20	20

Clean peppers, then cut them into 1/2-in. dice. Slice the mango into 1 x 1/2 in. (2.5 x 1.5 cm) pieces. Slice the white parts of the scallions into 1-in. (2.5-cm) lengths, reserving the green parts for other uses. Slice the water chestnuts into thin slices. Mix vegetables together and reserve.

(Continued on facing page)

Oil, peanut	2 tsp	10 ml
Ginger, minced	1 tsp	5 g
Reserved vegetables and mango	4 oz approx.	115 g approx.

Heat a wok or heavy skillet over high heat. Add the oil. When the oil is just below the smoking point add the ginger and stir-fry for 15–20 seconds. Add the vegetables and mango mixture and stir-fry for another minute. Remove vegetables from the pan and reserve in a warm place.

Oil, peanut	1 tsp	5 ml
Garlic, minced	1/2 tsp or to taste	3 g or to taste
Marinated chicken	4 oz	115 g

Add oil to the pan and, over high heat, stir-fry the garlic until it begins to color lightly. Add the chicken and several tablespoons of the marinade. Spread the chicken pieces over the surface of the pan so that they will cook quickly. Stir-fry the chicken for 1–2 minutes or until it is cooked through. Return the vegetables and mango to the pan and stir-fry for another minute.

Cornstarch	1 tsp	4 g
Chicken stock or water, cold	2 oz	60 ml

Mix ingredients together until smooth. Pour into center of pan and stir well. Cover pan and cook for another minute or until the liquids thicken.

Chicken with Red Chili and Green Bell Peppers

YIELD: 1 SERVING

Oil, peanut	1 tbsp	15 ml	*Heat oil in a wok or skillet over high heat and stir-fry the garlic until it begins to color lightly. Add the chicken and stir-fry for another minute or until the chicken is almost cooked through.*
Garlic, chopped	1 tsp	5 g	
Chicken breast, skinned and boned, then cut into 1/2-in. (1.5-cm) strips	4 oz	115 g	
Pepper, green bell, large dice	2 oz	60 g	*Add ingredients and stir-fry for another minute.*
Chili pepper, red, fresh, seeds and ribs removed, cut julienne	1 or to taste	1 or to taste	
Onion, sliced	1–2 slices	1–2 slices	
Oyster sauce	2 tsp	12 g	*Add the oyster, soy, and fish sauces. Stir-fry for another 1–2 minutes. Add the basil leaves, stir well, and remove from heat. Serve with white, boiled rice.*
Soy sauce, dark	1 tsp	5 ml	
Fish sauce	dash	dash	
Basil leaves, fresh, whole	6–8 depending on size	6-8 depending on size	

Chicken Teriyaki

YIELD: 1 SERVING

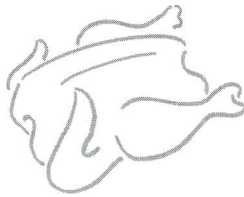

Chicken breast, skin on, boned	1, 6 oz	1, 170 g	*Using a sharp fork, pierce the chicken breast all over. Heat a thin film of oil in a small skillet over medium heat. Place the chicken skin side down in the skillet and sauté until the skin has browned. Turn the chicken to the other side, lower heat, and cook, covered for another 6–8 minutes or until the chicken is cooked through. When done, remove the chicken to a warm place and reserve.*
Oil, vegetable	as needed	as needed	
Teriyaki sauce (see recipe)	2–3 oz	60–90 ml	*Add the teriyaki sauce to the pan, stir to incorporate any pan juices, and bring to a boil. Cook at high heat for 30–40 seconds or until the sauce begins to thicken. Return the chicken to the pan. Cook uncovered for a minute or so, turning the chicken frequently to coat well. Continue until most of the teriyaki sauce has either been absorbed or reduced. To serve, cut the breast into slices and arrange fanlike on a warm plate. Serve with stir-fried vegetables and a side dish of white rice.*

Chicken with Ginger and Red Chili

YIELD: 1 SERVING

Oil, peanut	1 tbsp	15 ml	*Heat oil in wok or skillet over high heat and stir-fry until the garlic begins to color lightly.*
Garlic, chopped	1 tsp	5 g	
Chicken breast, skinned and boned, cut into 1/4-in. (0.75-cm) slices	4–5 oz	115–140 g	*Add the chicken and continue to stir-fry for another minute. Add the mushrooms and stir-fry for another 15–20 seconds.*
Mushrooms, white button, sliced	2–3	2–3	
Onion, red, sliced	1–2 slices	1–2 slices	*Add ingredients and stir-fry for 3–4 minutes or until the chicken is cooked through.*
Scallion, white and green parts, sliced in 1-in. pieces	1	1	
Gingerroot, fine julienne	1 tsp	5 g	
Chili pepper, red, fresh, julienne	1 or to taste	1 or to taste	
Soy sauce, light	2 tsp	10 ml	
Sugar	pinch	pinch	
Salt	pinch	pinch	

Marinated Chicken Kebabs

INDIA

YIELD: 10 SERVINGS

MARINADE

Oil, vegetable	4 oz	120 ml	*Combine ingredients in a stainless steel mixing bowl and reserve.*
Lemon juice, fresh-squeezed	4 oz	120 ml	
Soy sauce, dark	2 oz	60 ml	
Garlic, minced	1 tbsp	15 g	
Gingerroot, minced	1 tbsp	15 g	
Garam masala (see recipe)	1 tbsp	7 g	
Coriander, ground	1 tbsp	7 g	
Turmeric, ground	2 tsp	4 g	
Salt	1 tsp or to taste	5 g or to taste	
Pepper, black	1 tsp or to taste	2 g or to taste	
Pepper, cayenne	1/2 tsp or to taste	1 g or to taste	
Chicken breast meat, skinned and boned	4 lb	1.8 kg	*Cut chicken into 1 1/2-in. (4-cm) cubes. Lightly oil the skewers and thread 3 oz (90 g) of chicken on each. Cover all surfaces of the chicken with the marinade and place in a stainless steel pan. Cover and refrigerate for 3–4 hours before using.*
Oil, vegetable	as needed	as needed	
Skewers, stainless steel	as needed	as needed	

TO PREPARE AN INDIVIDUAL SERVING

Marinated chicken	2 skewers per serving	2 skewers per serving	*Grill over coals or under broiler flame, turning frequently, until the chicken is cooked through. While cooking, brush once or twice with a small amount of the marinade. Serve garnished with lemon wedges. Can also be served in smaller portions as an appetizer.*

Chicken with Basil

Jalapeño pepper, fresh, seeds and ribs removed, then chopped,	*1 or to taste*	*1 or to taste*	*Combine ingredients in a mortar and pestle or chop very fine with a knife. Reserve.*
Garlic, chopped	*1 tsp*	*5 g*	
Oil, peanut	*1 oz*	*30 ml*	*Heat oil in a wok or skillet over high heat and stir-fry the garlic and jalapeño puree for 10–15 seconds. Add the chicken and stir-fry for another minute.*
Chicken, ground	*4–5 oz*	*115–140 g*	
Red chili pepper, fresh, seeds and ribs removed, cut into quarters	*1*	*1*	*Add ingredients and continue to stir-fry for 2–3 minutes more or until the chicken is cooked through.*
Oyster sauce	*1 tsp*	*5 g*	
Fish sauce	*1 tsp*	*5 ml*	
Soy sauce, dark	*dash*	*dash*	
Basil leaves, fresh, depending on size	*4–5*	*4–5*	*Add the basil leaves and stir well. Serve over a bed of white, boiled rice. Garnish with fresh orange slices.*

Chicken Adobo

YIELD: 10 SERVINGS

MARINADE

Vinegar, white	8 oz	240 ml	*Combine ingredients and mix well.*
Garlic	1 tbsp	15 g	
Sugar	1 tbsp	15 g	
Salt	2 tsp	10 g	
Bay leaves, crumbled	3	3	
Pepper, coarsely ground	2 tsp	4 g	
Chickens	5, 2 1/2 lb each	5, 1.20 kg each	*Split each chicken in half down the backbone. Remove excess fat and skin; trim 1/4 in. (0.75 cm) of bone from the ends of the drumsticks. Fold wing under and place the split chickens in a single layer in a stainless steel roasting pan. Pour the marinade over the chicken, cover, and refrigerate for at least 4 hours or overnight. When marinated, place the chicken (skin side up) along with the marinade in a 350°F (175°C) oven and roast for 30–40 minutes or until the chicken is just done. Let cool and reserve in the refrigerator. (Do not overcook the chicken; if the chicken is slightly underdone it will be finished in the next stage of the cooking process.)*

TO PREPARE AN INDIVIDUAL SERVING

Marinated chicken	1/2 per serving	1/2 per serving	*Deep-fry the chicken at 350°F (175°C) until nicely browned and crisp on the edges. When done, drain on a towel to remove excess oil. Place chicken, skin side up, on a bed of shredded lettuce and garnish with alternating pieces of tomato and pineapple. Garnish with lemon wedge(s).*
Lettuce, shredded	as needed	as needed	
Tomato wedges	as needed	as needed	
Pineapple, fresh, cut in large cubes	as needed	as needed	
Lemon wedge(s)	1–2	1–2	

Barbecued Chicken Salad

YIELD: 10 SERVINGS

Oil, vegetable	*3 parts*	*3 parts*
Oil, sesame	*1 part*	*1 part*
Chicken breasts, skinned, boned, then slightly flattened	*10, 6 oz each*	*10, 170 g each*

Mix enough of these oils together to brush the chicken breast meat lightly on both sides. Grill over coals or broil 3–4 in. (8–10 cm) below the flame, turning once, until cooked through. Cooking time will vary depending on thickness of meat. Reserve.

SALAD DRESSING

Fish sauce	*4 oz*	*120 ml*
Vinegar, white	*4 oz*	*120 ml*
Lime juice, fresh	*4 oz*	*120 ml*
Peanuts, unsalted, roasted and crushed	*3 oz*	*80 g*
Sugar	*2 tbsp or to taste*	*30 g or to taste*
Chili pepper, ground	*1 tbsp or to taste*	*7 g or to taste*
Salt	*to taste*	*to taste*

Place ingredients in a small saucepan and slowly bring to a boil, stirring occasionally. When the liquids have reached the boiling point, remove from heat, let cool, and reserve until needed.

TO PREPARE AN INDIVIDUAL SERVING

Grilled chicken	*one piece*	*one piece*
Salad dressing	*as needed*	*as needed*
Tomato slices	*3–4*	*3–4*
Onions, sliced thin	*3–4*	*3–4*
Lettuce leaves	*as needed*	*as needed*
Cabbage, Savoy, uncooked, cut into very thin wedges	*2 wedges per serving*	*2 wedges per serving*
Cilantro leaves, fresh, chopped	*as needed*	*as needed*

Slice chicken breast meat into thin slices. Place the chicken, tomato and onion slices in mixing bowl with just enough salad dressing to coat the pieces lightly. Place a bed of lettuce on a chilled salad plate. Arrange the chicken slices in the center of the plate and surround with tomato and onion slices placed in an attractive pattern. Garnish the plate further by adding the cabbage wedges and a sprinkling of fresh, chopped cilantro leaves

Roast Duckling Cantonese Style

YIELD: 10 SERVINGS

SEASONING SAUCE

Soybean paste	8 oz	220 g
Rice wine or dry sherry	4 oz	120 ml
Sugar	3 oz	85 g
Salt	1 tsp	5 g
Star anise, crushed fine	5 whole	5 whole
Scallion, minced, white and green parts	5	5
Gingerroot, peeled and minced	2 oz	60 g
Garlic, minced	1 tbsp	15 g

Combine ingredients and reserve.

GLAZE MIXTURE

Malt sugar (maltose)	12 oz	340 g
Vinegar, white distilled	12 oz	360 ml
Water, boiling	4 oz	120 ml

Place the water in a small saucepan and bring to a boil. Add the malt sugar and vinegar. Simmer, stirring, for 2–3 minutes. Reserve.

Ducklings, cleaned and eviscerated, head and neck on	5, 2 3/4 lb each	5, 1.2 kg each
Reserved seasoning sauce		
Reserved glaze mixture		

Blanch ducklings in boiling water for 2–3 minutes. When cool enough to handle, tie a 2-ft (60-cm) length of butcher's twine firmly around the neck and under the wings of each bird. Cover the duck's cavity with a liberal coating of the seasoning sauce. Close the opening of each cavity with a skewer. Suspend the ducks by the neck over a tray to catch any drippings. Using a pastry brush, paint a thick coating of the glaze mixture over the entire surface of the ducks. Place them in the refrigerator. Let hang to dry for 4–6 hours.

(Continued on next page)

TO ROAST

Marinated ducklings		
Duck, chicken, or veal stock	*as needed*	*as needed*

Place the ducklings on a rack set over a drip pan, breast side down. Roast in a 400°F (200°C) oven for 30 minutes. Turn duck, lower heat to 350°F (175°C), and roast for another 40–45 minutes. Remove ducklings and reserve in a warm place. Place pan drippings in a saucepan. Degrease the liquid and add enough stock to make the total volume about 1 qt (1 L). Bring sauce to a boil, skim, then lower heat and simmer for 5 minutes, skimming as needed. Reserve.

TO SERVE

Duckling	*1/2 per serving*	*1/2 per serving*
Sauce	*2–3 oz per serving*	*60–90 ml per serving*

If duckling has cooled, place in a 350°F (175°C) oven until heated through. When reheated, use a cleaver to chop into 1-in. (2.5-cm) slices, cutting through the bone perpendicular to the breast bone. Reassemble to original shape after cutting then pour heated sauce on top.

Red Cooked Chicken

YIELD: 12 SERVINGS

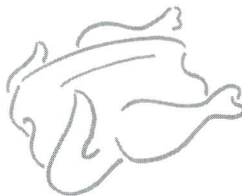

COOKING BROTH

Water	2 qt	2 L
Soy sauce, dark	1 1/2 pt	700 ml
Rice wine or dry sherry	4 oz	120 ml
Gingerroot, peeled, cut into thin slices	4 oz	115 g
Sugar	3 oz	85 g
Star anise, whole	1/2 oz	14 g
Tangerine peel, dried	3–4 pieces	3–4 pieces
Chicken, whole, trussed	3, 3 lb each	3, 1.4 kg each
Soy sauce	if needed	if needed
Water	if needed	if needed
Sesame oil	as needed	as needed
Chicken	1/4 per serving	1/4 per serving

Combine ingredients in a heavy saucepan large enough to hold the liquid and the chickens. Bring to a boil over medium heat, then lower heat and simmer, uncovered, for 30 minutes.

Wash and trim any excess fat or skin from the chickens. When the cooking liquid is ready, add the chickens, breast side down, and simmer, covered, for 1 hour. (If the liquid is not sufficient to cover, supplement with a 50/50 mixture of water and soy sauce.) When done, remove from heat. Keeping the pot covered, let the chicken cool completely in the cooking liquid.

Remove chickens from the broth and brush the surfaces with sesame oil. When serving, the chicken can be carved in joints, or cut through the bones (discarding the backbone) into bite-sized pieces. Spoon some of the cooking liquid over the chicken when serving. The broth can be refrigerated and used again. Bring to a rapid boil before reusing.

Duck Braised in Wine, Ginger, and Five-Star Anise

YIELD: 10 SERVINGS

Scallions, whole	15–20	15–20

Trim and wash the scallions. In a roasting pan just large enough to hold five split ducklings, distribute the scallions evenly over the bottom of the pan.

Ducklings	5, 2 3/4 lb each	5, 1.2 kg each
Five-spice powder	as needed	as needed
Oil, peanut	2 tbsp	30 ml

Split ducks down the spine and remove all excess fat and skin. Dust all surfaces with five-spice powder. Heat oil in a large heavy skillet over medium high heat until just below the smoking point. Sauté the duck halves, skin side down, until well browned. Turn the duck pieces and brown the other side. When done, place the duck in the roasting pan, skin side down on top of the scallions.

Rice wine	16 oz	470 ml
Water	8 oz	240 ml
Soy sauce	6 oz	180 ml
Sugar	4 oz	115 g
Gingerroot, thin sliced	3 oz	90 g
Garlic, chopped	1 tbs.	15 g
Peppercorns, black	1 tsp	2 g
Cinnamon stick	2, 3-in. pieces	2, 8-cm pieces
Star anise, whole	6	6

Combine ingredients in a small saucepan and bring to a boil. Lower heat and simmer for 2–3 minutes, then pour over the duck. Cover pan, and place in a 350°F (175°C) oven for 1 hour. Remove cover, turn duck skin side up, and cook for another 1/2 hour. When done, let cool, then remove duck to a clean tray and refrigerate. Strain the pan liquids and refrigerate. When broth has cooled sufficiently, degrease and reserve.

TO PREPARE AN INDIVIDUAL SERVING

Cooked duck	1/2 duck per serv- ing	1/2 duck per serv- ing
Reserved broth	as needed	as needed

Reheat duck, as needed, in a small amount of broth until heated through. Serve with rice and a cooked, leafy green vegetable. A small amount of the broth can be served separately on the side.

See color insert for photograph of recipe

Duck with Red Curry Sauce

YIELD: 1 SERVING

Oil, vegetable	*1 tsp*	*5 ml*	*Heat oil in a wok or small heavy skillet over medium heat. Add the curry paste and mix well. Add the coconut milk, bring to a simmer, and stir to blend thoroughly.*
Red curry paste	*1 tsp*	*6 g*	
Coconut milk	*4 oz*	*120 ml*	
Roasted duck, deboned, and cut into 1-in. (2.5-cm) pieces	*6 oz*	*170 g*	*Add the roasted duck, and remaining ingredients and simmer over low to medium heat for 5 minutes*
Stock, chicken	*2 tbsp*	*30 ml*	
Kaffir lime leaf	*1*	*1*	
Fish sauce	*1 tsp or to taste*	*5 ml or to taste*	
Sugar	*pinch*	*pinch*	
Salt	*pinch*	*pinch*	
Cherry tomatoes, cut in half	*2*	*2*	*Add the cherry tomatoes and basil leaves and simmer for another 2 minutes.*
Basil leaves, whole	*5–6*	*5–6*	

Roasted Crispy Duck

YIELD: 10 SERVINGS

Ducklings	5, 2 3/4 lb each	5, 1.2 kg each
Gingerroot, peeled and minced	3 tbsp	35 g
Cinnamon, ground	2 tbsp	15 g
Pepper, black	1 1/2 tbsp	10 g
Nutmeg, ground	1 tsp	2 g
Aluminum foil	as needed	as needed

TO PREPARE AN INDIVIDUAL SERVING

Roasted duck	1/2 half per serving	1/2 per serving
Soy sauce, light	as needed	as needed

Wash ducks, inside and out, then pat dry with towel. Blend the spice mixture. Take half of the mixture and spread it over the interior cavity of each duck. Rub the remaining spice mixture over the outer surfaces. Seal the cavity opening securely with a skewer.

Wrap each duck in a well-sealed, double layer of aluminum foil. Place them in a deep roasting pan and roast at 450°F (230°C) for 45 minutes. Remove aluminum foil and lower the oven temperature to 375°F (190°C). Using a sharp fork, puncture the skin in all places where there are fatty deposits. Place ducks on a rack set over the roasting pan. Return ducks to the oven and roast for another 20 minutes. When done, let cool and reserve until needed.

Brush all surfaces of duck with soy sauce. Place in a 500°F (260°C) oven, skin side up, until the skin is crisp and the duck is heated through. Duck may also be served cut through the bone into small pieces and reassembled. Accompany with fresh scallions, cucumber slices, and chopped lettuce. For dipping, serve a small bowl of dark soy sauce on the side.

Crisp Duck Twice Cooked

FLAVORING MIX

Chinese brown pepper-corns	1 1/2 oz	40 g
Salt	1 1/2 oz	40 g

In a heavy skillet or wok, toast the peppercorns over moderate heat for several minutes, shaking the pan frequently. When the peppercorns become very aromatic, place them in a spice mill or mortar and pestle and pulverize. If a mortar and pestle is not available, place peppercorns in a double folded towel and pulverize them using a heavy cleaver or skillet. Return peppercorns to the pan and add the salt. Mix well, and continue to toast, shaking the pan, for another minute or so. Remove from heat.

Rice wine	6 oz	180 ml
Soy sauce, dark	3 oz	90 ml
Gingerroot, grated	3 tbsp	40 g
Scallions, white and green parts sliced thin	4	4

Combine ingredients and add the toasted spices. Mix well and reserve.

Ducks	3, 4 lb each	3, 1.8 kg each

Remove excess fat. Rub flavoring mixture over the exterior surface and interior cavities of the ducks. Place ducks on tray and refrigerate for 3–4 hours.

TO PREPARE

Soy sauce	as needed	as needed
Flour	as needed	as needed

Place the ducks in a steamer and cook for 2 1/2 hours or until the ducks are very tender. When cool, brush with soy sauce and dust lightly with flour. Ducks may be prepared, in advance, to this point. When ready to serve, deep-fry the duck in hot oil for 4–5 minutes or until the skin is very crisp.

TO SERVE

Each duck may be cut in quarters to provide 4 servings from each. Smaller ducks may also be used and split in half, or ducks may be chopped through the bone into small pieces and served in portions combined with a variety of steamed or stir-fried vegetables or noodles.

Cornish Hens in Apricot Ginger Sauce

YIELD: 10 SERVINGS

Cornish hens	10	10	*Split hens in half and remove the skins. Fold wing tips under the breast. Place the hens in a stainless steel pan just large enough to hold them in a single layer. Sprinkle with the lemon juice, cover, and marinate in the refrigerator for several hours or overnight.*
Lemon juice, fresh squeezed	8 oz	240 ml	
Apricots, dried	1 lb	450 g	*Place apricots in a bowl and add enough boiling water to cover. Let soak until the apricots are plump and tender. Reserve.*
Boiling water	as needed	as needed	
Clarified butter	4 oz	120 ml	*In a heavy-bottomed skillet, heat clarified butter over medium high heat. Pat hens dry, then sauté until browned on both sides. Place hens, breast side up, in a small roasting pan. Reserve.*
Marinated hens			
Clarified butter	if needed	if needed	*Using the same pan, add a little clarified butter, if needed, and over medium heat, sauté the onions until browned lightly. Add the gingerroot and Mughal garam masala, and mix well. Cook, stirring for another minute.*
Onions, chopped fine	1 1/2 lb	680 g	
Gingerroot, peeled and chopped fine	3 tbsp or to taste	35 g or to taste	
Mughal garam masala (see recipe)	1 tbsp or to taste	7 g or to taste	
Tomatoes, peeled and chopped	2 lb	900 g	*Add ingredients to the skillet, mix well, and bring to a boil. Lower heat and simmer, uncovered, until the sauce has reduced and thickened a little. Add salt to taste.*
Reserved apricots, drained and chopped			
Stock, chicken	12 oz	350 ml	
Salt	to taste	to taste	
Reserved hens			*Distribute the sauce evenly over the hens, cover the roasting pan, and place in a 400°F (200°C) oven for 10 minutes. Lower oven temperature to 300°F (150°C), cover the pan with foil and roast until the juices run clear, approximately 30 minutes. Serve with the pan sauce and boiled rice.*

See color insert for photograph of recipe

Chicken Thighs with Garlic, Pepper, and Fresh Herbs

THAILAND

YIELD: 10 SERVINGS

MARINADE

Fish sauce	6 oz	180 ml
Oil, vegetable	3 oz	90 ml
Lime juice, fresh squeezed	3 oz	90 ml
Garlic, chopped	3 tbsp	35 g
Pepper, black, coarsely ground	1 tbsp	7 g
Sugar	2 tsp	10 g
Red pepper flakes	1 1/2 tsp or to taste	3 g or to taste
Coriander leaves, fresh, chopped	5–6 sprigs	5–6 sprigs
Chicken thighs	20, approx. 4 lb deboned	20, approx. 2 kg deboned

Combine ingredients and mix until the sugar is completely dissolved.

TO DEBONE

Make a long slit along the bone inside the upper portion of the thigh. Cut the meat free of the bone at either end then scrape or cut the meat from the bone. Remove bone, then re-shape the thigh. Using a small glass or stainless steel pan, place chicken meat, skin side up, in a single layer. Add the marinade and mix to cover all surfaces of the chicken evenly. Let marinate in the refrigerator for 4–6 hours before using.

TO PREPARE AN INDIVIDUAL SERVING

Oil, vegetable	1/2 oz	15 ml
Marinated chicken thighs	2 per serving	2 per servings
Salad greens, Romaine, Iceberg, chiffonade	as needed	as needed
Sprigs of fresh basil or coriander	as needed	as needed

In a small, heavy skillet, heat the oil over medium high heat. Sauté the chicken thighs skin side down until well browned and crisp, about 3–4 minutes. Lower heat, turn chicken to other side, and continue to sauté until meat is cooked through, or, after turning chicken, place in a hot oven for 5–6 minutes. When done, remove chicken from pan and place on absorbent towel to remove excess oil. Cut each thigh into 3 pieces on the diagonal. Reassemble thigh to original shape and place over a bed of salad greens. Garnish with sprigs of fresh basil or coriander.

195

POULTRY

Steamed Chicken with Lemon Sauce

MARINADE

Oyster sauce	6 oz	180 g
Lemon juice, fresh squeezed	6 oz	180 ml
Rice wine or dry sherry	4 oz	120 ml
Oil, peanut	2 oz	60 ml
Oil, sesame	1 oz	30 ml
Ginger juice (see recipe)	1 oz	30 ml
Cornstarch	4 tbsp	40 g
Sugar	1 tbsp	15 g
Salt	2 tsp or to taste	10 g or to taste
Pepper, white, fine ground	1 tsp or to taste	2 g or to taste

Combine ingredients and stir until the sugar and cornstarch are completely dissolved. Reserve.

Chicken breast meat	3 1/2– 4 lb	1.6–1.8 kg

Remove skin, trim all fat, then cut chicken into bite-sized pieces. Place in a stainless steel mixing bowl. Add the marinade and toss to coat the chicken pieces evenly. Cover, refrigerate, and allow to marinate for at least 1 hour before using.

TO PREPARE AN INDIVIDUAL SERVING

Marinated chicken	5–6 oz per serving	140–170 g per serving
Marinade	2 oz	60 ml
Cilantro leaves, fresh, chopped fine	as needed	as needed

Place the chicken and 2 oz (60 ml) of the marinade in an ovenproof individual serving, dish. Steam over boiling water in a covered pot fitted with a rack, or, in a steamer, for 6–8 minutes or until the chicken is cooked through. Garnish chicken with chopped cilantro and accompany with white rice.

Shredded Chicken with Onions

Y I E L D :   1   S E R V I N G

MARINADE

Egg white	From 1 small egg	from 1 small egg	Combine ingredients in a small mixing bowl. Stir until all of the cornstach is dissolved.
Rice wine	1 tsp	5 ml	
Cornstarch	pinch	pinch	
Salt	pinch	pinch	
Pepper, white	pinch	pinch	
Chicken breast meat	4–6 oz	115–170 g	Cut the chicken into 1/8-in. (0.5-cm) slices, then julienne each slice. Place chicken strips into a mixing bowl, toss well, and marinate for 15 minutes.

SAUCE

Chicken stock	3 oz	90 ml	Combine ingredients in a small mixing bowl. Stir until all of the cornstarch is dissolved. Reserve.
Soy sauce, light	1 tbsp	15 ml	
Chili oil	dash, or to taste	dash, or to taste	
Sesame oil	dash	dash	
Cornstarch	1 tsp	4 g	

TO PREPARE

Oil, vegetable	1 oz	30 ml	Heat a wok or heavy skillet over medium to high heat. Add the oil. When the oil is just below the smoking point add the chicken and stir-fry for 1–2 minutes or until the chicken is just cooked through. Remove the chicken from the pan and reserve in a warm place. Add the onion and stir-fry until the onions begin to color. Add the reserved sauce and bring to a boil. Return the chicken to the pan, raise the heat to high and cook, stirring, another minute or until the sauce thickens.
Marinated chicken			
Onion, cut root to stem, layers separated	1 medium	1 medium	
Reserved sauce			

Chicken Steamed with Tomatoes, Scallions, and Ginger

YIELD: 1 SERVING

FLAVORING MIXTURE

Gingerroot, fresh peeled, fine julienne	2 slices, 1/8-in. thick	2 slices, 0.5-cm thick	*Combine ingredients. Reserve.*
Fish sauce	1 tsp or to taste	5 ml	
Sesame oil	1 tsp	5 ml	
Sugar	pinch	pinch	
Salt	pinch	pinch	
Pepper, black, ground	pinch	pinch	
Chicken, breast meat, deboned, trimmed of all skin and fat	5 oz	140 g	*Cut the chicken into bite-sized pieces. Place in a heat-proof bowl along with the remaining ingredients.*
Tomato, peeled, cut into 6 wedges	1 medium	1 medium	
Scallion, white and tender green sections cut into thin rings	1	1	
Reserved flavoring mixture			*Add the flavoring mixture and toss to distribute evenly over the other ingredients. Steam over boiling water for 15 minutes or until the chicken is cooked through. Serve with white rice and a side dish of Nuoc Cham with garlic and chili (see recipe).*
Nuoc Cham with garlic and chili (see recipe)			

Chicken and Pork in Sweet Rice Wine

YIELD: 10 SERVINGS

Chicken breast, boned and skinned	10, 3–4 oz pieces	10, 90–115g pieces	*Flatten breast meat slightly between sheets of waxed paper and place in a stainless steel pan in a single layer. Add the ginger juice. Turn breast meat to ensure that each piece is well coated. Cover and refrigerate for at least 1 hour.*
Ginger juice (see recipe)	10 oz	300 ml	
Pork loin, boned and cut into 30 paper-thin slices	1 1/4 lb approx.	570 g approx.	*Chill pork well to facilitate slicing. Place pork slices in a stainless steel pan. Combine the remaining ingredients and mix until the cornstarch is completely dissolved. Pour over the pork and distribute evenly. Cover pan and refrigerate for 1 hour before using.*
Soy sauce	3 oz	90 ml	
Rice wine or dry sherry	3 oz	90 ml	
Cornstarch	1 tbsp	10 g	
Wood ear fungus or dried mushrooms	4 oz	115 g	*Soak in water for 1/2 hour or until soft, or, place in a small amount of boiling water for a few minutes. Reserve.*

BRAISING LIQUID

Rice wine	1 qt	1 L	*Combine ingredients and mix well until the sugar is dissolved. Reserve.*
Chicken stock	1 pt	470 ml	
Sugar	1 tbsp	15 g	
Salt	2 tsp	10 g	

(Continued on next page)

TO PREPARE AN INDIVIDUAL SERVING

Oil, peanut	1 tsp	5 ml
Reserved chicken breast		
Gingerroot, peeled and grated	1 tsp	5 g
Garlic, minced	1 tsp	5 g
Scallions, thin sliced	2	2
Reserved braising liquid	4–5 oz	120–145 ml
Reserved ginger juice marinade	1 oz	30 ml
Reserved pork slices	2 slices	2 slices
Wood ear fungus or dried Chinese mushrooms, sliced	1 oz	25 g

Heat oil in a wok or skillet over moderate heat. Add chicken breast and sauté until lightly browned. Add the gingerroot, garlic, and scallions. Turn chicken and sauté for another minute. Add the braising liquid and the ginger juice marinade. Bring to a boil, then reduce heat to low.

Add pork slices and a small amount of the soaked wood ear fungus or mushrooms. Cover and simmer for 3–5 minutes or until the chicken is cooked through and the pork is tender. Serve in deep bowls together with the cooking liquids.

Chicken Kebabs Marinated in Yogurt, Garlic, and Spices

YIELD: 10-12 SERVINGS

Chicken breast meat	4 lb	1.8 kg
Lemon juice, fresh squeezed	6 oz	180 ml
Salt	1 tsp	5 g
Pepper, white	1 tsp	2 g
Skewers	as needed	as needed
Reserved marinade		
Yogurt	6 oz	170 g
Garlic, minced	1 1/2 tbsp	20 g
Gingerroot, minced	1 tbsp	12 g
Coriander, ground	2 tbsp	14 g
Cumin, ground	1 1/2 tbsp	10 g
Turmeric, ground	1 tbsp	7 g
Red pepper flakes	1 tsp or to taste	1 g or to taste

TO PREPARE AN INDIVIDUAL SERVING

Chicken	6 oz per serving	170 g per serving

Cut chicken into 1-in. (2.5 cm) cubes and place in a stainless steel or glass bowl. Add the remaining ingredients and mix well to coat all of the pieces. Cover and refrigerate for hour. When done, place 6 oz (170 g) of chicken on each skewer. Place skewered chicken on a stainless steel tray. Reserve the marinade.

Combine these ingredients with the reserved marinade, then pour over the skewered chicken. Rotate the skewers to coat evenly. Cover and refrigerate overnight.

Place skewers on a well-oiled grill over medium high heat. Turn skewers from time to time to ensure even cooking.

Chicken Deep-Fried with Ginger Scallion Sauce

YIELD: 10 SERVINGS

MARINADE

Soy sauce	4 oz	120 ml
Gingerroot, peeled and minced	4 oz	115 g
Scallion, white and green parts, thin sliced	4 whole	4 whole
Peppercorns, Szechwan, crushed	1 tbsp	7 g
Sugar	2 tsp	10 g

Combine ingredients and mix until the sugar is completely dissolved. Reserve.

Chicken thighs and legs, bone in, skin on	6–7 lb	2.7–3.2 kg
Reserved marinade		

Remove excess fat and skin. Trim bone at the end of each drumstick. Place chicken in a stainless steel bowl and add the marinade. Toss to coat chicken pieces evenly. Cover and marinate under refrigeration, for several hours.

SAUCE

Garlic, minced	1 tbsp	15 g
Celery, minced	2 stalks	2 stalks
Coriander, stems and leaves, minced	4 sprigs	4 sprigs
Chicken stock	10 oz	300 ml
Soy sauce	5 oz	150 ml
Vinegar, white, distilled	2 oz	60 ml
Sesame oil	2 oz	60 g
Ketchup or tomato puree	3 tbsp	50 g
Sugar	1–2 tsp	5–10 g

Combine ingredients in a small saucepan and bring to a boil. Lower heat and simmer for 5 minutes. Strain and discard solids. Reserve in a warm place.

(Continued on facing page)

Marinated chicken	*9–11 oz per serving*	*255–310 g per serving*
Cornstarch	*as needed*	*as needed*
Oil, vegetable	*for deep-frying*	*for deep-frying*
Reserved sauce	*as needed*	*as needed*
Scallions, white and green parts sliced very thin	*as needed*	*as needed*

Coat chicken as needed with a dusting of cornstarch. Let chicken rest for 15 minutes. Deep-fry at 350°F (175°C) until well browned and cooked through. When done, drain on absorbent towels, then place on a warm plate. Spoon 2–4 tbsp (30–60 ml) of sauce on top along with a sprinkling of scallion.

Chicken and Cucumber Salad

YIELD: 10-12 SERVINGS

Chickens	2, 3 lb each	2, 1.3 kg each	*Clean chickens, removing all excess fat and loose skin.* Place chickens in a deep bowl with the soy sauce and marinate for 1 hour. Turn the chicken frequently.*
Soy sauce	8 oz	240 ml	
Oil, vegetable	for deep-frying	for deep-frying	*Heat oil to just below the smoking point and deep-fry the chicken until the skin is deep brown and crisp. (The chicken will be cooked through during the next stage of the cooking process.) Remove chickens from the oil and place them on a rack for steaming.*
Scallions, cut in 2-in. (5-cm) lengths	8	8	*Combine ingredients and place half of the mixture into the cavities of the chickens, the remainder over the surface. Place the chickens over boiling water in a steamer. Cover with a tight-fitting lid and steam for 1 hour. Remove chickens and let cool. Reduce the pan liquids to 4 oz (120 ml) and reserve.*
Gingerroot, peeled and cut into thin slices	2-inch piece	5-cm piece	
Peppercorns, brown	6 tbsp	40 g	
Water, boiling	12 oz	350 ml	

SEASONING SAUCE

Reserved chicken broth	4 oz	120 ml	*Combine ingredients and reserve.*
Soy sauce, light	4 oz	120 ml	
Vinegar, rice	2 oz	60 ml	
Sesame oil	2 oz	60 ml	
Garlic, minced	1 tbsp	15 g	
Reserved chicken			*When chicken is cool enough to handle, strip the meat, including the skin, from the bones. Tear into shreds and mix with the seasoning sauce. Place in the refrigerator and reserve until needed.*
Reserved sauce			

TO PREPARE AN INDIVIDUAL SERVING

Reserved chicken,	4 oz	115 g	*Place a mound of chicken on a cool plate surrounded with small cucumber spears.*
Cucumbers, cut into 1 x 1/4 in. (2.5 x .75 cm) strips			

*To reduce fat, skin may be removed and discarded.

Chung-King Chicken

YIELD: 2 SERVINGS

MARINADE

Egg white, lightly beaten	1 oz	30 ml
Cornstarch	1 tsp	4 g
Salt	pinch	pinch

Combine ingredients and stir until the cornstarch has completely dissolved.

Chicken breast, skinned and boned, cut into small dice	12 oz	340 g

Add the chicken to the marinade and stir to coat the pieces thoroughly. Marinate for 10–15 minutes.

SAUCE

Hoisin sauce	2 tbsp	30 ml
Sugar	2 tsp	10 g
Rice wine or dry sherry	1 tsp	5 ml
Gingerroot, peeled and crushed	1 tsp	4 g
Soy sauce	1 tsp	5 ml
Crushed red pepper flakes	pinch or to taste	pinch or to taste

Combine ingredients and mix until the sugar is completely dissolved. Reserve.

Snow peas	2 oz	60 g
Mushrooms, black, Chinese	4–5	4–5
Bell peppers, green and red	2 oz (1 oz each)	60 g (30 g each)

Trim the ends of the snow peas and remove the strings. Soak the mushrooms in a small amount of hot water. Discard the stems and slice caps into 1/4-in. (3/4-cm) strips. Cut the peppers into 1/4-in. (.75-cm) strips. Reserve.

TO PREPARE

Oil, peanut	1 tbsp	15 ml
Marinated chicken		

Heat wok or heavy skillet over high heat. Add the oil and reheat to just below the smoking point. Add the chicken and stir-fry for 1–2 minutes or until the chicken is cooked through. Remove chicken from the pan and reserve in a warm place.

Prepared vegetables

Stir-fry the vegetables briefly until they are hot but still very crisp.

Reserved sauce
Reserved chicken

Add the reserved sauce to the same pan and bring to a boil, stirring constantly. Return the chicken to the pan and stir-fry until all ingredients are well coated with the sauce and heated through.

Chicken Breast in Soy Sauce

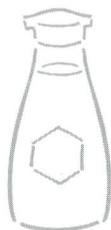

Ingredient			Method
Chicken breast, boned and skinned	1 piece, 4–6 oz	1 piece, 115–170 g	Trim any fat, then cover with a sheet of waxed paper or plastic wrap. Flatten slightly with a mallet or the side of a heavy cleaver. Dredge the chicken breast in cornstarch, shaking off any excess. Place oil in a heavy-bottomed sauté pan and heat over medium to high heat. Sear the chicken breast on one side, then turn it to the other side.
Cornstarch	as needed	as needed	
Oil, sesame	1 tbsp	15 ml	
Scallions, white and green parts cut in half, lengthwise then into 1-in. (2.5-cm) pieces	2	2	Add ingredients and mix well. Lower heat, cover pan, and simmer for 3–4 minutes or until the chicken is cooked through.
Garlic, minced	1 tsp or to taste	5 g or to taste	
Stock, chicken	2 oz	60 ml	
Soy sauce,* light	2 oz	60 ml	

*For variation, flavored soy sauces may be substituted.

Chicken with Cashews in Hoisin Sauce

YIELD: 1 SERVING

MARINADE

Dry sherry	1 tbsp	15 ml	*Combine ingredients in a small bowl and stir until the cornstarch is completely dissolved.*
Egg white, lightly beaten	2 tsp	10 ml	
Oil, sesame	1 tsp	5 ml	
Cornstarch	1 tsp	4 g	
Salt	pinch	pinch	
Pepper, white	pinch	pinch	
Chicken breast, cut into 1/2–3/4 in. (1.5–2.5 cm) cubes	4–6 oz	115–170 g	*Add the chicken and toss to coat pieces evenly. Marinate for 10–15 minutes.*
Oil, peanut	1 tbsp	15 ml	*Heat wok or skillet over high heat. Add oil and distribute evenly over surface of pan. When oil is just below the smoking point, add the scallions and garlic and stir-fry for 10–15 seconds.*
Scallions, white sections, sliced into 1/2-in. (1.5-cm) pieces	2	2	
Garlic, minced	1 tsp or to taste	5 g or to taste	
Marinated chicken			*Add the chicken, lower heat to medium, and continue to stir-fry for another 2 minutes or until the chicken is almost done. Remove contents of pan and reserve in a warm place.*
Garlic, minced	1/2 tsp	3 g	*Raise heat to high and add the garlic, let cook for a few seconds, then add the Hoisin sauce and stir. Return the chicken to the pan and stir-fry until the chicken is well glazed. Add the cashew nuts and scallions and heat through. Serve on a warm serving plate.*
Hoisin sauce	2 tbsp	35 g	
Cashew nuts, toasted	2 tbsp	15 g	
Scallions, green sections, cut into thin circles	2	2	

Chicken Stir-Fried with Snow Peas

YIELD: 1-2 SERVINGS

MARINADE

Egg white	of one large egg	of one large egg	Combine ingredients and stir until the cornstarch is completely dissolved.
Rice wine or dry Sherry	1 tbsp	15 ml	
Oil, peanut	1 tsp	5 ml	
Soy sauce	1 tsp	5 ml	
Cornstarch	1 tsp	4 g	
Salt	pinch	pinch	
Pepper, white	pinch	pinch	
Chicken breast, skin off and boned	4–6 oz	115–170 g	Trim all fat and tendons, then cut into 1/2-in. (1.5-cm) cubes. Place in a bowl with the marinade and toss to coat all pieces evenly. Marinate for 15 minutes.
Snow peas	3 oz	90 g	Trim stems, remove strings, and wash snow peas. Place in boiling water for 15–20 seconds, then place immediately into iced water. Reserve.

SAUCE

Chicken stock, cold	4 oz	120 ml	Combine ingredients and stir until the cornstarch is completely dissolved. Reserve.
Cornstarch	1 tsp	4 g	
Oyster sauce	1 tbsp	20 g	
Soy sauce	1 tsp	5 ml	

(Continued on facing page)

Oil, peanut or vegetable	to deep-fry	to deep-fry
Reserved marinated chicken		

Deep-fry the chicken cubes at 350°F (175°C) for 30 seconds. Remove from oil and reserve in a warm place.

Oil, peanut	1 tbsp	15 ml
Gingerroot, peeled	2 thin slices	2 thin slices
Reserved snow peas		

Place the peanut oil in a hot wok or skillet. Add the gingerroot and stir-fry until the aroma is released. Add the snow peas and continue to stir-fry until they are very hot. Place contents of the pan on a well-heated serving plate, covering the entire surface of the plate. Reserve in a warm place.

Scallions, white sections, sliced fine	2	2
Garlic, minced	1 tsp or to taste	5 g or to taste
Reserved chicken		
Sherry, dry	splash	splash

Using the same pan, adding a little oil if necessary, stir-fry the scallions and garlic over high heat for 5–10 seconds. Add the chicken and continue to stir-fry for another minute. Add the wine or sherry and stir well.

Reserved sauce		
Scallions, green sections, sliced fine	2	2

Add the sauce, lower heat, and cook until the sauce has thickened, then add the green sections of the scallions. When they have been incorporated with the other ingredients, place the entire contents of the pan on top of the bed of snow peas and serve.

Chicken Velvet

Chicken breast meat, skinless	2 lb	900 g
Cornstarch	1 tbsp	10 g
Ice water	1 tbsp	15 ml
Egg, whites only	2, large	2, large
Salt	1 tsp	5 g

Remove all tendons and bits of fat. Cut breast meat into large dice and place in a food processor fitted with the steel blade. Process the chicken to a fine puree. Add the remaining ingredients and, using the pulse action, blend thoroughly. Chicken Velvet is used to add texture and taste to soups. Prepare just prior to using and always keep refrigerated.

Chicken in Red Curry

YIELD: 10 SERVINGS

Chicken leg and thigh meat (or breast meat)	3 lb	1.4 kg	Remove all skin, bone, tendons, and fat. Cut chicken meat into 1-in. (2.5 cm) dice. Place coconut milk in a heavy-bottomed saucepan and bring to a boil over medium heat. Add the chicken. When the liquid returns to a boil, lower heat and simmer for 4–5 minutes or until the chicken is just cooked through. If breast meat is used, reduce cooking time. Remove from heat and reserve.
Coconut milk, thin	1 pt	480 ml	
Coconut milk (thick)	4 oz	120 ml	In a separate pot, combine the thick coconut milk and oil and bring to a boil. Add the curry paste, lower heat, and simmer for 5 minutes.
Oil, vegetable	3 oz	90 ml	
Red curry paste	2 tsp or to taste	20 g or to taste	
Fish sauce	3 tbsp or to taste	45 ml or to taste	Add ingredients and mix well.
Sugar, dark brown	1 tbsp or to taste	15 g or to taste	
Reserved chicken	as needed	as needed	Add the cooked chicken along with the liquids in which it was cooked. Bring to a boil, then lower heat and simmer for 1 minute. Let cool and reserve.

TO PREPARE AN INDIVIDUAL SERVING

Prepared chicken and sauce	5–6 oz per serving	140–170 g per serving	Reheat chicken and sauce as needed. Serve on a warmed plate. Garnish with 4–5 fresh basil or mint leaves and a sprinkling of lemon zest. Serve with white rice.
Basil or mint leaves, fresh	as needed	as needed	
Lemon zest	as needed	as needed	

211

POULTRY

Chicken with Stir-Fried Vegetables

YIELD: 1 SERVING

VEGETABLES

Broccoli	1 small stalk	1 small stalk
Cherry tomatoes	3	3
Onion	1 thick slice	1 thick slice
Scallion	1	1
Garlic	1 tsp	5 g
Chicken, thigh or breast meat, cut into small cubes	4 oz	115 g
Fish sauce*	1 tbsp	15 ml
Pepper, black, ground	as needed	as needed
Cornstarch	as needed	as needed
Oil, peanut or vegetable	as needed	as needed
Oil, peanut or vegetable	2 tsp	10 ml
Reserved onion, scallion, garlic and broccoli		
Water	2 oz	60 ml
Oyster sauce	1/2 tsp	3 ml
Fish sauce	1/2 tsp	3 ml
Cornstarch	1 tsp	3 g
Sugar	pinch	pinch
Reserved tomatoes		

*Vietnamese version of fish sauce is called nuoc mam. If unavailable, substitute Thai fish sauce, nam pla.

Cut and discard the thick, tough section of the broccoli stem. Remove the buds and cut them into small florets. Peel the remaining portion of the stalk, then cut it lengthwise into thin slices. Slice the cherry tomatoes and the onion in half. Slice the scallion, white and green parts, into 1-in. (2.5-cm) segments. Mince the garlic. Reserve.

Place the chicken in a mixing bowl and toss with the fish sauce and a sprinkling of pepper. When well-coated, dredge the chicken pieces in cornstarch. Shake off any excess and deep-fry at 375°F (190°C) until lightly browned. When done, drain on a clean towel, then place on a serving plate and reserve in a warm place.

Heat a wok or skillet over high heat. Add the oil and when just below the smoking point, stir-fry the onion, scallion, and garlic for 30–40 seconds. Add the broccoli and stir-fry for another minute. Add the water, reduce heat, cover, and cook for another minute or until the broccoli turns bright green.

Combine ingredients, with the exception of the tomatoes, and add to the pan. Stir well to incorporate thoroughly. Add the tomatoes and stir-fry briefly until sauce begins to thicken slightly. Pour these vegetables over the deep-fried chicken cubes. Serve on a bed of white rice.

Grilled Marinated Chicken and Leeks

YIELD: 10-12 SERVINGS

Chicken legs and thighs, boned	*4 lb (weight after boning)*	*1.8 kg (weight after boning)*

Cutting along the inner side of the legs and thighs, expose the bones and tendons. Remove them, then spread out the meat. Pierce each piece in several places with the tines of a sharp fork, then cover with plastic wrap and flatten the meat slightly with a heavy cleaver or a meat mallet. Place 3–4 small steel skewers, parallel to each other and approximately 1 in. (2.5 cm) apart, through each piece of chicken to retain the flattened shape. To facilitate turning while grilling, place the meat forward toward the pointed ends of the skewers. Place skewered chicken pieces on a stainless steel pan just large enough to hold them in one layer.

MARINADE

Leeks, small	*10–12*	*10–12*
Soy sauce, dark	*6 oz*	*180 ml*
Mirin	*6 oz*	*180 ml*
Sake	*6 oz*	*180 ml*
Lemon rind, julienne	*1/2 lemon*	*1/2 lemon*

Trim stem ends of the leeks. Cut the white sections crosswise into 2 pieces, then partially split them lengthwise and wash thoroughly. (Reserve the tender green parts for other uses.) Combine the leeks with the remaining ingredients and distribute evenly over chicken. Cover and marinate in the refrigerator for at least 1 hour, turning skewers once or twice.

TO PREPARE AN INDIVIDUAL SERVING

Skewered chicken	*5–6 oz per serving*	*140–170 g per serving*
Marinated leek	*2 sections per serving*	*2 sections per serving*

Grill chicken over medium hot coals or under broiler for 3–4 minutes per side, turning once. Start the cooking process with the skin side of the chicken closest to the source of heat. Leek may also be grilled at this time. When done, place chicken on a cutting board, remove skewers, and slice into 3 or 4 pieces. Reassemble the meat as closely as possible to the shape it had when it was skewered. Place on a heated plate and garnish with the grilled leek.

Chicken Patties

YIELD: 10 SERVINGS

SEASONING MIXTURE

Soy sauce	3 oz	90 ml	*Combine ingredients thoroughly.*
Sesame oil	2 oz	60 ml	
Scallion, white and green parts, minced	2	2	
Gingerroot, peeled and minced	2 oz	60 g	
Garlic, minced	2 oz	60 g	
Sesame salt (see recipe)	2 oz	60 g	
Salt	1 tsp or to taste	5 g or to taste	
Pepper, black	to taste	to taste	
Chicken, ground	3 lb	1.4 kg	*Place chicken in a mixing bowl and add the seasoning mixture. Blend thoroughly, then form into 2–3 oz (60–90 g) round, flat patties. Refrigerate until needed.*

TO PREPARE

Oil, vegetable	as needed	as needed	*Pan-fry, broil, or grill over coals on a lightly oiled surface.*
Chicken patties	as needed	as needed	

Serve patties on a bed of lettuce accompanied by fresh cucumber spears or slices. Garnish with very thin threads of hot, fresh red chili pepper. Serve Yank Nyam Jang (see recipe) dipping sauce on the side.

Crisp-Fried Marinated Chicken

YIELD: 10-12 SERVINGS

MARINADE

Water	8 oz	240 ml
Soy sauce, light	4 oz	120 ml
Rice wine	2 oz	60 ml
Cornstarch	2 tbsp	20 g
Salt	1 tbsp	15 g
Sugar	1 tbsp	15 g
Five-spice powder	1 tbsp	7g

Combine ingredients and stir until the sugar is completely dissolved.

Chicken parts, legs, thighs, bone in	6 lb	2.7 kg

Place chicken parts in a stainless steel tray and pour the marinade on top. Toss to coat the pieces evenly. Cover and refrigerate overnight.

TO PREPARE AN INDIVIDUAL SERVING

Cornstarch	as needed	as needed
Oil	for deep-frying	for deep-frying
Marinated chicken	9 oz per serving	270 g per serving

Remove the chicken parts from the marinade and let drain. Lightly dredge in cornstarch. Deep-fry in 350°F (175°C) oil until cooked through and golden brown.

Chicken Steamed with Asparagus

YIELD: 10 SERVINGS

MARINADE

Rice wine or dry sherry	4 oz	120 ml
Soy sauce, light	3 oz	90 ml
Sugar	3 tbsp	45 g
Gingerroot, chopped fine	2 tbsp	25 g

Combine ingredients in a glass or stainless steel container large enough to hold 3 1/2 lb (1.6 kg) of chicken breasts.

Chicken breast, skinned and deboned	3 1/2 lb	1.6 kg

Trim chicken breasts to remove all fat and skin. Cut into uniform, bite-sized pieces. Add to the marinade, toss well to distribute the marinade evenly, then cover and refrigerate for 45 minutes to 1 hour.

Asparagus	2 lb	900 g

Break off the tough, woody parts of the stems. Using a vegetable peeler, strip the outer skin from the lower portions of the asparagus. Slice on the diagonal, into pieces 1 1/2 in. (4 cm) long. Reserve.

TO PREPARE AN INDIVIDUAL SERVING

Marinated chicken	5–6 oz	140–170 g
Rice flour	as needed	as needed
Reserved asparagus	2–3 oz	60–90 g
Salt	as needed	as needed

Dredge the chicken pieces in rice flour. Place the asparagus on the bottom of a heat-proof serving dish. Arrange the chicken pieces on top and sprinkle lightly with the salt. Place in steamer and cook for 10–15 minutes or until the chicken is cooked through. Cooking time will vary depending on the thickness of the chicken breast meat.

Chicken with Red Peppers and Ginger

YIELD: 1 SERVING

Oil, peanut	1 oz	30 ml	*Heat a wok or skillet over high heat. Add the oil and gingerroot. When the oil has reached a high temperature, just below the smoking point, add the chicken and red peppers. Stir-fry for 1 minute.*
Gingerroot, peeled and cut julienne	1–2 slices	1–2 slices	
Chicken breast, skinned and deboned; cut into bite-sized pieces	1, 5–6 oz	1, 140-170 g	
Red bell pepper, cut into 1/2-inch (1.5-cm) squares	2 oz	60 g	
Chicken stock	3 oz	90 ml	*Add ingredients and stir well. Reduce heat, cover, and cook for 3–4 minutes or until the chicken is cooked through.*
Soy sauce, dark	1 tbsp	15 ml	
Chili flavored oil	1 tsp or to taste	5 ml or to taste	
Sugar	1/2 tsp	3 g	
Pepper, black, fine ground	pinch	pinch	
Cornstarch	2 tsp	7 g	*Mix the cornstarch with enough water to make a thin paste. Add this to the chicken, raise heat, and cook briefly until the sauce has thickened.*
Water	as needed	as needed	

Chicken with Cashews and Chili Pepper

YIELD: 1 SERVING

Chicken breast, skinned and deboned	1, 5–6 oz	1, 140–170 g	*Place chicken breast between sheets of waxed paper and flatten slightly with the side of a cleaver or meat mallet. Cut chicken into thin slices approximately 1 x 3 in. (2.5 x 8 cm). Dust lightly with all-purpose flour.*
Flour, all-purpose	as needed	as needed	
Oil, peanut	1 oz	30 ml	*Heat wok or heavy skillet over high heat. Add the oil and heat to just below the smoking point. Stir-fry the chicken until it browns lightly.*
Garlic, minced	1/2 tsp	2 g	*Add ingredients and stir-fry briefly until the garlic becomes aromatic.*
Chili peppers, red, fresh, cut lengthwise into quarters	1 or to taste	1 or to taste	
Scallion, white parts only, cut into 1-in. (2.5 cm) pieces	2–3 depending on size	2–3 depending on size	*Add ingredients and continue to stir-fry for another 1–2 minutes or until the chicken is cooked through. Serve with white rice.*
Onion	1/4-in. slice cut in half	0.75-cm slice cut in half	
Oyster sauce	1 tbsp	20 g	
Soy sauce, light	1 tbsp	15 ml	
Soy sauce, dark	dash	dash	
Sugar	1 tsp	5 g	
Cashew nuts, roasted, unsalted	1 oz	30 g	

Chicken and Bamboo Shoot with Hoisin Sauce

YIELD: 1 SERVING

Ingredient	US	Metric	Method
Chicken breast, skinned and deboned then cut into small cubes	5–6 oz	140–170 g	*Combine ingredients and stir well. Let marinate for 10 minutes.*
Hoisin sauce*	1 tbsp	20 g	
Rice wine or dry sherry	1 tbsp	15 ml	
Soy sauce, dark	2 tsp	10 ml	
Red pepper flakes	pinch, or to taste	pinch, or to taste	
Chicken stock	2 oz	60 ml	*Combine ingredients and reserve.*
Bamboo shoot, canned, sliced 1/8-in. (0.5 cm) thick	2 oz	60 g	
Gingerroot, minced	1/2 tsp	2 g	
Scallion, white and green parts, sliced in 1-in. (2.5 cm) pieces	1	1	
Oil, peanut	1 tbsp	15 ml	*Heat wok or skillet over high heat. Add oil. When oil has been heated to just below the smoking point, add the chicken with the marinade, and stir-fry for 1–2 minutes. Add the remaining ingredients and continue to stir-fry for another 2 minutes or until the chicken is just cooked through.*
Reserved chicken			
Reserved bamboo shoot/scallion mixture			

*Hoisin sauce is available from commercial sources.

Barbecued Chicken Breast

YIELD: 10 SERVINGS

Chicken breasts, skin on, deboned	10, 6–8 oz each	10, 170–230 g each	Trim excess skin or fat from the breasts. Place a single layer in a stainless steel pan. Refrigerate.
MARINADE			
Cilantro, fresh, leaves and stems	10 sprigs	10 sprigs	Finely chop ingredients in a food processor fitted with the steel blade.
Gingerroot, peeled and minced	2 oz	60 g	
Lemongrass, tender white stems chopped fine	2 oz	60 g	
Curry powder	3 tbsp	20 g	
Pepper, white	3 tbsp	20 g	
Sugar	1 tbsp	15 g	
Soy sauce, light	16 oz	470 ml	With the processor running, slowly add half of the soy sauce. Turn off the processor and add the remaining soy sauce. Stir well. Pour the marinade over the chicken and distribute evenly. Cover and refrigerate overnight.
CHILI SAUCE			
Vinegar, white distilled	16 oz	470 ml	Combine ingredients in a small saucepan and bring to a boil, stirring, over medium heat. Lower heat and simmer until liquid begins to thicken slightly. Remove from heat and let cool.
Sugar	4 oz	115 g	
Red chili, ground	2 oz or to taste	60 g or to taste	
Garlic, minced	1 1/2 tbsp	20 g	
Salt	3/4 tbsp or to taste	10 g or to taste	
TO PREPARE AN INDIVIDUAL SERVING			
Chicken breast	1	1	Remove chicken breast from marinade and grill slowly over coals or under the broiler flame, basting with the marinade two or three times. Serve with a small side dish of chili sauce on the side. Garnish plate with a fine julienne of carrot, and daikon, or white cabbage.
Chili sauce	as needed	as needed	
Carrot, julienne	as needed	as needed	
Daikon, julienne	as needed	as needed	
White cabbage, shredded	as needed	as needed	

220

Tea-Smoked Duck

YIELD: VARIABLE, DEPENDING ON USE

Duck breasts	10, 10 oz each	10, 280 g each
Stock, chicken	as needed	as needed
Salt	as needed	as needed
Pepper, black	as needed	as needed

Poach the duck breasts in chicken stock until they are cooked medium to rare. Drain and pat dry. Reserve the stock for other uses. Sprinkle a liberal amount of salt and pepper on both sides and place on the rack of a smoker (see Cooking Processes— Pan Smoking in Chapter 1).

Moistened aromatic
  wood chips, as pre-
  ferred
Green tea leaves

Place duck breasts directly on a rack positioned several inches over the tea leaves and wood chips to ensure that the food does not come into direct contact with the smoking agent. Smoked duck breasts may be served sliced, warm or cold as an entree, diced, in salads; as a garnish along with other ingredients in soups; or on rice or noodle dishes.

See color insert for photograph of recipe

CHAPTER SEVEN

Meats

Beef Stir-Fried with Chili Peppers

YIELD: 1 SERVING

Beef, tenderloin	5–6 oz	140–170 g	*Cut the meat into thin slices, then julienne. Mix*
Soy sauce, dark	1 tbsp	15 ml	*the remaining ingredients in a small mixing bowl.*
Rice wine	1 tbsp	15 ml	*Add the meat and marinate for 10–15 minutes.*
Cornstarch	1 tbsp	10 g	
Chili peppers, fresh,	1 green	1 green	*Slice the chilies in half lengthwise. Remove the seeds*
New Mexican, or	1 red	1 red	*and membranes, then cut the chilies into long, thin*
Anaheim for a milder			*shoestrings. Heat a wok or a heavy skillet over*
taste			*medium to high heat. Add the oil and, when just*
Sugar	1 tsp	5 g	*below the smoking point, add the chilies, sugar, and*
Salt	1/2 tsp or to taste	3 g or to taste	*salt. Stir-fry for 15–20 seconds. Remove the chilies and reserve.*
Garlic, peeled, sliced thin	1 tsp	5 g	*Using the same pan, stir-fry the garlic until it begins to brown lightly. Add the beef and continue*
Marinated beef			*to stir-fry until the meat loses its red color. Return the peppers to the pan and stir-fry for another 20–30 seconds. Serve with white rice.*

Anise-Flavored Braised Beef

YIELD: 10-12 SERVINGS

Ingredient	US	Metric	Method
Beef, rump, top round or eye round	4 lb	1.8 kg	*Tie meat into uniform shape with butcher's twine. Rub lightly with salt. Heat a heavy-bottomed stew pot or wok over high heat. Add the oil. When very hot, sear the meat on all sides. Remove meat to a warm place.*
Salt	as needed	as needed	
Oil, peanut	3 tbsp	45 ml	
Gingerroot, peeled and sliced 1/8-in. (0.5-cm) thick	4 slices	4 slices	*Add ingredients to the pot and stir-fry for 20–30 seconds.*
Garlic, peeled and smashed	2 medium cloves	2 medium cloves	
Chicken stock	as needed	as needed	*Return meat to the pot and add ingredients. Use as much chicken stock as needed to bring the liquid contents of the pot 1 inch above the meat. Bring liquids to a boil, lower heat, cover, and simmer for 2 hours or until the beef is very tender. When done, remove meat, wrap in foil, and place under weights to compress meat and make it easier to slice. Let rest for at least 1 hour. Strain the stock and reserve. Serve meat hot or cold along with a small amount of the cooking liquid. Slices of meat can be reheated in the cooking liquid, if desired. Extra stock can be reserved for other purposes.*
Soy sauce, light	6 oz	180 ml	
Soy sauce, dark	6 oz	180 ml	
Rice wine or dry sherry	2 oz	60 ml	
Star anise	4 whole	4 whole	
Sugar	2 oz or to taste	60 g or to taste	

Bulgogi

YIELD: 10 SERVINGS

Beef, tenderloin or sirloin, chilled	3 lb	1.4k g	*Cut the meat across the grain, into thin slices. Slice again into thin strips 2–3 in. (5–8 cm) in length. Place in a stainless steel mixing bowl.*
Soy sauce, light	6 oz	180 ml	*Combine ingredients and stir until the sugar is completely dissolved.*
Soy sauce, dark	4 oz	120 ml	
Sesame oil	2 oz	60 ml	
Sugar	2 oz	60 g	
Pepper, fine ground	1 tsp	2 g	
Garlic, minced	3 oz	85 g	*Add ingredients and mix thoroughly. Pour over meat and toss to coat slices evenly. Cover and marinate for 15–20 minutes. Cook 4–5 oz (115–140 g) portions to order over high heat on a tabletop grill, charcoal grill, or sauté in a lightly oiled skillet. Accompany with Korean barbecue sauce (see recipe) for dipping. Serve with boiled white rice.*
Gingerroot, peeled and minced	3 oz	85 g	
Scallions, minced	3 oz	85 g	
Sesame seeds, toasted and ground	1 tbsp	6 g	

Cold Beef
with Anise-Flavored Aspic

YIELD: 10-12 SERVINGS
(DOUBLE THIS YIELD IF USED AS AN APPETIZER)

Beef shin meat	4 lb	1.8 kg	*Trim all fat, gristle, and outer membrane. Tie meat with butcher's twine to obtain a uniform shape.*
Beef stock	to cover by 2 in.	to cover by 5 cm	*Place beef in a stew pot and cover with stock. Add the star anise and bring to a boil. Lower heat, partially cover, and simmer for 2 hours.*
Star anise	8 whole	8 whole	
Soy sauce, dark	4 oz	120 ml	*Add ingredients and continue to simmer for another hour or until the meat is very tender. When done, remove meat from cooking liquid, let cool, then wrap in aluminum foil. Place in refrigerator, under weights, for 5–6 hours. Reduce the stock to 8 oz (240 ml) then strain the liquid into a shallow tray. When cool, place in refrigerator to gel. When serving, use this aspic cut into small cubes as a garnish for the cold sliced beef.*
Sugar, brown	2 oz	60 g	
Gingerroot	2-in. piece	5-cm piece	
Salt	to taste	to taste	

Stir-Fried Flank Steak with Vegetables

YIELD: 10-12 SERVINGS

MARINADE			
Water	4 oz	120 ml	*Combine ingredients and stir until the cornstarch is dissolved.*
Soy sauce, dark	3 oz	90 ml	
Rice wine or dry sherry	2 oz	60 ml	
Sesame oil	2 tsp	10 ml	
Cornstarch	2 tsp	7 g	
Flank steak, trimmed of all fat and membrane	2 1/2 lb	1.15 kg	*Chill meat to just above the freezing point, then cut across the grain into slices no more that 1/4 in. (0.75 cm) thick. Cut each slice into 2- to 3-in. (5- to 8-cm) pieces. Toss meat with the marinade. Marinate at least 20–30 minutes. Reserve.*
Tomatoes, firm, cut into 1/2-in.(1.5-cm) dice	1 lb	450 g	*Prepare vegetables and reserve.*
Onion, cut into 1/2-in. (1.5-cm) dice	1 lb	450 g	
Green bell pepper, seeded and cut into 1/2-in. (1.5-cm) dice	1/2 lb	225 g	
Mushrooms, white, button, sliced	1/2 lb	225 g	
Snow peas, trimmed, strings removed, blanched for 10–15 seconds then refreshed in iced water	1/4 lb	115 g	

(Continued on next page)

FLAVORING MIXTURE

Chicken stock	1 qt	1 L
Soy sauce, dark	4 oz	120 ml
Chinese black vinegar	2 oz	60 ml
Rice wine or dry sherry	1 oz	30 ml
Ketchup	4 tbsp	70 g
Sugar	4 tbsp	60 g
Salt	to taste	to taste

Combine ingredients and reserve.

TO PREPARE AN INDIVIDUAL SERVING

Oil, peanut	1 tbsp	15 ml
Reserved meat	3–4 oz	85–115 g
Onion	1 1/2 oz	40 g
Green pepper	1 1/2 oz	40 g
Tomato	1 1/2 oz	40 g
Mushrooms	1/2–1 oz	15–30 g
Flavoring mixture	3–4 oz	90–120 ml

Heat a wok or skillet over high heat. When just below the smoking point, add the oil and let pan return to high temperature. Add the meat and stir-fry for 1 minute or until the slices lose all red color. Remove the meat to a warm place. Add the onions to the pan and stir-fry for another minute or until they become slightly soft. Add the peppers, tomato, and mushrooms. Stir-fry for another minute. Add the flavoring mixture and, stirring, bring to a boil.

Cornstarch	1/2 tsp	5 g
Water, cold	as needed	as needed
Reserved meat		
Blanched snow peas	as needed	as needed

Mix the cornstarch with enough water to make a smooth paste, then add to the vegetables. Stir-fry until the sauce begins to thicken. Return the meat to the pan along with a few snow peas. Stir-fry to coat all of the ingredients with the sauce and heat through. Serve with boiled white rice.

Pork Flavored with Anise and Ginger

YIELD: 10-12 SERVINGS

Ingredient	US	Metric
Chicken stock	1 pt	470 ml
Soy sauce, light	6 oz	180 ml
Soy sauce, dark	3 oz	90 ml
Gin	2 oz	60 ml
Sugar, light brown	2 oz	60 g
Cinnamon stick	4-in. piece	10-cm piece
Gingerroot, sliced 1/4 in. (1 cm) thick	5–6 pieces	5-6 pieces
Scallions	5	5
Star anise	3 whole	3 whole

Combine ingredients in a small stock pot and bring to a boil over medium to high heat.

Ingredient	US	Metric
Pork loin, trimmed of fat, boned and tied	3 1/2 lb	1.6 kg

Add the pork and return the cooking liquid to a boil. Lower heat and simmer, partially covered, for 1 1/2 hours, or until the meat is very tender. Turn the meat several times during the cooking period. When done, remove meat from cooking liquid and wrap in foil. Let cool under a weighted tray to make slicing easier. Degrease and strain the cooking liquids and use as a sauce, if desired. Serve sliced or diced in combination with rice, vegetable, or noodle dishes.

Deep-Fried Pork Cutlet (Tonkatsu)

YIELD: 10 SERVINGS

SAUCE

Worcestershire sauce	6 oz	180 ml
Ketchup	6 oz	170 g
Soy sauce	to taste	to taste
Japanese mustard powder	to taste	to taste
Sake	to taste	to taste

Combine ingredients to taste or use commercially prepared Tonkatsu sauce.

Pork chops, loin, boned, with a very thin rim of fat left on	10, 5–6 oz each	10, 140–170 g each
Salt	as needed	as needed
Pepper, black	as needed	as needed
Flour	as needed	as needed
Egg, beaten	as needed	as needed
Bread crumbs, toasted, slightly coarse	as needed	as needed

Score the thin rim of fat in 4–5 places to prevent the chop from curling. Lightly salt and pepper the chops on both sides, then dredge in flour. Shake off any excess flour, then dip in the beaten egg. Next, press the chops firmly into the bread crumbs making sure that all surfaces are well coated. Place them on a sheet pan covered with parchment paper and refrigerate for an hour before using.

(Continued on facing page)

Oil, vegetable	*for deep-frying*	*for deep-frying*
Pork chop	*1 per serving*	*1 per serving*
Cabbage, bok choy or other similar variety, shredded thin	*as needed*	*as needed*
Sauce	*as needed*	*as needed*
Lemon wedges	*2*	*2*

Deep-fry the chop in 350°F (175°C) oil, turning once or twice, until cooked through and golden brown, approximately 4–5 minutes. The coating should be quite crisp. Drain on a clean towel, then cut into 1-in. strips, keeping the original shape of the chop. Place shredded cabbage over half of a warm serving plate. Place the chop on top of the cabbage toward the center of the plate. Serve the sauce in a separate small dish for dipping or pour a generous band of the sauce directly over the centers of the pork strips. Garnish with several lemon wedges.

KATSUDON: A VARIATION

Oil, vegetable	1 tbsp	15 ml
Onion, chopped	10 oz	280 g
Dashi (see recipe)	20 oz	600 ml
Sake	4 oz	120 ml
Soy sauce, dark	4 oz	120 ml
Sugar	1–2 tbsp or to taste	15–30 g or to taste
Scallions, chopped	as needed	as needed

Prepare the cutlets in the same manner. Omit the shredded cabbage or Bok Choy and serve over a bed of sticky rice with the following sauce.

Heat oil in a wok or heavy-bottomed skillet over medium heat. Add onions and sauté, stirring frequently until the onions are soft.

Add ingredients and simmer for 5 minutes. Let cool, reserve, and reheat as needed. Garnish with chopped scallions and serve on the side.

Roast Pork Canton Style No. 1

YIELD: 10-12 SERVINGS

Sugar	6 oz	170 g	*Dissolve sugar in water and boil until the liquid has the consistency of a heavy syrup. Remove from heat and reserve.*
Water	10 oz	300 ml	
Pork, fresh, leg, trimmed of all fat, skin, and membrane	3 1/2 lb	1.6 kg	*Cut pork into 2-in. (5-cm) square strips, then cut each strip into 6-in. (15-cm) lengths.*
MARINADE			
Soy sauce, dark	6 oz	180 ml	*Place the pork in a stainless steel pan. Pour the marinade on top, then toss to coat the pieces well. Cover and refrigerate for 3–4 hours turning occasionally.*
Wine, dry sherry or rice wine	3 oz	90 ml	
Hoisin sauce	3 oz	90 ml	
Oil, peanut	2 oz	60 ml	
Reserved syrup	2 oz	60 ml	
Gingerroot, peeled and chopped fine	2 tbsp	25 g	
Scallions, white and green parts sliced thin	5–6	5–6	
Red food coloring (optional)	a few drops	a few drops	
Marinated pork			*Roast pork on a rack for 20–25 minutes in a 400°F (200°C) oven. Turn the pieces and baste with the marinade. Roast for 10 minutes more. When done, remove from oven and brush with a 50/50 mixture of sesame oil and syrup. Reserve. Serve sliced hot or cold, or use in combination with steamed vegetables, noodles, or rice. Can also be served in small cubes as a garnish for soups.*
Marinade	as needed	as needed	
Sesame oil	as needed	as needed	
Syrup	as needed	as needed	

Roast Pork Canton Style No. 2

YIELD: 10-12 SERVINGS

MARINADE

Five spice powder	2 tbsp	15 g
Peppercorns, brown Chinese, finely ground	4 tbsp	30 g
Gingerroot, grated or finely chopped	2.5 oz	70 g
Soy sauce, light	6 oz	180 ml
Oyster sauce	3 oz	90 ml
Rice wine or dry sherry	2 oz	60 ml
Sesame oil	1 oz	30 ml
Sugar	4 oz	115 g
Red food coloring (optional)	1/2 tsp	15 ml
Pork loin or tenderloin	4 lb	1.8 kg
Honey	4 tbsp	40 g

Combine ingredients and mix until the sugar is dissolved. Reserve.

Cut pork along the grain into strips 2 in. (5 cm) wide and 1 in. (2.5 cm) thick. Place in a glass or stainless steel tray. Add the marinade and coat the pork strips well. Cover meat and refrigerate for at least 4 hours or overnight. Traditionally, these pork strips are roasted suspended from individual hooks placed near the top of a barbecue oven. If this is not feasible, place strips on a wire rack set over a roasting pan to catch the drippings. Reserve the marinade. Roast at 450°F (230°C) for 10 minutes. Add the honey to the marinade and mix well. Brush this mixture over the pork. Lower heat to 325°F (165°C) and roast for another 20 minutes, basting frequently. Use as an entree or in combination with stir-fried or steamed vegetables, as a garnish for soup or serve with fried rice or noodles.

Skewered Beef and Scallions

YIELD: 10 SERVINGS

SEASONING MIXTURE

Soy sauce, dark	6 oz	180 ml	Combine ingredients and mix well. Reserve.
Rice wine	2 oz	60 ml	
Sesame oil	1 oz	30 ml	
Sugar	3 tbsp	45 g	
Garlic, minced	2 tbsp	30 g	
Scallions, white and green parts minced	4	4	
Beef, top round	2 3/4 lb	1.25 kg	Cut meat into 1/4-in. (.75-cm) thick slices. Score the meat lightly at 1/2-in. (1.5-cm) intervals with the tip of a sharp knife. Do not cut all the way through the meat. Cut each slice into pieces approximately 3 in. (8 cm) long and 1/2 in. (1.5 cm) wide.
Scallions, white and part of green sections, if needed	as needed	as needed	Trim bulb ends of scallions, then cut the white sections into lengths a bit shorter than the beef strips. This is to compensate for the beef shrinkage during cooking. Reserve the tender green parts for other uses.
Skewers, bamboo Reserved seasoning sauce	as needed	as needed	Alternate the beef slices with the scallions. String them together in this alternating pattern by passing the skewer though the wide upper section of the beef strip and the end of the scallion opposite the bulb part. Each skewer should contain 4 strips of beef separated by 3 scallion sections. Place the prepared skewers in a glass or stainless steel tray. Distribute seasoning sauce evenly over the beef and scallions and marinate for several hours, turning once or twice.

TO PREPARE AN INDIVIDUAL SERVING

Oil, vegetable	2 tsp	10 ml	Heat a skillet over high heat, then add oil. When oil is just below the smoking point, fry the beef and scallions, turning once, until done as desired. If prepared over a grill, baste once on each side with the seasoning sauce.
Skewered beef and scallion	45 oz per serving	115 g per serving	

See color insert for photograph of recipe

Beef with Bean Curd and Leek

YIELD: 1-2 SERVINGS

SAUCE

Chicken stock, cold	4 oz	120 ml
Sherry	2 tbsp	30 ml
Soy sauce	2 tbsp	30 ml
Cornstarch	1 tsp	4 g
Sugar	1 tsp	5 g
Salt	pinch	pinch

Combine ingredients and stir until the cornstarch is completely dissolved. Reserve.

Bean curd	3 oz	90 g

Cut bean curd into 1/2-inch (1.5-cm) cubes and soak for 15 minutes in water that is just below the boiling point.   Drain and reserve.

Oil, peanut	1 tbsp	15 ml
Beef, lean, ground twice	4 oz	115 gg
Leek, white part, washed and shredded fine	1 small	1 small

Heat wok or skillet over high heat. When very hot, add the oil and distribute it evenly over the surface of the pan. Add the beef and stir-fry until it loses color. Add the leek and continue to stir-fry for another 30–40 seconds.

Black beans, fermented	2 tsp	20 g
Bean paste, hot	1 tsp	10 g
Garlic, minced	1 tsp	5 g
Gingerroot, minced	1 tsp	4 g
Chili pepper, fresh, red, minced	1/2 tsp or to taste	4 g or to taste
Pepper, black	to taste	to taste

Add ingredients to the pan and stir-fry for another 30 seconds.

Reserved sauce
Reserved bean curd

Add the sauce and bring to a boil. Lower heat and simmer for another minute. Add the bean curd and gently incorporate it with the other ingredients. Simmer until the sauce has thickened. Serve immedietely.

Beef Curry

YIELD: 10 SERVINGS

Oil, vegetable	2 oz	60 ml	*Heat oil over high heat in a heavy-bottomed stew pot. Add beef cubes and brown on all sides. When done, remove meat and reserve in a warm place.*
Beef, top round or chuck, cut into 1 1/2-in. (4-cm) cubes	4 lb	1.8 kg	
Oil, vegetable	1 oz	30 ml	*Using the same pot, add oil, if needed, and fry the onions over medium heat, stirring, until they are a deep brown color.*
Onion, cut into small dice	2 lb	900 g	
Gingerroot, peeled and minced	4 tbsp	50 g	*Add the gingerroot and garlic and cook, stirring, for 1 minute. Add the remaining ingredients and cook for another 15–20 seconds, stirring constantly.*
Garlic, minced	1 1/2 tbsp	25 g	
Coriander, ground	2 1/2 tbsp	18 g	
Cumin, ground	1 tbsp	7 g	
Turmeric, ground	1 tbsp	7 g	
Pepper, cayenne	1 tsp or to taste	2 g or to taste	
Salt	to taste	to taste	
Stock, beef	1 1/2 qt	1.4 L	*Add stock and deglaze the pan. Add the beef and tomatoes and bring the liquids to a boil. Lower heat, cover the pot partially, and simmer for 1 1/2–2 hours or until the meat is very tender. When done, adjust seasonings to taste. Cool, then refrigerate. To serve, reheat portions in the sauce. Serve with boiled potatoes or rice. Garnish with chopped, fresh cilantro leaves.*
Tomatoes, fresh preferred, peeled, seeded, and chopped fine	1 1/2 lb	680 g	
Reserved beef			

Beef with Orange and Chili Flavor

YIELD: 1 SERVING

Beef fillet, semi-frozen	6 oz	170 g
Soy sauce, dark	2 tbsp	30 ml
Oil, vegetable	1 tbsp	15 ml
Scallion, white and green part, sliced thin	1	1
Gingerroot, peeled and grated	1 tsp	4 g
Cornstarch	pinch	pinch
Oil, peanut	1 oz	30 ml
Chili peppers, red, dried	2 or to taste	2 or to taste
Chinese brown peppercorns	1 tsp	2 g
Orange peel, dried	2–3 pieces	2–3 pieces
Reserved beef		
Soy sauce, light	1 tbsp	15 ml
Sesame oil	1 tsp	5 ml

Slice beef into very thin, uniform slices. Use an electric slicing machine if available. (Chilling the beef will make it easier to slice.) Slice each piece again into 1 x 2 in. (2.5 x 5 cm) strips.

Combine ingredients in a mixing bowl. Mix until the cornstarch is completely dissolved. Add the beef slices and toss to cover the beef evenly. Let stand for 15 minutes.

Heat wok or skillet over high heat. Add the oil and heat until it is just below the smoking point. Add the chili peppers, peppercorns, and orange peel. Stir-fry until the peel begins to brown lightly. Remove all contents of the pan and reserve.

Return the beef to the pan and stir-fry until the edges are crisp. Add the soy sauce and sesame oil and stir. Return the chili peppers, peppercorns, and orange peel to the pan. Continue to stir-fry until heated through.

Stewed Beef Ribs
with Chestnuts and Gingko Nuts

YIELD: 10-12 SERVINGS

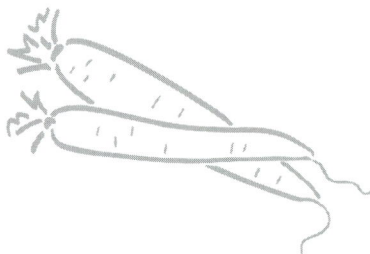

Beef, short ribs	8 lb	3.6 kg	*Cut the short ribs into 2–3 in. (5–7.5 cm) pieces.*
Rice wine	6 oz	180 ml	*Trim any excess fat then score the ribs diagonally,*
Sugar	4 oz	115 g	*almost to the bone, at 1-in. (2.5-cm) intervals.*

Combine the sugar and rice wine and stir until the sugar is completely dissolved. Distribute this mixture over the meat, covering all surfaces evenly. Allow to marinate for 30 minutes.

SEASONING MIXTURE

Soy sauce, dark	8 oz	240 ml	*Combine ingredients and mix well. Reserve.*
Sesame oil	2 oz	60 ml	
Scallions, chopped, white and green parts	10	10	
Salt	1 tsp or to taste	5 g	
Pepper, black	1 tsp or to taste	2 g	

Onions, medium	1 lb	450 g	*Cut onions in half, then slice thin, root to stem. Peel*
Chestnuts,* fresh, peeled	30	30	*chestnuts. Cut the carrot and white radish into*
Carrot, peeled	3/4 lb	340 g	*pieces resembling the peeled chestnuts. Steam dates*
White radish (daikon), peeled	3/4 lb	340 g	*until soft, then remove skins and seeds. Chop or julienne the trimmings. Reserve.*
Jujubes (Chinese red dates)	30	30	

Available fresh in season; year round, in cans.

(Continued on facing page)

Gingko nuts,* shelled	40	40
Oil	as needed	as needed

Soak the gingko nuts in hot water to loosen the skins. Heat a skillet with a small amount of oil and stir-fry the gingko nuts until they turn pale green. Reserve.

Marinated ribs		
Seasoning sauce		
Water or beef stock	as needed	as needed
Reserved vegetables		
Reserved gingko nuts		

Dip ribs into the seasoning sauce then place them in a stew pot with enough water or stock to cover. (Reserve the seasoning mixture to adjust flavor later.) Bring the liquid to a boil over high heat, then lower heat, cover partially, and simmer for 30–40 minutes or until the meat is tender but still firm. Add the vegetables, with the exception of the gingko nuts, and simmer for another 10–15 minutes or until the vegetables are tender. Add the gingko nuts 10 minutes before completion of cooking. Adjust flavor of liquids with some of the seasoning mixture, if necessary. When done, uncover and cook over high heat until most of the liquid has evaporated and the contents of the pot begin to glaze.

Pine nuts, chopped fine

Serve in a deep, heated bowl. Sprinkle chopped pine nuts on top.

Available fresh in season; year round, in cans.

Marinated Beef with Snow Peas

YIELD: 10-12 SERVINGS

MARINADE

Oyster sauce	4 oz	120 ml	*Combine ingredients and mix until the cornstarch and sugar are completely dissolved.*
Rice wine or dry sherry	4 oz	120 ml	
Soy sauce, dark	2 oz	60 ml	
Ginger juice	1 tbsp	15 ml	
Oil, sesame	1 tbsp	15 ml	
Sugar	1 tsp	5 g	
Salt	1 tsp	5 g	
Pepper, white, fine ground	1 tsp	2 g	
Cornstarch	2 tbsp	20 g	
Flank steak	3 lb	1.4 kg	*Chill flank steak to facilitate slicing. Trim all fat and membrane. Cutting across the grain on the diagonal, slice into very thin slices. Cut the slices into pieces approximately 2 x 1/2 in. (5 x 1.5 cm). Place in a stainless steel mixing bowl and add the marinade. Toss well to coat pieces evenly. Cover and refrigerate for at least 1 hour before using.*
Snow peas	1 1/2 lb	680 g	*Wash, trim stems, and remove strings. Cut each pod in two on the diagonal. Reserve.*

(Continued on facing page)

Oil, peanut	*2 tsp*	*2 ml*
Ginger, chopped fine	*1 tsp or to taste*	*4 g or to taste*
Snow peas	*2–3 oz*	*60–90 g*

Heat a wok or heavy skillet over high heat. Add the oil and heat to just below the smoking point. Add the ginger and stir-fry briefly until it becomes aromatic. Add the snow peas and continue to stir-fry for 30–40 seconds. Remove the contents of the pan and reserve in a warm place.

Oil, peanut	*1 tsp (if needed)*	*5 ml (if needed)*
Garlic, minced	*1/2 tsp or to taste*	*3 g or to taste*
Marinated flank steak	*4–5 oz*	*115 g*

Add oil to pan and add the garlic. Stir-fry for 10–20 seconds or until the garlic begins to color lightly. Add the flank steak and 1 tbsp (15 ml) of the marinade and stir-fry until the meat loses all color. Return the snow peas and ginger and stir-fry for another 30 seconds.

Chicken broth	*3 oz*	*90 ml*
Cornstarch	*1 tsp*	*4 g*
Oyster sauce	*1 tsp*	*5 ml*

Combine ingredients thoroughly and pour into the center of the pan. Stir-fry for another minute or until the liquids thicken.

Braised Beef in Tomato Yogurt Sauce

YIELD: 10-12 SERVINGS

Tomatoes, fresh preferred if in season (otherwise used canned Italian), peeled, seeded, and chopped	2 lb	900 g	*Place ingredients into the bowl of a food processor fitted with the steel blade. Process to a smooth puree. Reserve.*
Yogurt	6 oz	170 g	
Gingerroot, peeled and minced	3 tbsp	30 g	
Garlic minced	2 tbsp	30 g	
Oil, vegetable	2 oz.	60 ml	*Heat oil over high heat in a heavy-bottomed, deep, braising pan. Add beef cubes and brown on all sides. When done remove meat and reserve in a warm place.*
Beef, top round or chuck, trimmed and cut into 1 1/2-in. cubes	4 lb	1.8 kg	
Oil, vegetable	1–2 oz	30–60 ml	*Using the same pan, add a small amount of oil, if needed, and fry the onions over medium heat, stirring, until they are a deep brown color.*
Onion, cut into small dice	2 lb	900 g	
Cardamom, ground	2 tsp	4 g	*Add spices and cook, stirring, for about a minute or until they become aromatic. Lower heat and add the reserved tomato mixture and the beef stock, scraping up any browned bits still clinging to the pan. Bring to a boil over medium heat. Lower heat and simmer for 5 minutes.*
Turmeric, ground	2 tsp	4 g	
Cloves, ground	2 tsp	4 g	
Pepper, cayenne	1 tsp	2 g	
Salt	1 tsp or to taste	5 g or to taste	
Reserved tomato mixture			
Stock, beef	1 qt	1 L	
Reserved beef cubes	as needed	as needed	*Return the beef to the pan, stir well, and cover with a tight lid. Place the pan in a 350°F (175°C) oven for 2 hours or until the meat is very tender. Add a small amount of beef stock, from time to time, if needed. When done, adjust seasonings. Let cool and refrigerate until needed. Before reheating for individual servings, remove any fat that has congealed on top. Serve with boiled rice and garnish with chopped fresh cilantro leaves.*
Stock, beef			

See color insert for photograph of recipe

Glazed Pork Ribs

YIELD: 10-12 SERVINGS

Pork spare ribs	*8 lb*	*3.6 kg*	*Using a band saw or butcher's saw, cut the ribs across the bone into 2–4 in. (5–10 cm) lengths, then into smaller pieces cutting between the bones.*
Soy sauce, dark	*16 oz*	*470 ml*	*Place ingredients in a heavy-bottomed saucepan*
Rice wine or dry sherry	*8 oz*	*240 ml*	*large enough to hold the ribs. Add the ribs and*
Sugar	*6 oz*	*170 g*	*enough water to cover to depth of 1 inch (2.5 cm).*
Gingerroot, peeled and cut into 1-in. pieces	*3 oz*	*90 g*	*Bring to a boil over high heat. Cover pot partially, lower heat to a simmer and cook for 30 minutes, turning ribs occasionally. Uncover pot and discard*
Scallions, green and white parts, cut in half	*8*	*8*	*the gingerroot and scallions. Turn heat to high and reduce the liquid until it has become thick and*
Water	*as needed*	*as needed*	*glazes the ribs. Turn ribs frequently to coat them evenly. Ribs are done when well glazed.*

Braised Lamb in a Cream Sauce

YIELD: 10 SERVINGS

Ingredient	US	Metric	Method
Almonds, blanched, slivered	2 oz	60 g	Place the almonds into the bowl of a food processor fitted with the steel blade. Chop the almonds as fine as possible. Add the remaining ingredients and puree.
Onion, sliced	1 lb	450 g	
Yogurt	8 oz	225 g	
Gingerroot, peeled and sliced	1 oz	30 g	
Heavy cream	1 pt	470 ml	Add ingredients and blend them with the yogurt mixture using the pulse action of the processor. Reserve.
Coriander, ground	2 tbsp or to taste	15 g or to taste	
Cardamom, ground	1 tbsp or to taste	7 g or to taste	
Salt	2 tsp or to taste	10 g or to taste	
Pepper, black	1 tsp or to taste	2 g or to taste	
Clarified butter	2 oz	60 ml	Heat clarified butter over medium heat in a braising pan just large enough to hold the lamb cubes. Add the lamb and brown lightly. Add the reserved yogurt/cream mixture and stir to coat the lamb cubes. Lower heat, and slowly bring liquids to a boil. Cover the pan and cook over very low heat for 1 1/2 hours, stirring occasionally, or until the meat is very tender. When done, adjust seasonings to taste.
Lamb, leg, trimmed of all fat, cut into 2-in. (5-cm) or smaller, cubes	3 lb	1.4 kg	
Potatoes,* boiling, cut into 1-in. cubes (optional)	2 lb	900 g	

*Potatoes may be added to the pot 20–30 minutes before completion. Add 4–6 oz (120–180 ml) of milk to pan if needed. Serve with rice pilaf or potatoes. If preparing individual servings to order, use cooked potato cubes and add when reheating individual portions.

Lamb Braised in Savory Yogurt Sauce

YIELD: 10-12 SERVINGS

MARINADE

Onion, coarsely chopped	1 1/2 lb	680 g
Gingerroot, minced	3 tbsp	35 g
Coriander, ground	2 tbsp	15 g
Salt	2 tsp or to taste	10 g or to taste
Red pepper flakes	1 tsp or to taste	2 g or to taste

Place ingredients into the bowl of a food processor fitted with the steel blade and puree.

Yogurt	2 lb	900 g
Clarified butter	4 oz	120 ml

Add ingredients to the processor bowl. Using the pulse action, blend thoroughly. Reserve.

Lamb leg	3 1/2 lb	1.5 kg

Trim all fat from meat, then cut into 1 1/2-in. (4-cm) cubes. Combine the meat with the marinade and cover. Refrigerate overnight.

Marinated meat		
Marinade		
Stock, lamb, chicken stock, or water	8 oz or as needed	240 ml or as needed

Place the meat with the marinade in a deep casserole. Bring to a boil over medium to low heat, stirring occasionally. Lower heat, cover, and simmer for 1–1 1/2 hours or until the lamb is very tender. Stir frequently to prevent sticking. When meat is done, remove from heat and reserve together with the cooking liquids.

Clarified butter	2 oz	60 ml
Garlic, minced	1 tbsp	15 g
Cumin, ground	1 tbsp	7 g
Cardamom, ground	2 tsp	4 g
Mughul garam masala (see recipe)	2 tsp	4 g
Heavy cream	12 oz	350 ml or
Salt	to taste	to taste

In a small skillet, heat the clarified butter over high heat. Add the garlic and sauté very briefly until slightly colored. Add the cumin, cardamom, and mughul garam masala. Sauté, stirring, for a few seconds, then add the heavy cream and heat through. Do not boil. Adjust salt if necessary. Mix well and remove from heat. Combine this mixture with the lamb and the pot liquids and mix well. Let cool and reserve. To serve, reheat over low heat, in single portions or as needed.

Lamb Scallops with Scallions

YIELD: 1 SERVING

TO PREPARE THE SCALLOPS

Lamb, leg, boned	*as needed*	*as needed*	*Trim meat of all fat, gristle, and tendons. Place in freezer long enough for the meat to become firm but not frozen. Chilling time will vary depending on thickness of meat. When well chilled, slice the meat into thin scallops, then into bite-sized pieces. Reserve, refrigerated.*

TO PREPARE AN INDIVIDUAL SERVING

Lamb, scallops	*4–5 oz*	*115–140 g*	*Place meat in a stainless steel bowl and add the soy sauce and wine. Toss to coat pieces evenly. Marinate for 10 minutes.*
Soy sauce	*1 tbsp*	*15 ml*	
Shaohsing wine or dry sherry	*1 tbsp*	*15 ml*	

SAUCE

Soy sauce	*2 tbsp*	*30 ml*	*Combine ingredients and reserve.*
Shaohsing wine or dry sherry	*2 tbsp*	*30 ml*	
Oil, sesame	*1 tsp*	*5 ml*	
Cornstarch	*1 tsp*	*3 g*	
Sugar	*pinch*	*pinch*	
Salt	*pinch*	*pinch*	

See color insert for photograph of recipe

(Continued on facing page)

Oil, peanut	*1 tbsp*	*15 ml*
Garlic, sliced thin	*3/4 tsp*	*3 g*
Marinated lamb		
Reserved sauce		
Scallions, white and green parts cut into 1 1/2-in. (4-cm) julienne	*2*	*2*

Heat wok or skillet over high heat. When the pan is very hot add the oil and distribute it evenly over the pan. Add the garlic and stir-fry for 10–15 seconds or until it just begins to color. Add the lamb and continue to stir-fry for another 20–30 seconds. Add the sauce and stir-fry until the sauce is thoroughly incorporated, then add the scallions and stir-fry until they are heated through.

Oil, sesame	*as needed*	*as needed*

When done, place lamb on a warm serving plate and sprinkle lightly with sesame oil.

Lamb Sauté with Garlic and Scallions

YIELD: 1 SERVING

Soy sauce, light	2 tbsp	30 ml
Oil, peanut	1 tbsp	15 ml
Rice wine or dry sherry	1 tbsp	15 ml
Chinese brown pepper-corns, toasted and ground	1 tsp	2 g
Sesame oil	1 tsp	5 ml
Salt	pinch	pinch
Cornstarch	as needed	as needed

Combine ingredients and mix thoroughly. Use enough cornstarch to make a thin paste.

Lamb, leg, chilled	6 oz	170 g

Slice meat as thin as possible across the grain. Then slice again into thin strips. Place meat in a bowl with the soy sauce mixture and toss to coat meat evenly. Let stand for 15 minutes.

Oil, peanut	1 tbsp	15 ml
Scallions, white and green parts sliced into 1/2-in. (1.5-cm) pieces	3	3
Garlic, sliced thin	2 medium cloves	2 medium cloves

Heat wok or skillet over high heat. Add oil, then stir-fry the scallions and garlic briefly until the garlic begins to color lightly. Remove these ingredients from the pan and reserve. Do not let the garlic brown.

Marinated lamb		
Soy sauce	1 tbsp	15 ml
Rice wine or dry sherry	1 tbsp	15 ml
Sesame oil	1 tsp	5 ml

Using the same pan, stir-fry the lamb until lightly browned, then add the soy sauce, rice wine, and sesame oil. Stir several times. Return the scallions and garlic to the pan. Stir-fry briefly until all ingredients are heated though.

Grilled Lamb Liver Kebabs

YIELD: 10-12 SERVINGS

Lamb or calf's liver	3 3/4 lb	1.7 kg	*Remove all membrane and outer skin. Cut liver into 1-in. cubes. Lightly oil the skewers, then thread 3 oz (90 g) of liver on each. Place them in a stainless steel pan.*
Oil, vegetable			
Skewers, small stainless steel or bamboo			
Oil, vegetable	4 oz	120 ml	*Combine ingredients and distribute evenly on all surfaces of the liver. Cover and refrigerate for 2–3 hours before using.*
Lemon juice	4 oz	120 ml	
Garlic, minced	1 1/2 tbsp	20 g	
Salt	2 tsp or to taste	10 g or to taste	
Pepper, cayenne	1 tsp or to taste	2 g or to taste	

TO PREPARE AN INDIVIDUAL SERVING

Marinated liver	2 skewers per serving	2 skewers per serving	*Grill liver over hot coals or under broiler flame until slightly charred on the outside and medium rare on the inside. Prepare a balanced mixture, to taste, of chopped onion, tomato, and fresh chili peppers. Serve liver on the skewers topped with several tablespoons of the vegetable mixture. Garnish plate with several lemon wedges. When prepared in smaller portions, this can be served as an appetizer.*
Onion, chopped	as needed	as needed	
Tomato, chopped	as needed	as needed	
Chili pepper, fresh, green, minced	as needed	as needed	

Pork Chops in Sweet Ginger Sauce

YIELD: 10 SERVINGS

SAUCE

Rice wine or dry sherry	12 oz	350 ml	Combine ingredients in a small saucepan. Bring to a boil over medium heat. Lower heat and simmer for 15 minutes. When done, strain, let cool, and reserve.
Soy sauce	12 oz	350 ml	
Sugar	10 oz or to taste	280 g or to taste	
Gingerroot, peeled and shredded	3 oz	90 g	
Garlic, sliced thin	3 tbsp	45 g	
Pork chops	20, 4 oz each	20, 115 g each	Bone in, fat trimmed, leaving a thin rim on edge of meat. Score fat in 4–5 places to prevent curling. Reserve.

TO PREPARE AN INDIVIDUAL SERVING

Oil, sesame	1 tbsp	15 ml	Heat oil in a heavy skillet over medium to high heat. When oil is just below the smoking point, add the chops and sear on both sides. Lower heat, cover pan, and cook until the chops are cooked through. Add the reserved sauce and raise the heat to high. Cook, uncovered, turning the chops frequently, until they are glazed and the sauce has almost completely evaporated. Remove chops and reserve in a warm place.
Pork chops	2 per serving	2 per serving	
Reserved sauce	2–3 oz per serving	60–90 ml per serving	
Chili peppers, fresh, red, fine julienne	as needed	as needed	Using the same pan, add a total weight of 2–3 oz (60–90 g) of a mixture of hot and sweet peppers. The ratio of hot to sweet peppers can be varied according to taste. Stir-fry over high heat until slightly softened. Place peppers on top of chops along with any remaining pan juices.
Red bell peppers, fine julienne	as needed	as needed	
Green bell peppers, fine julienne	as needed	as needed	

Deep-Fried Pork Cutlets

YIELD: 10 SERVINGS

SEASONINGS

Rice wine or dry sherry	10 oz	300 ml	*Combine ingredients.*
Gingerroot, peeled and grated	3 oz	85 g	
Scallions, minced fine, white and tender green parts	3	3	
Salt	2 tsp	10 g	
Pepper, white	1 tsp or to taste	2 g or to taste	
Pork loin, center cut, boned and trimmed	4 lb	1.8 kg	*Cut into 3-oz (90-g) slices. Place meat between sheets of waxed paper and flatten with a meat mallet or heavy cleaver. Make small incisions around the edges of each chop to prevent curling. Rub the seasoning mixture on all surfaces of the pork cutlets. Place the seasoned cutlets, stacked, in a stainless steel tray. Cover and refrigerate until needed. Allow at least 1 hour for seasonings to flavor meat before using.*
Cornstarch	as needed	as needed	*Place the cornstarch, eggs, and bread crumbs each in a separate flat container. Dip the cutlets in that order. Press the cutlets into bread crumbs to coat well. (Cutlets may be prepared in quantity up to this point and refrigerated for later use. Store, separated by waxed paper, in refrigerator.) Deep-fry at 375°F (190°C) until golden brown and cooked through. When done, drain on absorbent paper or a clean kitchen towel. Slice each fillet into 1-in. (2.5-cm) strips, cutting against the grain, then reassemble to original shape and place on a warmed plate.*
Egg, beaten	as needed	as needed	
Bread crumbs, coarse	as needed	as needed	
Seasoned pork fillets	6 oz per serving	170 g per serving	
Spiced salt (see recipe)	as needed	as needed	*Serve spiced salt and soy sauce in small, separate bowls, for dipping.*
Soy sauce, dark	as needed	as needed	

Pork Fillet with Bamboo Shoots and Mushrooms

YIELD: 1   SERVING

Egg white, beaten	1 medium	1 medium
Salt	pinch	pinch
Cornstarch	as needed	as needed
Pork fillet, loin or tenderloin	4 oz	115 g

Combine ingredients using enough cornstarch to make a thin paste.

Slicing across the grain, cut the pork into very thin slices. Place in a small mixing bowl and toss with the egg white mixture until the meat is well coated. Let stand for 15 minutes.

FLAVORING MIXTURE

Chicken stock	2 oz	60 ml
Soy sauce, light	1 tbsp	15 ml
Rice wine or dry sherry	1 tbsp	15 ml
Salt	pinch	pinch
Cornstarch	1/2 tsp	3–4 g

Combine ingredients and reserve.

Oil, peanut	1 tbsp	15 ml
Scallions, white and green parts sliced thin	2	2
Gingerroot, fine julienne	1 tsp	4 g
Mushrooms, fresh (of choice)	2 oz	60 g
Bamboo shoot, sliced thin	1 oz	30 g
Sesame oil (optional)	as needed	as needed

Heat wok or skillet over high heat. Add the oil and reheat to just below the smoking point. Briefly stir-fry the scallions and ginger until they become aromatic. Add the pork and continue to stir-fry until the pork loses its raw color. Remove all contents from the pan and reserve. Next, stir-fry the mushrooms and bamboo shoots for 20–30 seconds, add the flavoring mixture and stir. Return the pork to the pan and bring liquids to a boil. Lower heat and simmer until the sauce begins to thicken. Add a sprinkle of sesame oil just prior to serving (optional)

Pork Roasted with Honey

YIELD: 4 1/2 POUNDS (2 KG)

MARINADE

Honey	4 oz	115 g
Chicken stock	4 oz	120 ml
Soy sauce, dark	3 oz	90 ml
Oyster sauce	2 oz	60 ml
Hoisin sauce	2 oz	60 ml
Rice wine	2 oz	60 ml
Five-spice powder	2 tsp or to taste	4 g or to taste
Pepper, white, ground	1 tsp or to taste	2 g or to taste

Combine ingredients thoroughly. Reserve.

Pork tenderloins, 8–12 oz (225–340 g) each	5 lb	2.25 kg

Trim the tenderloins of any fat or membrane, then place in a roasting pan just large enough to hold them. Distribute the marinade evenly over all surfaces. Cover and refrigerate. Allow to marinate for 8 hours, turning occasionally.

Marinated pork
  tenderloin

Roast the pork with the marinade in a 425°F (220°C) oven for 30 minutes, or until the pork has reached an internal temperature of 150°F (65°C). While roasting, turn and baste every 5–10 minutes. When done, let cool, then refrigerate.

Note: Pork roasted in honey can be served in a variety of ways: as an entree, an appetizer, as a garnish in soups, or in combination with noodles or rice and/or vegetables in other stir-fried preparations.

Pressed Beef Served Cold

YIELD: 10-12 SERVINGS

Beef, brisket*	3 1/2 lb	1.6 kg
Water or beef stock	as needed	as needed
Onion, diced	1 lb	450 g
Carrot, sliced	12 oz	340 g

Place meat in a pot with enough water or stock to cover. Bring to a boil over medium to high heat. Lower heat and simmer for 1 hour, skimming as necessary. Add the vegetables and simmer for another hour or until the meat is very tender. Let meat cool in liquid. Remove meat and wrap in a clean cloth. Refrigerate overnight, under weights. Strain and reserve the stock for other uses.

SAUCE

Soy sauce, light	10 oz	300 ml
Vinegar, rice	4 oz or to taste	120 ml or to taste
Scallion, white and green parts, finely sliced	4	4
Garlic, minced	1 1/2 tbsp or to taste	20 g or to taste
Sugar	2 tsp or to taste	10 g or to taste
Sesame salt (see recipe)	to taste	to taste
Pepper, black	to taste	to taste

Combine ingredients thoroughly and reserve.

TO SERVE

Pressed beef	as needed	as needed
Lettuce leaves, shredded	as needed	as needed
Reserved sauce		

Arrange thinly sliced beef over a bed of shredded lettuce leaves. Serve with a small amount of the sauce on top. Sauce may also be presented separately in a small side dish.

*Traditionally made with beef shank, this preparation can be served as part of a buffet, or, as an appetizer or an entree accompanied with rice. If using beef shank, prior to cooking, trim all silver skin and remove the tendons.

Short Ribs in a Sweet Broth

Short ribs, cut into 4-in. (10-cm) lengths	8 lb	3.6 kg
Water or beef stock	3–4 qt	3–4 L

Trim excess fat from ribs and place in a soup pot. Add water or stock to cover by 2 inches and bring to a boil. Lower heat to a simmer, cover partially, and cook for 1 hour or until the meat is very tender. Skim the broth as needed while cooking until no more scum rises to the surface and the liquid is clear. When done, remove the short ribs and reduce the liquid to 2 1/2 quarts (2.3 L). Degrease the broth and return the short ribs to the pot.

Onion juice	6 oz	180 ml
Pear juice, fresh	6 oz	180 ml
Garlic, thin sliced	1 tbsp	15 g
Scallions, green and white parts, thin sliced	4–5	4–5
Sesame seeds, toasted	3 tbsp	20 g
Sesame oil	3 tbsp or to taste	45 ml
Sugar	2 tsp or to taste	10 g or to taste
Salt (optional)	2 tsp or to taste	4 g or to taste
Pepper, black, fine ground	to taste	to taste

Add ingredients, stir well, and simmer for 5–6 minutes. Taste and adjust seasonings if necessary. Let cool and reserve until needed.

TO SERVE

Reserved ribs and broth	as needed	as needed
Pine nuts	as needed	as needed

Reheat broth and ribs. Place a portion of ribs with the bones in a heated, deep soup bowl. Add 7–8 oz (200–240 ml) of the broth and sprinkle pine nuts on top as a garnish.

Steak with Daikon, Carrot, and Ginger

YIELD: 10 SERVINGS

MARINADE

Soy sauce, dark	4 oz	120 ml	*Combine ingredients and reserve.*
Mirin	2 oz	60 ml	
Garlic, minced	1 tbsp	15 g	
Steaks, sirloin or rib	10, 8 oz each	10, 220 g each	*Trim excess fat. Place each steak between sheets of waxed paper and pound lightly with a mallet or heavy cleaver to flatten steaks slightly. Lightly score the surfaces of the meat with the point of a sharp knife to aid the penetration of the marinade. Spread the marinade over all surfaces of the steaks. Cover, then refrigerate for at least 1 hour before cooking.*
Rice vinegar	4 oz	120 ml	*Combine the rice vinegar and sugar in a mixing bowl and stir until the sugar is dissolved. Cut the daikon and carrot into 2-in. (5-cm) rounds then cut each round into thin slices lengthwise. Cut these slices into very thin matchsticks. Mix these ingredients together, then toss in the vinegar and sugar dressing. Let stand for at least 1 hour before serving.*
Sugar	2 oz	60 g	
Daikon, peeled	6 oz	170 g	
Carrot, peeled	6 oz	170 g	
Gingerroot, peeled	2 oz	60 g	

TO PREPARE AN INDIVIDUAL SERVING

Oil, vegetable	1 tsp	5 ml	*Heat the oil in a skillet over high heat until just below the smoking point.* Sauté the steak until done as desired. Slice steak preserving its original shape, into 1-in. (2.5-cm) strips cutting on the diagonal against the grain. Place steak on a well-heated plate. Use a slotted spoon to drain excess dressing and place a small mound of the drained daikon mixture next to the meat. Garnish with fresh sprigs of watercress.*
Steak, marinated			
Scallion, green part, sliced thin	1	1	
Daikon mixture	as needed	as needed	

*Steak may be brushed lightly with oil and grilled or broiled.

Stuffed Cabbage
with Tomato Ginger Sauce

YIELD: 10-12 SERVINGS

STUFFING

Oil, vegetable	2 oz	60 ml
Lamb, trimmed of fat, ground twice	2 1/2 lb	1.15 kg

Heat the oil in a heavy skillet over medium heat. Add the meat and brown, stirring, to break up any lumps. When done, remove from pan and reserve.

Onions, minced	1 1/2 lb	680 g
Gingerroot, peeled and minced	2 tbsp	25 g
Garlic, minced	2 tbsp	30 g
Chili pepper, green, fresh, seeds and ribs removed, then minced	1 tbsp or to taste	6 g or to taste

Add ingredients to the pan and sauté, stirring, for 1–2 minutes over medium heat. Do not allow the onions or garlic to brown.

Reserved meat		
Turmeric	1 tsp	2 g
Stock, beef	6 oz	180 ml
Salt	2 tsp or to taste	10 g or to taste

Return the meat to the pan. Add the turmeric, stock, and salt to taste. Blend all ingredients thoroughly. Cook over medium heat, stirring occasionally, until all of the liquid has evaporated. When done, remove from heat.

Cilantro leaves, fresh, chopped fine	6–8 sprigs	6–8 sprigs
Garam masala (see recipe)	2 tbsp	14 g
Lemon juice, fresh squeezed	2 tbsp	30 ml

Add ingredients and distribute the seasonings evenly. Break up any lumps that may form. When done, the meat should be fairly dry and have the even texture of very coarse meal. Taste and adjust seasonings if necessary. Reserve.

(Continued on next page)

Cabbage leaves Reserved meat	*Number needed will vary depending on size. Average entree serving will contain 2–3 cabbage leaves stuffed with approx. 4 oz (115 g) of the meat mixture.*	

Select cabbage that will produce the needed number of fresh, unblemished leaves of uniform size. Reserve any leftover cabbage leaves from the centers of the cabbage heads for use in the accompanying sauce. Remove just enough of the core to separate the outer leaves. Briefly immerse the remainder of the cabbage in boiling water to loosen the next layers. When all of the usable leaves have been separated, blanch them for 1–2 minutes or until they become flexible enough to roll. Thick sections of the leaves can be pared down with a vegetable peeler. When done as desired, plunge them immediately into cold water then drain. Place several spoonfuls of the meat mixture (amount will vary depending on the size of the cabbage leaf) close to the stem end of the leaf. Roll the leaf toward the thinner end, tucking in the sides as you roll. Reserve the completed rolls, seam side down.

Oil, vegetable	*1 oz*	*30 ml*
Onion, thin slices	*1 1/2 lb*	*680 g*
Cabbage leaves reserved for sauce, shredded		
Tomatoes, peeled and chopped	*1 1/2 lb*	*680 g*
Tomato paste	*2 tbsp*	*30 g*
Gingerroot, peeled and minced	*2 tbsp*	*24 g*
Stock, beef	*24 oz*	*700 ml*
Salt	*to taste*	*to taste*
Pepper, black	*to taste*	*to taste*

Heat oil over medium heat in a heavy casserole just large enough to hold the stuffed cabbage rolls and the sauce. Sauté the onions until they are soft. Add the remaining ingredients, mix well, and bring to a boil. Lower heat and simmer for 5 minutes. Adjust seasonings if necessary. Remove half of the contents of the pot. Pack the stuffed cabbage rolls in the pot as closely together as possible. Distribute the ingredients just removed from the pot evenly over the top of the cabbage rolls. Place a heavy plate on top. Cover the pot and cook in a 350°F (175°C) oven for 45 minutes. When done, let cool, then refrigerate. Reheat individual portions as needed. Serve with boiled rice.

Beef with Asparagus in Oyster Sauce

YIELD: 10 SERVINGS

MARINADE

Chicken stock or water	4 oz	120 ml
Oil, peanut	2 oz	60 ml
Soy sauce	2 tbsp	30 ml
Shaohsing wine or dry sherry	2 tbsp	30 ml
Potato or cornstarch	1 tbsp	3 g
Salt	1/2 tsp	3 g
Sugar	1/2 tsp	3 g
Pepper, black	pinch	pinch
Beef, top or bottom round, skirt or fillet	2 1/2 lb	1.15 kg

Combine ingredients and mix until the potato or cornstarch is completely dissolved.

Chill meat to make slicing easier. Trim meat of all fat then cut into very thin slices. Cut each slice into strips, then cut the strips into pieces about 1 1/2 in. (4 cm) long. Place in a mixing bowl and add the marinade. Stir to coat the meat thoroughly. Cover and refrigerate for at least 30 minutes before using.

TO PREPARE AN INDIVIDUAL SERVING

Oil, peanut	1 tbsp	30 ml
Garlic, minced	1 tsp	5 g
Gingerroot, minced	1 tsp	5 g
Scallions, white parts only cut into 1-in. (2.5-cm) pieces	2	2

Heat wok or skillet over high heat. When very hot add the oil and distribute it evenly over the surface of the pan. When the oil is just below the smoking point add the garlic, gingerroot, and scallions and stir-fry for 5–10 seconds.

(Continued on next page)

Marinated beef	4 oz	115 g	*Add the beef and continue to stir-fry over high heat*
Shaohsing wine or dry sherry	*as needed*	*as needed*	*for another minute. Add a splash of the wine, stir for another few seconds, then remove contents of pan to a warm serving dish leaving a small amount of liquid in the pan.*
Asparagus, cleaned, root ends peeled, then cut into 1-in. (2.5-cm) lengths	2 oz	60 g	*Using the same pan, add the asparagus and stir-fry for a minute. Lower heat, cover, and let steam for another minute. Raise heat, then add the potato starch which has been thoroughly dissolved in the stock and oyster sauce.*
Stock, chicken	2 tbsp	30 ml	
Oyster sauce	1 tbsp	15 ml	
Potato or corn starch	1/2 tsp	3 g	
Reserved beef			*Return the beef to the pan and add the scallions.*
Scallions, green parts cut into 1-in. (2.5-cm) lengths	2	2	*Stir-fry briefly until heated through.*

Beef with Hot Chili Peppers and Mushrooms

YIELD: 1 SERVING

Ingredient			Method
Cornstarch	1/2 tsp	4 g	*Dissolve the cornstarch in enough water to make a thin paste.*
Water, cold	as needed	as needed	
Flank steak, well chilled	3–4 oz	85–115 g	*Slicing across the grain and at an angle, cut the flank steak into thin slices. Then cut the slices into bite-size pieces. Place the meat in a small mixing bowl and add the cornstarch mixture. Mix well to coat the pieces of meat uniformly. Reserve.*
Jalapeño peppers	1 green	1 green	*Slice peppers into quarters or eighths. Remove seeds and ribs for a milder taste. Reserve.*
	1 red	1 red	
Oil, vegetable	1 tbsp	15 ml	*Heat a wok or skillet over high heat then add the oil. Stir-fry the onions and garlic until the garlic just begins to brown. Add the flank steak, red and green jalapeño peppers, and mushroom slices. Stir to mix these ingredients, then add the oyster sauce. Continue to stir-fry for 1–2 minutes or until the beef is cooked through, but not overcooked. Add the basil leaves and stir-fry until they wilt slightly. Serve over a bed of boiled or steamed white rice.*
Onion, cut in 2 pieces	1/2 small	1/2 small	
Garlic, chopped	1 small clove	1 small clove	
Mushrooms, white button, sliced	2–3 medium	2–3 medium	
Oyster sauce	1 tbsp	15 ml	
Basil leaves, whole, fresh	5–6	5–6	

Shredded Brisket with Quail Eggs and Chilies

YIELD: 10 SERVINGS

Quail eggs	15	15	*Cook eggs in gently simmering water for 7–8 minutes. Turn eggs frequently to center yolks. When done, place in cold water until cool. Remove shells, slice each egg in half, and reserve covered in the refrigerator.*
Beef, brisket, trimmed	3 1/2 lb	1.6 kg	*Cut beef into 2-in. (5-cm) square pieces. Place in a stew pot with enough water or stock to cover. Bring to a boil, skim, then lower heat and simmer for 1 1/2 hours or until the beef is very tender and can be shredded easily. Remove meat and let cool.*
Water or beef stock	to cover	to cover	
Soy sauce, dark	12 oz	350 g	*Add the soy sauce, sugar, and garlic cloves to the stew pot and simmer for 5 minutes. Add the chili peppers and simmer for another 5 minutes. Remove from heat. When the meat is cool enough to handle, shred it into strands by pulling it apart along the grain. Return the meat to the pot. When liquids have cooled, refrigerate covered until needed.*
Sugar	3 oz	80 g	
Garlic cloves, peeled	30 medium	30 medium	
Chili peppers, fresh (New Mexican, or Anaheim, for a milder taste), sliced into quarters	6–7 red 6–7 green, depending on size	6–7 red 6–7 green, depending on size	

TO SERVE

Reserved meat and chilies	approx. 5–6 oz per serving	approx. 140–170 g per serving	*Remove any fat that has congealed on the top. Reheat portions, as needed, including a proportionate amount of the cooking liquid. Serve the meat in a warm, deep bowl along with some of each of the peppers, 3 garlic cloves, and 3 halves of quail egg per serving. Accompany with boiled white rice.*
Reserved quail eggs			

Lamb with Leeks

YIELD: 1 SERVING

MARINADE

Chicken stock	2 tbsp	30 ml
Soy sauce, dark	2 tbsp	30 ml
Sugar, brown	1/2 tsp	3 g
Five-flavor powder	pinch	pinch

Combine ingredients in a small mixing bowl.

Lamb, shoulder or leg	6 oz	170 g

Slice lamb across the grain into thin strips approximately 1 x 3 in(2.5 x 8 cm). Place strips in marinade and mix well. Let stand for 10–15 minutes.

Leek	1 small	1 small

Cut off green parts and reserve for other purposes. Split the white section down the middle and wash thoroughly. Cut into 2-in. (5-cm) segments then julienne fine.

Oil, peanut	2 tsp	10 ml
Garlic, sliced thin	1 medium clove	1 medium clove
Salt	pinch	pinch
Marinated lamb		
Julienned leeks		

Heat wok or skillet over high heat. Add the oil. When the oil is just below the smoking point add the garlic and salt and stir-fry for 10–15 seconds. Add the lamb, the marinade, and the julienned leek. Stir-fry over high heat for 2–3 minutes, then serve.

Lamb Grilled with Mint and Cumin

YIELD: 10 SERVINGS

MARINADE

Oil, vegetable	4 oz	115 g
Lemon juice	4 oz	115 g
Mint leaves, fresh, chopped fine	8–9 sprigs	8–9 sprigs
Garlic. minced	1 1/2 tbsp	25 g
Gingerroot, peeled and minced	1 tbsp	12 g
Cumin, ground	1 tbsp	7g
Paprika, ground	1 tbsp	7 g
Salt	1 tsp	5 g
Pepper, cayenne	1/2 tsp or to taste	1 g or to taste
Clove, ground	1/2 tsp	1 g

Combine ingredients and reserve.

Lamb leg, boned and butterflied	4 lb (weight after boning and trimming)	1.8 kg (weight after boning and trimming)

Remove the bone and all fat. Rub the marinade over all surfaces of the meat. Place in a stainless steel pan, cover, and refrigerate for 8 hours. Turn the meat occasionally.

Marinated leg of lamb

Before grilling, bring the lamb to room temperature. Wipe the meat with a clean kitchen towel to remove any of the solids contained in the marinade. Grill the meat over coals or under the broiler flame until internal temperature in thickest part of the meat reaches 140°F (60°C). Grill longer if well-done meat is desired. Remove meat from grill, cover with foil, and let rest for 20–30 minutes before carving.

Spiced Lamb Patties Grilled on Skewers

YIELD: 10 SERVINGS

Lamb, ground twice	3 lb	1.4 kg
Yogurt	8 oz	225 g
Flour, chickpea	4 tbsp	40 g
Garlic, minced	1 tbsp	15 g
Poppy seeds, white, ground	2 tbsp	12 g
Gingerroot, peeled and minced	1 tbsp	12 g
Coriander, ground	1 tbsp	7 g
Cumin	1 tsp	2 g
Cardamom, ground	1 tsp	2 g
Yogurt	8 oz	225 g
Salt	to taste	to taste

TO PREPARE AN INDIVIDUAL SERVING

Skewered lamb patties	4–5 oz per serving	115–140 g per serving
Clarified butter	as needed	as needed

Mix ingredients together by hand or with an electric mixer. Sauté a spoonful of the mixture in a small amount of clarified butter or vegetable oil.* Adjust seasonings if necessary. Shape the meat into sausage-shaped patties and thread onto oiled, stainless steel skewers. Cover and refrigerate until needed.

To give the meat patties a uniform thickness, roll the skewered meat on a flat surface that has been brushed with clarified butter. Grill over coals or under a broiler flame until crisp on the outside but still moist on the inside. Garnish with fresh, thin slices of onion and wedges of lemon or lime.

*Meat preparation can also be piped from a pastry tube directly onto a hot, oiled grill in 3–4 in. (8–10 cm) lengths.

Marinated, Grilled Sirloin

YIELD: 10 SERVINGS

MARINADE		
Scallions, white and green parts, sliced thin	10	10
Oil, sesame	6 oz	180 ml
Garlic, minced	3 tbsp	45 g
Sugar	3 oz	85 g
Sesame seeds	2 oz	60 g
Salt	1 tsp or to taste	5 g or to taste
Pepper, black, fine ground	1 tsp or to taste	2 g or to taste
Steak, sirloin	10, 8 oz each	10, 220 g each

Combine ingredients and reserve.

Place steaks in a single layer in a stainless steel tray. Distribute the flavoring mixture evenly over both sides of the steaks. Marinate for at least 2 hours before using. Grill over coals or broil under flame until done as desired.

Meatballs in Mushroom Sauce

YIELD: 10-12 SERVINGS

Beef, chuck, ground twice	4 lb	1.8 kg	*Combine ingredients thoroughly then shape into 2–3 oz (60–80 g) meatballs. (Cut meatball size in half if used as an appetizer or for a cocktail buffet.)*
Garlic, minced	2 tbsp	30 g	
Sesame seeds, toasted	1 tbsp	6 g	
Oil, sesame	1 tbsp	15 ml	
Salt	2 tsp.	10 g	
Oil, vegetable	as needed	as needed	*Heat oil to a depth of 1/2 in. (1.5 cm) in a heavy skillet. Roll the meatballs in flour to lightly coat. Shake off any excess flour. Fry the meatballs, turning frequently, until they are cooked through and well browned on all sides. Reserve.*
Flour	as needed	as needed	
Meatballs			

SAUCE

Oil, sesame	2 oz	60 ml	*Heat oil in a saucepan over high heat. Add ingredients and sauté until they begin to brown lightly.*
Onion, small sized, cut into quarters; each quarter separated into individual segments	3/4 lb	340 g	
Scallion, white and green parts cut on the diagonal into 1-in. (2.5-cm) pieces	6	6	
Garlic, sliced	4–5 cloves	4–5 cloves	

(Continued on next page)

Mushrooms, white common, caps and stems, sliced thin	*1 lb*	*450 g*
Carrot, round, thin slices	*1/2 lb*	*220 g*
Beef stock	*1 qt*	*1 L*
Soy sauce, dark	*2 oz*	*60 ml*
Pepper, black, fine ground	*1/2 tsp or to taste*	*1 g or to taste*

Add the mushrooms and carrots and sauté for another 20–30 seconds. Add the beef stock and soy sauce and bring to a boil. Lower heat, add pepper, and simmer, uncovered, for 20 minutes. Adjust seasoning if necessary.

Cornstarch	*2 tbsp*	*20 g*
Beef stock, cold	*as needed*	*as needed*

Mix the cornstarch and as much cold beef stock as needed to make a smooth, thin paste. Slowly stir this mixture into the simmering sauce and cook until it begins to thicken. Let cool and reserve until needed. To serve, reheat meatballs in the sauce over medium heat. Bring temperature to just below the boiling point and simmer until heated through.

Pork Curry

YIELD: 10-12 SERVINGS

MARINADE			
Onion, small dice	1 lb	450 g	
Garlic, minced	4 tbsp	60 g	
Gingerroot, minced	2 tbsp	25 g	
Vinegar, white, distilled	6 oz	180 ml	
Sesame oil	2 tbsp	1 oz	

Combine ingredients and mix well. Reserve.

Pork, leg, cut into 1 1/2-in. (4-cm) cubes	3 1/2 lb	1.6 kg	

Trim all fat and skin from meat. Place meat in a glass or stainless steel container and add the marinade. Toss well to coat uniformly. Cover and reserve in the refrigerator for 4–6 hours.

Oil, peanut	2 tbsp	30 ml	
Water or chicken stock	as needed	as needed	

When meat has marinated sufficiently, remove from marinade and sauté in peanut oil until lightly browned. (Reserve pan.) Transfer the meat to a stew pot, along with any remaining marinade and enough water or chicken stock to cover. Bring to a boil, then lower heat and simmer, partially covered, for 1 1/2 hours or until the meat is very tender. Add additional water or stock, if needed.

Shallots, diced	2 oz	60 g	
Red chilies, fresh, chopped fine	2 tbsp or to taste	12 g or to taste	
Turmeric, ground	2 tsp or to taste	4 g or to taste	
Shrimp paste	2 tsp or to taste	20 g or to taste	
Salt	to taste	to taste	

When the pork has cooked sufficiently, sauté these ingredients over moderate heat for 2–3 minutes using the same pan in which the pork was browned. Add a ladle of the pork cooking liquid to the sauté pan and deglaze the pan. Transfer the entire contents of the sauté pan to the simmering pork and cook for another 5 minutes. Adjust seasonings if necessary.

Grilled Pork Ribs

YIELD: 10 SERVINGS

Pork, spare ribs	8 lb	3.5 kg	*Saw the ribs through the bone into 2–3 in. (5–7.5-cm) lengths. Separate into small sections by cutting through the meaty parts. Score the meat, almost to the bone, every 1/2 in.(1.25 cm).*
Ginger juice (see recipe)	6 oz	180 ml	*Combine ingredients and mix until the sugar is completely dissolved. Rub this mixture over all surfaces of the ribs and refrigerate for 1 hour.*
Sugar	3 oz	85 g	

SEASONING MIXTURE

Soy sauce, dark	6 oz	180 ml	*Combine ingredients thoroughly then rub over all surfaces of the ribs. Cover and refrigerate for 2 hours. To serve, place sections of rib on skewers, approximately 12 oz (340 g) per portion, and grill over hot coals or under a broiler flame. Garnish with lemon slices, grilled scallions, and whole garlic cloves which have been roasted or grilled separately.*
Sugar	2 oz	60 g	
Sesame oil	2 oz	60 g	
Scallions, white and green parts chopped fine	6	6	
Garlic, minced	4 tbsp	60 g	
Pepper, black	1 tbsp or to taste	8 g or to taste	

Short Ribs in a Sweet Sauce

YIELD: 10–12 SERVINGS

Beef, short ribs	8 lb	3.5 kg	Cut ribs into 3-in. (7.5-cm) lengths. Trim excess fat. Score an "X" in the meat portion, cutting almost to the bone. Place the ribs in a stainless steel pan large enough to hold them in a single layer.
Soy sauce	8 oz	240 ml	Combine ingredients in a mixing bowl and stir until the sugar is completely dissolved. Pour over the ribs, then turn the ribs in the marinade to coat evenly. Marinate for at least 2 hours before cooking.
Sesame oil	2 oz	60 ml	
Scallions, white and green parts, sliced thin	6	6	
Sugar	4 oz	115 g	
Sesame seeds, toasted	2 oz	60 g	
Pepper, black, fine ground	1 tsp	2 g	

TO PREPARE

Short ribs	10–12 oz per serving	280–340 g per serving	Grill over coals or broil under flame until done as desired. Baste with the marinade, once or twice on each side, while cooking.

Savory Grilled Beef Salad

YIELD: 10 SERVINGS

Flank steak	2 1/2 lb	1.15 kg	*Trim all fat and tough membrane from meat. Grill over coals or broil 2–3 in. (5–7.5-cm) from flame, medium rare, or as preferred. Reserve.*
DRESSING			
Cooked rice	6 tbsp	6 tbsp	*Place ingredients in a food blender or processor fitted with the steel blade and puree. Pour into a mixing bowl.*
Lime juice, fresh	10 oz	300 ml	
Fish sauce	4 oz	120 ml	
Sugar	1 tsp or to taste	5 g or to taste	
Chili powder	1 tsp or to taste	2 g or to taste	
Shallot, sliced thin	3 oz	90 g	*Add ingredients to the dressing and mix well. Adjust seasonings if necessary.*
Mint leaves, fresh, chopped	10 sprigs	10 sprigs	
Cilantro leaves, fresh, chopped	10 sprigs	10 sprigs	
Lemon grass, tender white parts sliced thin	4 tbsp	25 g	
TO SERVE			
Grilled beef, sliced thin	3–4 oz per serving	90–115 g per serving	*Place beef slices in a mixing bowl with just enough dressing to coat. Toss well. Place a bed of shredded lettuce on a chilled plate. Top this with slices of meat placed in an attractive pattern. Sprinkle with chopped scallion. Garnish with wedges of tomato and cucumber slices or other seasonal garden vegetables.*
Dressing	as needed	as needed	
Scallion, white and tender green parts, chopped	1 per serving	1 per serving	
Lettuce, shredded	as needed	as needed	

Steak with Daikon,
Scallion, and Lemon

YIELD: 1 SERVING

CONDIMENT

Daikon radish, grated	3 oz	85 g
Soy sauce, dark	2 tsp	10 ml
Scallion, green part, sliced thin	1	1

Combine ingredients and reserve at room temperature.

Oil, vegetable	as needed	as needed
Steak, boneless sirloin, trimmed	6–8 oz	170–220 g
Reserved condiment		
Lemon wedges	as needed	as needed

Brush steak lightly with oil. Grill over coals or under broiler flame until done as desired. Rare is recommended. When done, slice the steak into 1-in. (2.5-cm) strips cutting on an angle. Reassemble the steak to its original shape and place on a warm plate. Distribute the daikon and scallion mixture evenly over the top of the steak. Garnish with lemon wedges served on the plate.

See color insert for photograph of recipe

Flavorings and Condiments

Barbecue Sauce

YIELD: APPROXIMATELY 1 PINT (475 ML)

Soy sauce, light	10 oz	300 ml
Rice wine	4 oz	120 ml
Scallions, minced	2 oz	60 g
Garlic, minced	2 tbsp	30 g
Sesame seeds, toasted and ground	2 tbsp	4 g
Chili sauce	to taste	to taste

Combine ingredients and let rest 6–8 hours or overnight before using.

Used with grilled meats and as a table condiment.

279

FLAVORINGS AND CONDIMENTS

Nuoc Cham

YIELD: APPROXIMATELY 1 PINT (475 ML)

No. 1

Fish sauce	8 oz	240 ml	*Place these ingredients, with the exception of the water, into the bowl of a food processor fitted with a steel blade and puree. Add the water in small amounts to taste, and mix well.*
Garlic	4 medium cloves	4 medium cloves	
Dried small red, hot, chili peppers	6 or to taste	6 or to taste	
Sugar	4 tbsp	60 g	
Lime juice	2 tbsp	30 ml	
Water	6 oz or to taste	180 ml or to taste	

No. 2

Fish sauce (nuoc mam)	4 oz	120 ml	*Combine ingredients.*
Lime juice, fresh squeezed	2 oz	60 ml	
Vinegar, white distilled	1 oz	30 ml	
Garlic, puree	1/2 oz	15 g	
Chili flakes, dried	2 tsp or to taste	4 g or to taste	
Water	8 oz	240 ml	*Dissolve the sugar in the water. Add to the other ingredients and mix well. When serving as a dipping sauce, add a small amount of finely shredded carrot for color.*
Sugar	4 oz	115 g	

This popular Vietnamese condiment is used as a dipping sauce for fried foods, rice, noodles, and other vegetable dishes.

Chojang—A Vinegar Dipping Sauce

YIELD: 1 PINT (475 ML)

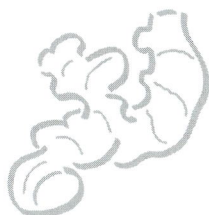

Soy sauce, dark	14 oz	415 ml
Vinegar, rice or cider	2 oz	60 ml
Sesame seeds, toasted	2 tsp	12 g
Gingerroot, peeled and minced	1 1/2-in. piece	4-cm piece
Red pepper flakes	2 tsp or to taste	6 g or to taste
Sugar	2 tsp	10 g

Combine ingredients and mix well. Store in refrigerator in a tightly closed container.

Used as a dipping sauce for vegetables, fish, and meats. Also used as a flavoring agent. Other ingredients such as chili peppers, scallions, garlic, and/or cilantro, may be chopped fine and added to taste.

Coconut Milk: Thick and Thin*

(used in many southeast Asian countries)

YIELD: APPROXIMATELY 22-24 OZ (650-700 ML)

THICK

Coconut,** dried grated, unsweetened	5 oz	140 g
Water, or, a 50/50 mixture of water and milk, or, for a richer product, whole milk	1 qt	950 ml

Place the liquid in small saucepan and bring to a boil. If using milk be sure to scald first. Add the coconut, cover the pan, and remove from heat. Let stand until cool. Strain through a fine sieve. Press to extract as much of the liquid as possible. Reserve the remaining coconut to make "thin" coconut milk.

THIN

Coconut used to make "thick" coconut milk	1 qt	1 L
Water, or, a 50/50 mixture of water and milk, or, for a richer product, whole milk		

Yield: approximately the same as above

Repeat the same process as above. Reserve the liquid and discard the depleted coconut.

*Unsweetened coconut milk is readily available in both thick and thin consistencies from commercial sources, either canned or frozen.

**Fresh coconut meat can be used if obtained from ripe coconuts.

Note: Do not confuse the liquid contained within the coconut with coconut milk. Coconut milk is obtained through the above process.

Skewered Beef and Scallions, page 236

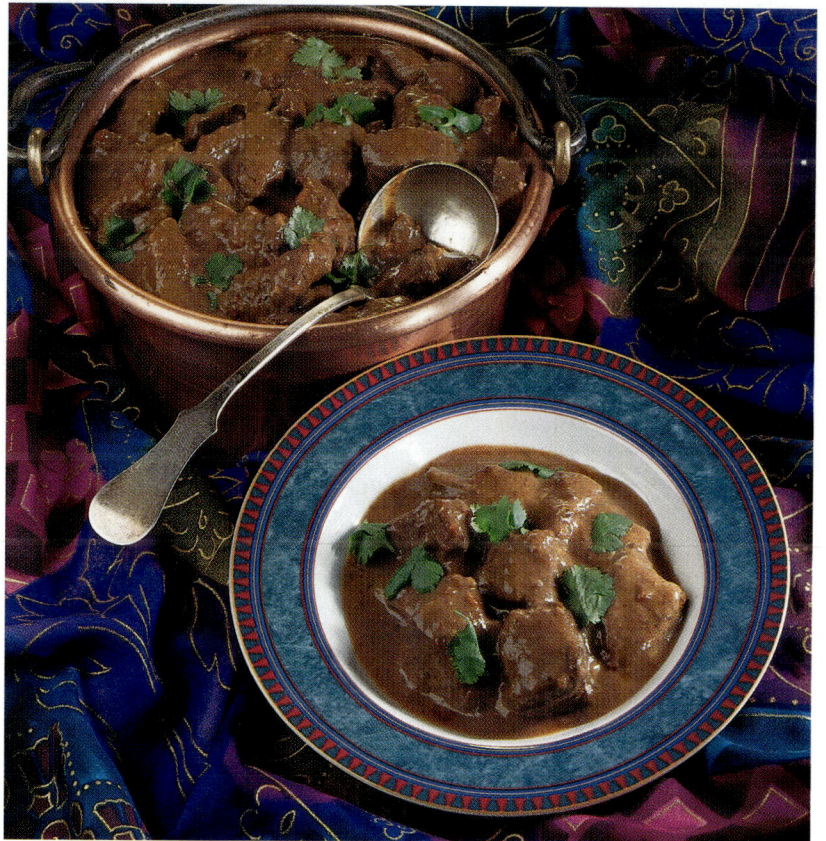

Braised Beef in Tomato Yogurt Sauce, page 244

Lamb Scallops with Scallions, page 248

Steak with Daikon, Scallion, and Lemon, page 275

Pineapple and Currant Chutney, page 291

Red and Green Chilies in Vinegar, page 294

Fried Rice with Pork, Corn, and Red Beans, page 320

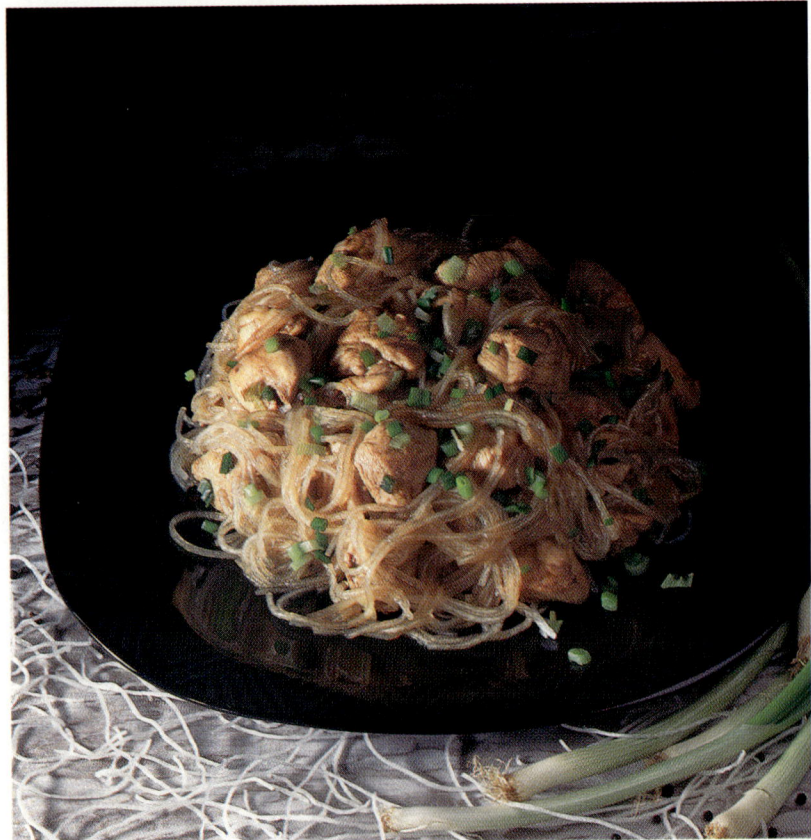

Chicken with Cellophane Noodles, page 341

Steamed Stuffed Mushrooms with Udon Noodles in Broth, pages 27 and 357

Shanghai Noodles with Bean Sprouts, page 358

Spring Snow with Mixed Fruits, page 362

Mango with Rabadi, page 370

Garlic-Flavored Coconut Milk

YIELD: 1 PINT (475 ML)

Oil, vegetable	1 tbsp	15 ml
Garlic, minced	2 tsp	10 g
Coconut milk, thick	1 pt	470 ml

Heat oil in a small saucepan over medium heat. Add garlic and sauté until it begins to color lightly. Add the coconut milk and heat to just below the simmering point. Remove from heat and cool. Strain and discard any solids. Reserve under refrigeration. Especially useful as a sauce with shrimp and other seafoods.

GARAM MASALA (MASALA=SPICE BLENDS)

The blend of a variety of dry-roasted, ground spices used in the cuisine from colder, northern sections of India. Four traditional spices, cardamom, cinnamon, cloves, and black pepper, are commonly found in its preparation. Spices such as coriander, cumin, dried chilies, a variety of peppers, mace, as well as other flavoring agents, are also used according to individual taste. In most preparations, the spices are toasted prior to grinding. Toasting serves to intensify the flavors. Garam masalas are usually added near the end of the cooking period.

There are two methods for toasting:

1. Place a thin layer of the spices in a dry, heavy skillet. Place skillet on the stovetop over low heat for about 15 minutes, stirring occasionally.

2. Place a thin layer of the spices on a baking sheet and toast in a 200°F (90°C) oven for 30 minutes, stirring occasionally (crush the cinnamon sticks and bay leaves before toasting).

When the spices have darkened in color and give off a noticeable aroma, grind them in a clean coffee mill or spice grinder, then pass them through a fine-meshed sieve to eliminate any of the larger pieces. It is best to prepare garam masala in small batches. It can be stored in an airtight container for up to 3 months.

The following proportions are only approximations and may be adjusted to suit individual taste.

No. 1

Black peppercorns	1 oz	30 g
Green cardamom pods	1 oz	30 g
Black cardamom pods	1 oz	30 g
Cumin seeds	1 oz	30 g
Black cumin seeds	1 oz	30 g
Cloves, whole	1 oz	30 g
Cinnamon sticks, 3 in. (8 cm) in length	2	2
Bay leaves	10	10

Toast, then grind to a powder.

No. 2
MUGHUL GARAM MASALA

Black cardamom pods	4 oz	115 g
Cloves, whole	1/2 oz	15 g
Peppercorns, black	1/2 oz	15 g
Nutmeg, grated	1 tbsp	7 g
Cinnamon stick, crushed, 3 in. (8 cm) in length	3	3

Break open pods, discard the skins, and combine the seeds with the remaining ingredients. Toast, then grind to a fine powder.

No. 3

Coriander seed	12 oz	340 g
Cumin seeds	6 oz	170 g
Pomegranate seeds	1 oz	30 g
Cloves, whole	1 oz	30 g
Black peppercorns	1 oz	30 g
Green peppercorns	1 oz	30 g
White peppercorns	1 oz	30 g
Fennel seed	1 tbsp	5 g
Bay leaf, crushed	4	4
Chili pods dried	6	6
Saffron threads	pinch	pinch

Toast spices.

Nutmeg, ground	1/2 oz	15 g
Mace, dried	10 blades	10 blades

Add the nutmeg and mace, then grind all of the ingredients into a fine powder.

Fish Sauce (Nuoc Mam)
Flavored with Lime Juice

YIELD: 1 PINT (475 ML)

Fish sauce	6 oz	180 ml
Lime juice, fresh squeezed	6 oz	180 ml
Water	4 oz	120 ml
Garlic, minced	1 tbsp	10 g
Sugar	6 oz or to taste	170 g or to taste
Chilies, fresh, red or green, seeded, ribs removed, sliced very thin	2–3 or to taste	2-3 or to taste

Combine ingredients and reserve in the refrigerator for several hours before using.

This is used as a dipping sauce or as a seasoning in cooked dishes. It is an essential flavoring agent in the Vietnamese kitchen. If unavailable, fish sauce from Thailand can be substituted.

Fish Sauce with Chili (Prik Nam Plaa)

YIELD: 1 PINT (475 ML)

Fish sauce	12 oz	350 ml
Lime juice, fresh squeezed	4 oz	120 ml
Small green chilies,* fresh, sliced into very thin rings	20	20
Shallot, sliced thin	1 oz	30 g
Sugar	2 tsp	10 g

Combine ingredients. Sprinkled on foods in very small amounts, this condiment adds a flavor that is both salty and hot.

Used to brighten the taste of rice and a wide variety of other foods.

VARIATION: FISH SAUCE WITH SLICED CHILIES AND LEMON

Fish sauce	16 oz	470 ml
Lemon juice, fresh squeezed	2 tbsp	30 ml
Small, hot chilies, thinly sliced	2 tbsp	12 g

Combine ingredients. Variation: omit the lemon juice and add thinly sliced garlic cloves or shallots.

*If available, use the very small, fiery, bird's eye chilies, a favorite in Thai cuisine. If not, use other hot chili, chopped fine.

Flavored Soy Sauces

YIELD: 1 PINT (475 ML)

SHERRY OR RICE WINE FLAVORED

Soy sauce	8 oz	240	*Mix until the sugar is dissolved.*
Beef stock	4 oz	120	
Sherry, dry or rice wine	4 oz	120	
Sugar	1 tsp	5 g	*Mix until the sugar is dissolved.*

VINEGAR FLAVORED

Soy Sauce	10 oz	300 ml	*Combine ingredients and mix until the sugar is dissolved.*
Vinegar, white distilled or rice wine vinegar	6 oz	180 ml	
Sugar	1 tsp	5 g	

CHILI FLAVORED

Chili sauce	8 oz	225 g	*To create interesting variations in taste, these flavored soy sauces may be substituted for soy sauce when preparing savory meat and vegetable dishes.*
Soy sauce, light	8 oz	240 ml	
Gingerroot, minced	2 tbsp	25 g	
Garlic, minced	1 tbsp	15 g	
Sugar	1 tbsp	15 g	

Hot Chili Oil

YIELD: 8 OUNCES (240 ML)

Peanut oil	8 oz	240 ml
Dried red chilies	4–5 or to taste	4–5 or to taste

Place oil in a small, heavy-bottomed saucepan. Heat oil to just below the smoking point, then remove from heat. Open chilies and remove seeds and ribs. If a hotter flavor is desired, do not remove the seeds and ribs. Break into small pieces and add to the oil. Let rest until cool. Strain, pour into a glass jar, and seal tightly.

A hot, clear oil used in small amounts to flavor soups and sauces. Available from commercial sources in bottles.

Marinated Carrot and Sweet Radish

YIELD: APPROXIMATELY 2 POUNDS (900 G)

Carrot, thin sliced	1 lb	460 g
White radish, thin sliced	1 lb	460 g
Water	16 oz	480 ml
Vinegar, white, distilled	2 oz	60 ml
Sugar	2 oz	60 g
Salt	1 oz	30 g

Mix carrot and white radish in equal proportions in a glass or stainless steel container. In a small bowl, combine the remaining ingredients and mix until the sugar is completely dissolved. Pour this over the vegetables. Cover and allow to marinate for at least 2 hours before serving. To serve, remove vegetables from the marinade with a slotted spoon, let drain briefly, then serve in a side dish.

Pepper-Salt Seasoning

Peppercorns, Chinese, brown	4 oz	115 g
Salt	8 oz	230 g

Place peppercorns in a dry wok or skillet over moderate heat and toast, stirring, for 2–3 minutes or until the peppercorns become aromatic. Place the toasted peppercorns in a spice mill or mortar and grind fine. Return them to the pan and add the salt. Stir-fry for another 1–2 minutes or until the ingredients are thoroughly mixed and aromatic. Let cool, then place in a tightly sealed jar.

Used as a flavoring in a variety of cooked dishes.

Pineapple and Currant Chutney

YIELD: APPROXIMATELY 3 POUNDS (1.4 KG)

Pineapple, fresh	3 lb clean meat	1.4 kg clean meat	Cut pineapple into 1/4-in. (0.75-cm) slices, then cut each slice into 1-in. (2.5-cm) pieces. Reserve with the juice.
Clarified butter	2 oz	60 ml	Heat clarified butter in a heavy-bottomed saucepan over medium heat. When butter is hot, but below the smoking point, add the chilies, coriander, and cumin. Fry, stirring, until the chilies begin to darken in color. Remove pan from heat.
Chilies, whole red, dried	2–3	2–3	
Coriander seeds	1 tbsp	6 g	
Cumin seeds	1 tbsp	6 g	
Reserved pineapple and juice			Add pineapple and its juices, clove, cardamom, and cinnamon to the pan. Stir to combine ingredients, then return pan to heat. Bring mixture to a slow boil over moderate heat. Lower heat and simmer, stirring to prevent sticking, until the fruit is soft and most of the juice has evaporated. Remove the chilies and the cinnamon stick and discard.
Clove, powdered	1 tsp	2 g	
Cardamom seeds, pods removed; crushed	1 tsp	2 g	
Cinnamon stick	2-in. piece	5-cm piece	
Sugar, dark brown	12 oz	340 g	Add the sugar and currents and mix well. Continue to simmer, stirring, until the mixture is very thick and the fruit is glazed. Adjust seasonings to taste if necessary. Let cool, then refrigerate until needed.
Currants	4 oz	115 g	

See color insert for photograph of recipe

Ponzu Sauce

Lemon juice, fresh squeezed	8 oz	240 ml
Soy sauce, dark	6 oz	175 ml
Vinegar, rice	2 oz	60 ml
Mirin, brought to a boil to burn off the alcohol	2 oz	60 ml
Kelp (Kombu)	1, 2-in. sq. piece	1, 5-cm sq. piece
Dried bonito flakes	1/2 oz	10 g

Combine ingredients and let stand in a cool place for one full day. Strain through a double layer of cheesecloth. Discard solids. Place in a sealed container and refrigerate.

Used as a dipping sauce with sushi or other vinegared dishes.

Red Curry Paste

YIELD: APPROXIMATELY 1 POUND 12 OUNCES (800 G)

Chilies, dried	*4 oz*	*115 g*
Shrimp, dried, ground	*4 oz*	*115 g*
Garlic, stir-fried, until lightly browned	*4 oz*	*115 g*
Shallots, stir-fried until lightly browned	*2 oz*	*60 g*
Oil, vegetable	*4 oz*	*120 ml*
Sugar, palm*	*4 oz*	*115g*
Fish sauce	*3 oz*	*90 ml*
Tamarind juice, medium concentrated	*2 oz*	*60 ml*

Using a mortar and pestle, pound ingredients until they form a uniform mass. An electric blender may also be used; the texture will be somewhat different, but acceptable.

Heat the oil in a wok over medium heat. Add this mixture and stir-fry for several minutes.

Add ingredients and continue to stir-fry until the curry paste has a uniform red color. Adjust seasonings to achieve a good sour, sweet and salty balance.

An essential ingredient for making Thai curry dishes. Curry pastes are readily available, made in Thailand, from commercial sources.

*If unavailable, substitute brown sugar.

Red and Green Chilies in Vinegar

YIELD: VARIABLE

Red chilies, fresh, hot	*3 parts*	*3 parts*	*Wash chilies, remove stems, and slice into very thin rings. Add vinegar as needed.*
Green chilies, fresh, hot	*2 parts*	*2 parts*	
Vinegar, white, distilled	*to cover by 1/2 in.*	*to cover by 1.5 cm*	*Used as a table condiment for a wide variety of dishes.*

See color insert for photograph of recipe

Sesame Salt

YIELD: 8 OUNCES (230 G)

Sesame seeds, toasted	*8 oz*	*220 g*	*Place toasted sesame seeds in a blender or spice mill and grind fine. Add the salt and blend.*
Salt	*2 tsp*	*10 g*	

Spicy Red Bell Pepper Sauce

YIELD: APPROXIMATELY 2 1/4 POUNDS (1 KG)

Butter, whole, and	1 oz	30 g	*Place ingredients in a heavy-bottomed saucepan*
Oil, vegetable, 50/50 mixture	1 oz	30 g	*and cook, covered, over low heat until very soft.*
Red bell pepper, chopped	2 lb	900 g	
Chili pepper, jalapeño or other green, fresh, hot pepper	6 oz	170 g	
Salt	to taste	to taste	*Puree in a food processor. Add salt and pepper to*
Pepper, white	to taste	to taste	*taste.*

Teriyaki Sauce

YIELD: 24 OUNCES (720 ML)

Soy sauce, dark	8 oz	240 ml	*Combine ingredients in a small, heavy-bottomed*
Mirin	8 oz	240 ml	*saucepan over medium heat. Bring to a boil.*
Sake	8 oz	240 ml	*Remove from heat, let cool. Store in a sealed con-*
Sugar	2 oz	60 g	*tainer under refrigeration, until needed.*

Used as a glaze and sauce for pan fried and broiled meats, poultry, and fish.

Yank Nyum Jang— A Dipping Sauce

YIELD: 1 PINT (475 ML)

Soy sauce	9 oz	270 ml	*Combine ingredients and mix well. Reserve.*
Vinegar, white distilled	5 oz	145 ml	
Sesame oil	2 oz	60 ml	
Garlic, pureed	1 tbsp	15 g	
Sesame seeds, toasted	1 tbsp	6 g	
Sugar	1 tbsp	15 g	
Cayenne pepper	to taste	to taste	

TO SERVE

Reserved sauce	as needed	as needed	*Pour 1–2 oz (30–60 ml) per serving into a small dish and garnish with a sprinkling of thinly sliced scallion.*
Scallions, sliced thin, green and white parts	as needed	as needed	

Chinese Beef Marinade

YIELD: APPROXIMATELY 1 1/2 PINTS (700ML)

Oil, vegetable	6 oz	180 ml
Water	6 oz	180 ml
Soy sauce, light	5 oz	150 ml
Rice wine or dry sherry	3 oz	90 ml
Soy sauce, dark	2 oz	60 ml
Sesame oil	2 oz	60 ml
Cornstarch	4 tbsp	40 ml
Sugar	3 tbsp	45 g
Gingerroot, minced	2 tbsp	25 g
Garlic, minced	1 tbsp	15 g
Salt	1 tbsp	15 g
Egg whites, beaten	4	4

Combine ingredients, mix well, and store, covered in the refrigerator, in a glass or stainless steel container. This marinade is used for beef cut into thin slices, strips or shreds. This amount should be sufficient to marinate up to 8 lb (3.5 kg) of beef cut in this manner.

Curry Paste

YIELD: APPROXIMATELY 12 OUNCES (340 G)

Pepper, black, coarsely ground	2 tsp	4 g
Caraway seeds, ground	2 tsp	4 g
Coriander seeds, ground	2 tsp	4 g
Cayenne pepper	1 tsp or to taste	2 g or to taste
Onion, large dice	8 oz	230 g
Lemon zest	1 lemon	1 lemon
Lime zest	1 lime	1 lime
Garlic minced	2 tbsp	30 g
Oil, vegetable	2 oz	60 ml
Anchovy paste	1 tbsp	20 g
Coriander leaves, fresh, chopped fine	10 sprigs	10 sprigs
Salt	to taste	to taste

Thoroughly blend ingredients.

Place ingredients in the bowl of a food processor fitted with the steel blade. Puree until very smooth. Add the spices and mix until thoroughly blended.

Add ingredients and mix by hand.

Ginger Juice

(used in many Asian and southeast Asian countries)

YIELD: APPROXIMATELY 1 PINT (475 ML)

Rice wine or dry sherry	12 oz	340 ml
Gingerroot, peeled and grated	6 oz	170 g

Combine ingredients and heat to just below the boiling point. Let cool, then store, refrigerated, in a glass or stainless steel container overnight. Strain the liquid through a double layer of cheesecloth, then squeeze the grated gingerroot to extract all liquid. Store, refrigerated, in a tightly covered glass or stainless steel container.

OTHER METHODS FOR MAKING GINGER JUICE

1. Peel and finely grate very fresh gingerroot. Place in a double layer square of cheesecloth. Gather the corners together and twist to express the juice.

2. Mix rice wine and finely grated gingerroot in the same proportions as above and refrigerate. Strain before using.

Marinade for Grilled Meats

YIELD: APPROXIMATELY 1 1/2 PINTS (700 ML)

Mirin or sweet sherry	10 oz	300 ml	*Combine ingredients and stir until the sugar is completely dissolved.*
Soy sauce, dark	6 oz	180 ml	
Sesame oil	3 oz	90 ml	
Vinegar, white dis-tilled	3 oz	90 ml	
Sugar	2 tbsp	30 g	
Miso	2 oz	60 g	

Peanut Curry Sauce

YIELD: 1 1/2 QUARTS (1.5 L)

Coconut milk	1 qt	1L	*Combine ingredients and blend thoroughly.*
Peanut butter	8 oz	230	
Red curry paste	4 oz	115 g	
Sugar	4 oz	115 g	
Tamarind juice	4 oz	120 ml	
Salt	to taste	to taste	

Peanut Sauce

YIELD: APPROXIMATELY 3 POUNDS (1.4 KG)

Ingredient	US	Metric	Method
Roasted peanuts, unsalted	1 lb	450 g	*Place peanuts into the bowl of a food processor fitted with the steel blade. Chop the peanuts as fine as possible. Reserve.*
Oil, vegetable	2 oz	60 ml	*Heat oil in a wok or heavy skillet over medium heat. Add the shallots and garlic. Stir-fry for 30–40 seconds or until they begin to color lightly.*
Shallots, minced	5–6	5–6	
Garlic, minced	1 tbsp	15 g	
Water	1 qt	1 L	*Add ingredients and bring to a boil, stirring. Lower heat and simmer for 20 minutes or until the sauce has thickened to a batter-like consistency. Stir frequently. Remove from heat and cool.*
Sugar	1 1/2 tbsp or to taste	20 g or to taste	
Pepper, cayenne	1 tsp or to taste	2 g or to taste	
Salt	1 tsp or to taste	5 g or to taste	
Reserved peanuts			
Pepper, black, fine ground	to taste	to taste	*Using a wire whisk, add ingredients to taste.*
Lime juice, fresh squeezed	to taste	to taste	

Scallion Oil

YIELD: 1 PINT (475 ML)

Peanut oil	16 oz	470 ml
Scallions, white sections, split in half lengthwise	20	20

Heat oil in a wok or heavy skillet over low to medium heat. Fry scallions until they are golden, then remove them from the oil and reserve for stock. When oil has cooled but still warm, strain through a fine sieve and pour into a jar. Cover and store in a cool place. Not necessary to refrigerate.

Spiced Salt Seasoning

YIELD: 1 POUND (450 G)

Salt	14 oz	400 g
Five-spice powder	2 oz	60 g

Place salt in a dry wok or heavy skillet and heat through, stirring constantly, over moderate heat. Remove from heat and add the five-spice powder and mix thoroughly. Store in a tightly sealed jar.

Sweet and Sour Sauce

YIELD: APPROXIMATELY 1 1/4 PINTS (600 ML)

Sugar	10 oz	280 g
Vinegar, white distilled	15 oz	440 ml
Salt	3 oz	90 g

Combine ingredients in a small, heavy-bottomed saucepan and heat over medium heat, stirring, until the sugar is dissolved. Bring to a simmer. Adjust for salt. Let cool, then place in a tightly sealed jar and refrigerate until needed.

Used in combination with other sauces or to marinate vegetables, especially cucumbers.

Yakitori Sauce

YIELD: APPROXIMATELY 1 QUART (900 ML)

Oil, vegetable	as needed	as needed
Chicken, leg bones	4	4
Soy sauce, dark	20 oz	590 ml
Sake	12 oz	355 ml
Mirin	6 oz	180 ml
Tamari sauce	2 oz	60 g
Sugar rock	6 oz	170 g

Rub a light film of oil over the bones. Roast bones in a 400°F (200°C) oven or over a slow grill until they are crisp and well browned.

Combine ingredients in a heavy-bottomed saucepan. Add the roasted bones and, stirring, bring to a boil over medium heat. Lower heat and simmer until the volume of liquids has reduced by one quarter. Remove from heat and let cool. Discard the bones, then strain the liquids through a double layer of cheesecloth and place in a sealed container. Store in the refrigerator.

Note: Yakitori is used to enhance the flavor of grilled foods. Foods may be dipped directly into the sauce toward the end of the cooking process, or the sauce may be applied with a brush. If used as a dip while cooking, and the same batch is to be used again, bring the sauce to a boil, strain, then allow to cool before storing in the refrigerator. This sauce is readily available commercially.

Rice and Noodles

RICE   More than half the world's population depends on rice as a staple food. While Americans eat about 10 pounds of rice per year per capita, Asians, on the average, consume upward of 300 pounds. In most Asian cultures, rice is unquestionably the foundation upon which the national cuisine rests. It is at the very center of each meal. Easy to cultivate, rice is inexpensive to purchase and, when served in combination with other proteins, has the curious ability to increase the individual nutritional values. Thousands of varieties of rice are cultivated throughout the world. Rice will grow where other grains such as wheat will not and will yield more per cultivated acre than either corn or wheat. When served with rice, meats, vegetables, fish and other seafood, soups and rich flavored sauces, yogurt, and legumes are often treated as accompaniments or garnishes. Hence, Asian portion sizes for rice do not usually correlate with portion sizes for American or European dishes.

All Asians do not eat the same kind of rice; the Chinese and Indians prefer a long-grained rice, while Japanese and Koreans choose the short-grain variety. Natural flavor, while subtle, also plays a role. Thais are partial to a long-grain rice that has the faint taste of jasmine while the slightly sweet, nutty flavor of Basmati rice is the favorite throughout India.

Rice is a versatile food which lends itself to a wide variety of uses in all menu categories from savory dishes to sweet. Uncooked, it is ground into flour for cakes, puddings, and noodles. Fermented, it provides the basic substance from which Sake, the national wine of Japan, is produced. The grain is also used to produce a delicate vinegar whose natural flavor marries well with other flavoring agents.

Despite the multitude of varieties, rice is packaged in three categories based on length: long-grain; medium grain, and short grain. Long-grain rice, also known as Carolina, is one of the most widely used varieties; because of its tendency to stay separate and fluffy when cooked, it is a good all-purpose rice. Short-grain, on the opposite end of the spectrum in terms of size and characteristics, is a glutinous rice which is almost round in shape. It contains more starch, resulting in a stickier and more tender texture when cooked, thereby making it ideal for sushi and other Japanese dishes. The glutinous qualities of short grain rice also make it the rice of choice for puddings, savory fillings, sweets and coatings. Medium-grain rice has characteristics which fall somewhere in between the long and short varieties, both in its size and glutinous qualities.

Most Asians prefer to use polished or white rice. The recipes in this book assume the use of this kind of rice. When harvested, all varieties of rice are brown. The extent to which the newly harvested rice is processed determines whether the finished product emerges as white rice or brown rice. Contrary to popular belief, brown rice is not rice that has been left in its pristine, natural state. Its outer husk has been removed, but the bran immediately inside the husk remains. Brown rice is the rice of choice for the health-conscious; it contains more of the grain's vitamins, minerals, and starch, a good percentage of which is lost in the milling or polishing process used to produce white rice. (Needless to say, the more the product undergoes commercial processing, fewer the nutrients that remain.)

Rice is most often cooked by the absorption method. The size and shape of the grain, the duration of time that has elapsed since it was harvested, and the particular texture desired when cooked are major factors in determining the amount of water that will be needed. It becomes important, therefore, to understand the unique properties of whatever rice product you choose to use. Brown rice, for example, can require up to twice the amount of water as white rice and can also take a significantly longer period of time to cook. Converted rice, on the other hand, is a fast-cooking and more convenient product to use. Partially cooked through a steaming process and then dehydrated, the price of this convenience is the loss of many of the nutrients. Some of these "lost" nutrients are returned to the grain through an additional process which "enriches" it before marketing. The final product, however, is unsatisfactory in terms of taste and texture when compared to unconverted white or brown rice, and its use, therefore, is not recommended. "Instant" or "minute" rice products also have been precooked and dried. The grains are cracked to allow water to permeate instantly, thereby speeding up the cooking process. As with "converted" rice, the end product, while predictable, is usually disappointing.

Every variety of rice has its own individual characteristics. Length, shape, fragrance, and texture are the primary dictates when selecting which rice to use. Other factors, however, such as the ratio of liquid to rice and the duration of the actual cooking, are key in determining the ultimate texture and flavor.

COOKING RICE

It is to be expected that a staple as important as rice would encourage the development of a large body of information regarding its preparation. This becomes very apparent as one reviews the methodology of the various Asian cultures, each of which professes its particular method to be the best way of producing the "perfect" rice. And, since each cuisine differs in the specific uses of its "perfect" rice, and since form follows function, everyone is undoubtedly correct. We in the West tend to treat rice as a side dish, as an alternative to the potato or other starch, rather than "at the center of the plate." Perhaps the time has come to treat this important food with some of the care it so rightly deserves and has deservedly received for ages from the cooks of Asia.

THE RATIO

Two parts liquid to one part rice is the generally accepted ratio when cooking rice. This ratio, of course, is more the exception than the rule. As stated previously, many factors can affect the ratio of rice to liquid. In some Asian countries, rice is well rinsed in cold water before cooking to remove any debris. Some claim this ensures a fluffier texture, because it removes some of the material remaining from the polishing process. Rinsing also reduces the amount of starch in the rice. A high starch content can inhibit the separation of the grains. Some Asian cooks always soak rice for a period of time ranging from one to eight hours before cooking. This process not only rids the rice of some of its starch and some of its nutrients, it also serves to soften the grains through the absorption of water, thereby lessening the cooking time. Rice that has been soaked usually requires less liquid to cook. If using an imported rice, such as Basmati, one of India's most fragrant long-grain rices, it is recommended that the rice be rinsed in several changes of cold water and then soaked for about one-half hour, using twice the volume of water to rice. Further, some suggest that the soaking water be used in the cooking process.

The primary method for cooking rice, absorption, requires a specific ratio of rice to water and very slow cooking. As stated earlier, the rule of thumb is two parts water to one part rice. *However, water absorption varies according to the type and age of the rice used.* Here are guidelines for cooking some of the most commonly found varieties of rice. Since the yield in terms of serving portions depends upon specific use, only volume yields are given.

Variety	Uncooked rice	Water	Simmer approx.	Volume yield
Long-grain, white	1 part	1.75-2 parts	18–20 minutes	2.5-3 parts
Long-grain, brown	1 part	2.5 parts	45 minutes	3-4 parts
Short-grain, white	1 part	1.5-1/75 parts	20 minutes	3 parts
Medium-grain, white	1 part	1.5-1.75 parts	20 minutes	3 parts
Basmati*	1 part	1.75 parts	25 minutes	3 parts

*Soak or rinse this rice before cooking.

The amount of liquid can also be varied to achieve different results. This and the length of cooking time will affect the texture of the finished product.

When cooking rice on top of the stove, be sure to use a heavy pot with a tight-fitting lid. This will ensure an even heat absorption and keep any steam created in the cooking process from escaping. Measure the liquid into the pot and bring to a boil. Add the rice and return the liquid to a boil over high heat. Stir to keep grains from sticking to the bottom of the pot; then cover with a tightly fitting lid, reduce the heat to its lowest point, and cook, without stirring or uncovering, until all of the liquid has been absorbed. Rice can be kept warm by covering the pot with a clean, absorbent towel and placing it in a colander over barely simmering water.

Two additional methods of cooking rice, one old and one new, deserve to be mentioned here. The first is to boil the rice in an unspecified, large amount of water until half cooked, then to drain, return to the pot, and finish cooking, covered, in a slow oven or over very low heat on top of the stove. Modern technology has provided us with the second means: automatic electric or gas-fired rice cookers. Automatic rice cookers are manufactured in a variety of sizes from small, electric residential models to very large, gas-fired commercial models which are used in restaurants. Using automated controls, these cookers produce perfectly cooked rice and have the capability of keeping the rice warm over a long period of time.

Regardless of the method used, keep in mind that the goal in cooking rice is to use the minimum amount of liquid to produce the desired texture. And, where rice is concerned, the texture is most important.

Sushi Rice

YIELD: VARIABLE

VINEGAR DRESSING

Rice vinegar, unflavored	3 oz	90 ml
Sugar	2 oz	60 g
Salt	1 tbsp	5 g
Rice, short grain, Japanese or Korean	1 3/4 lb	800 g
Kelp (konbu), washed	3–4 in. square	8–10 cm square
Water	1.5 qt	1.4 L

TO MIX

Cooked, hot rice
Reserved vinegar dressing

Heat vinegar in a small pan over low heat. When warm, add the sugar and salt and stir until they are dissolved. Reserve at room temperature.

Wash rice several times in enough fresh water to cover. When the water remains clear, drain and place the rice in a medium sized, heavy-bottomed pot. Add 1.5 qt (1.4 lt) of fresh water, place the kelp on top of the rice, and heat over medium heat until the water simmers. Remove the kelp and discard. Cover pot with a tight-fitting lid and boil for 2–3 minutes. Lower heat and cook for another 15 minutes or until all of the water has been absorbed. Do not stir rice. Remove pot from heat and let stand, covered, in a warm place for 15 minutes.

Place rice in a large, shallow mixing bowl. Quick cooling of the rice will result in the firmer texture that is desired for sushi. Using a flat wooden spatula or spoon, toss rice gently to cool. Try not to mash the grains in this process. At the same time sprinkle the vinegar dressing evenly over the rice. When the rice has reached room temperature, place in a container and cover with a damp towel to keep it from drying out. Sushi rice should not be refrigerated and should be used the same day that it is made.

Beef Bowl Rice

YIELD: 10 SERVINGS

FLAVORING MIXTURE			*Combine ingredients and reserve.*
Water	1 pt	470 ml	
Soy sauce, dark	8 oz	240 ml	
Mirin	8 oz	240 ml	
Hot cooked rice	15 cups	15 cups	
TO PREPARE AN INDIVIDUAL SERVING			
Oil, vegetable	1 tsp	15 ml	*Heat a heavy-bottomed skillet or wok over high heat. Add oil and heat to just below the smoking point. Add onion or scallion and stir-fry until soft. Add the beef slices and continue to stir-fry until the meat loses its red color. Add the flavoring mixture and stir-fry for another minute.*
Onion, sliced thin, or scallions cut diagonally into 1-in. (2.5 cm) pieces	1 oz	30 g	
Beef, top or bottom round chilled, then sliced very thin	2–3 oz	60–90 g	
Reserved flavoring mixture	3 oz	90 ml	
Ginger juice	1 tbsp	15 ml	*Remove pan from heat and stir in the ginger juice. Place a portion of hot cooked rice into a deep, heated bowl. Place the beef and the pan juices on top. Serve immediately.*
Hot cooked rice	1 1/2 cups per serving	1 1/2 cups per serving	

Rice and Chicken Biriyani

YIELD: 10-12 SERVINGS

Yogurt	1 1/2 lb	680 g	*Combine ingredients.*
Onion, grated	1 lb	450 g	
Garlic, minced	3 tbsp	45 g	
Gingerroot, minced	2 tbsp	25 g	
Chili, green, fresh, seeds and ribs removed, chopped fine	2 tbsp or to taste	12 g or to taste	
Cilantro leaves, fresh, chopped	2 tbsp	6 g	
Chicken, breast meat, skinned and boned	2 lb	900 g	*Cut chicken into 1-in. (2.5 cm) cubes. Place in a stainless steel mixing bowl and add the marinade. Toss well to coat pieces evenly. Cover and refrigerate for 4–6 hours.*
Marinade			
Clarified butter	4 oz	120 ml	*In a heavy-bottomed saucepan, heat the clarified butter over medium heat. Add the spices, mix well, and cook until the aroma of the spices is released. Add the rice and stir well. Toast rice, stirring frequently, until it begins to color lightly.*
Cardamom, ground	1/2 tsp	1 g	
Cloves, ground	1/2 tsp	1 g	
Rice, Basmati, washed and drained	1 1/4 lb	600 g	

(Continued on next page)

Chicken stock	1 qt	1 L	In a separate pot, bring the stock to a boil. Remove from heat, add the saffron and salt. Stir until dissolved. Add this to the toasted rice and bring to a boil. Lower heat to a simmer and cover with a tight-fitting lid. Cook for about 15 minutes or until the rice is cooked but not completely tender.
Saffron, powdered	1 tsp	2 g	
Salt	2 tsp or to taste	10 g or to taste	

Clarified butter	as needed	as needed	In a buttered baking pan, layer the rice, chicken, fried onion, sliced eggs, and peas, finishing with a layer of rice on top. Add whatever liquids remain in the pan. If all of the liquid has been absorbed, add an additional 4–6 oz (120–170 ml) of stock. Cover pan and place in a 300°F (150°C) oven for 30–40 minutes or until the rice is tender, the chicken cooked through, and all of the liquid has been absorbed.
Partially cooked rice			
Reserved marinated chicken			
Onion, sliced thin and fried crisp	1 lb	450 g	
Eggs, hard boiled, sliced	6	6	
Peas, fresh or frozen	6 oz	170 g	

Almonds, sliced and toasted			When serving, garnish each portion with a sprinkling of almonds and raisins.
Raisins, lightly fried in clarified butter			

Fried Rice with Roast Pork and Shrimp

YIELD: 10-12 SERVINGS

Rice, short grain	2 lb	900 g	*Cook rice according to standard procedure. When done remove lid, cover with an absorbent towel, return the lid and let cool.*
Water	2 qt	1.9 lt	
FLAVORING MIXTURE			*Combine ingredients and reserve.*
Soy sauce, light	2 oz	60 ml	
Soy sauce, dark	2 oz	60 ml	
Sugar	2 tsp	10 g	
Salt	1 tsp	5 g	
Pepper, black	1 tsp	2 g	
Shrimp, cleaned, peeled and deveined	8 oz	230 g	*Prepare the shrimp. Combine the remaining ingredients and marinate the shrimp for 15–20 minutes.*
Ginger juice	4 tbsp	60 ml	
Cornstarch	2 tbsp	20 g	
Salt	1 tsp	5 g	
Oil, vegetable	1 tbsp	15 ml	*Heat wok or heavy skillet over high heat. Add oil. When the oil is hot add half the egg mixture. Tilt the pan so that the egg covers as much of the surface as possible to form a thin pancake. When set, turn to the other side and cook briefly. Remove from pan, let cool, roll then cut into very thin strips. Repeat this process with the remaining egg. Reserve.*
Eggs, lightly beaten with 2 tbsp (30 ml) of water	6 large	6 large	
Oil, vegetable	if needed	if needed	*Reheat wok or skillet. Add a little oil, if needed. Stir-fry the shrimp, pork, peas, and scallion until the shrimp turns pink. Add the flavoring mixture and stir well. Add the cooked rice and continue to stir-fry over medium heat until the rice is well coated and heated through. Garnish with the reserved egg strips and chopped cilantro leaves.*
Reserved shrimp			
Roast pork, small dice	6 oz	170 g	
Green peas, cooked	4 oz	115 g	
Scallion, chopped, white and green sections	4–5	4–5	
Reserved flavoring mixture			
Reserved cooked rice at room temperature			
Reserved egg strips			
Cilantro leaves, chopped	as needed	as needed	

Fried Rice with Chicken and Chili Peppers

YIELD: 2 SERVINGS

Dried cayenne peppers	1–3 or to taste	1–3 or to taste	Place peppers in a small mixing bowl and add very hot water to just cover. Soak peppers for 15 minutes or until very soft. Drain and chop fine. Reserve.
Oil, vegetable	1 tbsp	15 ml	Heat wok over high heat. Add the oil and heat until the oil is just below the smoking point. Add the garlic and cayenne peppers and stir-fry briefly until the garlic begins to color lightly.
Garlic, minced	1 tbsp	15 g	
Reserved cayenne peppers			
Chicken breast meat, sliced thin, then into bite-sized pieces	6 oz	170 g	Add the chicken and stir-fry until the chicken begins to brown lightly. Add the remaining ingredients and continue to stir-fry for another 30–40 seconds.
Oyster sauce	2 tbsp	60 ml	
Jalapeno pepper, stem, seeds and ribs removed then sliced into thin strips	1	1	
Cooked rice	1 cup	1 cup	Add the rice and stir-fry for another minute, then add the fish sauce and sugar. Continue to stir-fry until the rice is heated through.
Fish sauce	1 tbsp	15 ml	
Sugar	1 scant tsp	4 g	
Basil leaves	10–15 depending on size	10–15 depending on size	Add the basil leaves and cook, stirring, until they are slightly wilted.
Coriander leaves	3–4 sprigs	3–4 sprigs	Place on a heated plate and garnish with coriander leaves and slices of fresh cucumber.
Cucumber slices	as needed	as needed	

Rice with Crab Meat

YIELD: 2 SERVINGS

Oil, vegetable	1 tbsp	15 ml	Heat wok or heavy skillet over high heat. Add the oil and distribute it evenly over the pan. Stir-fry the garlic until it begins to brown lightly. Add the cooked crab meat and stir-fry for another 10–15 seconds.
Garlic, chopped fine	2 tsp or to taste	10 g or to taste	
Crab meat, cooked	6–8 oz	170–230 g	
Onion, medium dice	2 oz	60 g	Add ingredients and stir-fry briefly to incorporate.
Soy sauce, light	1 tbsp	15 ml	
Fish sauce	1 tbsp	15 ml	
Sugar	2 tsp	10 g	
Egg, beaten	1	1	Add the egg and scramble with the other ingredients.
Rice, cooked	2 cups	2 cups	Add the rice and tomato and continue to stir-fry until heated through and well mixed. Adjust seasonings if necessary. Spoon rice mixture on the center of a warmed plate.
Tomato, peeled, large dice	12 oz	340 g	
Pepper, black	as needed	as needed	Garnish plate with ingredients. Serve the flavored fish sauce on the side.
Cucumber slices	as needed	as needed	
Cilantro leaves, whole	as needed	as needed	
Scallions, whole, green section ends trimmed	as needed	as needed	
Fish sauce with sliced chilies (see recipe)	1 small side dish	1 small side dish	

Rice with Mixed Vegetables and Chicken

YIELD: 10 SERVINGS

Ingredient	US	Metric	Method
Rice, Japanese, short grain, brown	16 oz	450 g	*Place rice in a bowl. Add water to cover by 1–2 in. (2.5–5 cm). Wash rice several times using fresh, cold water. When the water remains clear after washing, drain rice, then place in a colander and let sit for 45–60 minutes.*
Snow peas	8 oz	225 g	*Remove strings and trim ends. Cut into fine julienne lengthwise, then into 1-in. (2.5-cm) lengths. Blanch in boiling water for 10–15 seconds then plunge immediately into iced water. Cool briefly, then drain and reserve.*
Chicken,* dark meat, skin, tendons, and fat removed. Cut into 1/4-in. (0.75-cm) dice	8 oz	225 g	*Blanch chicken in boiling water for about 15 seconds. Place in ice water just long enough to cool, then drain and reserve.*
Carrot, cut into 1-in. (2.5 cm), fine julienne	4 oz	115 g	*Prepare vegetables and reserve.*
Green beans, cut into 1-in.(2.5 cm), fine julienne	4 oz	115 g	
Mushroom, white, button, sliced thin	6 small	6 small	
Dashi (see recipe)	1.25 qt	1.2 L	*Combine ingredients in a heavy-bottomed pot and bring to a boil. Cover, reduce the heat to low, and cook until the rice is tender.*
Soy sauce	4 oz	120 ml	
Mirin	2 oz	60 ml	
Reserved chicken, rice, and all vegetables except the snow peas			
Reserved snow peas			*Add the snow peas and the sake and mix well. Do this quickly so that the temperature does not drop too much. Cover pan with a clean towel, then with the lid. Remove pan from heat and let sit for 10–15 minutes before serving.*
Sake	2 oz	60 ml	

*Diced grilled meats or white, firm-textured fish may be substituted for the chicken. When using fish, add uncooked fish at the same time as the snow peas.

Rice with Spicy Beef

YIELD: 1 SERVING

Soy sauce, light	2 tsp	10 ml	*Mix the soy sauce and pepper in a small mixing bowl. Add the beef and mix to coat. Marinate for 10–15 minutes.*
Pepper, black, ground	pinch	pinch	
Beef,* chilled, cut into very thin slices, then coarsely chopped	3–4 oz	90–115 g	
Pepper, jalapeño, chopped fine	2 tsp	4 g	*Combine the jalapeño pepper with the garlic. Heat wok over high heat. Add oil and distribute it evenly. Stir-fry the pepper and garlic mixture briefly until the aroma is released.*
Garlic, minced	2 tsp	4 g	
Marinated beef			*Add the marinated beef and flavoring ingredients and continue to stir-fry until the meat is cooked through. Taste and adjust flavorings if necessary.*
Oyster sauce	2 tsp	10 ml	
Fish sauce	2 tsp	10 ml	
Sugar	1 tsp	5 g	
Soy sauce, dark	dash	dash	
Red chilies, fresh, cut on the diagonal	5–6 thin slices	5–6 thin slices	*Add ingredients and toss to incorporate.*
Basil leaves, fresh, whole	5–6, depending on size	5–6, depending on size	
Rice, cooked	1 cup	1 cup	*Place a mound of warm rice on one side of a heated plate, the beef mixture on the other. Garnish with 1–2 fresh basil leaves. Serve with a side dish of flavored fish sauce (see recipe).*
Beef mixture			
Basil leaves	1-2	1-2	
Flavored fish sauce	as needed	as needed	

*Pork or chicken may be used instead of beef.

Savory Rice Cooked in Coconut Milk

YIELD: 10-12 SERVINGS

Ingredient	US	Metric	
Rice, long grain	1 1/2 lb	700 g	*Rinse rice until water is clear. Drain and reserve.*
Coconut milk, thin	1.75 qt	1.6 L	*Combine ingredients in a saucepan large enough to cook the rice. Bring to a boil and add the rice. Stir well. Cover pan with a tight-fitting lid and lower heat to its lowest point. Cook for about 20 minutes or until the rice is done. Remove from heat and place a clean towel over open pot. Return lid and let sit for 5–10 minutes. Gently fluff the rice with a fork to separate the grains before serving.*
Onion, small dice	8 oz	230 g	
Garlic, minced	1 oz	30 g	
Shrimp paste	1 tsp	4 g	
Lemon zest	1/2 lemon	1/2 lemon	
Coriander, ground	1 tbsp	6 g	
Cumin, ground	2 tsp	4 g	
Turmeric, ground	2 tsp	4 g	

Chicken and Fried Rice

YIELD: 1 SERVING

Oil, vegetable	2 tsp	10 ml	Heat wok or heavy skillet over high heat. Add the oil. Add the chicken and garlic and stir-fry until the chicken becomes white.
Chicken breast meat, boned, skin removed, sliced into thin strips lengthwise	4 oz	115 g	
Garlic, minced	1 tsp	5 g	
Scallion, chopped	1	1	Add the scallion and stir-fry until it becomes slightly softened, then add the egg. Stir-fry until the egg just begins to set. Add the rice, tomato, and the flavoring ingredients. Stir-fry until all ingredients are heated through.
Egg, beaten	1	1	
Rice, cooked	1 cup	1 cup	
Cherry tomatoes, cut into halves	2	2	
Soy sauce, light	1 tsp	5 ml	
Fish sauce	splash or to taste	splash or to taste	

TO SERVE

Cucumber slices	as needed	as needed	Place chicken/rice mixture on the center of a warm plate. Garnish with cucumber slices lime slices and prik nam plaa (see recipe).
Lime slices	as needed	as needed	
Prik nam plaa (see recipe)	as needed	as needed	

Fried Rice with Pork, Corn, and Red Beans

YIELD: 10 SERVINGS

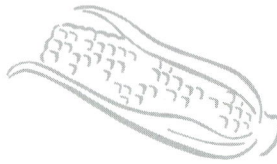

Corn kernels, fresh, stripped from the cob	8 oz	225 g	*Blanch the corn and snow peas in boiling water until cooked through but still crisp. Place in iced water until cool. Drain and combine with the cooked kidney beans. Reserve.*
Snow peas, trimmed	8 oz	225 g	
Kidney beans, cooked	8 oz	225 g	
Oil, vegetable	3 oz	90 ml	*Heat wok or large, heavy skillet over high heat. Add the oil. When the oil is just below the smoking point add the garlic and stir-fry briefly. Add the pork and continue to stir-fry until the pork loses its raw color.*
Garlic, minced	3 tbsp	45 g	
Pork, ground twice	1 1/2 lb	680 g	
Rice, cooked	10 cups	10 cups	*Add ingredients and stir-fry until heated through.*
Reserved vegetables			
Fish sauce	to taste	to taste	
Sugar	to taste	to taste	
Pepper, black, ground	to taste	to taste	

TO SERVE

Rice mixture	as needed	as needed	*Cover one-half of a warmed plate with a generous mound of the rice mixture. Place the crisp fried egg on the other side. Garnish with cucumber slices and tomato wedges placed around the edge of the plate topped with a sprinkling of chopped scallion and cilantro leaves. Serve a small dish of the flavored fish sauce on the side.*
Egg, fried, edges crisp	1 per serving	1 per serving	
Cucumber, half slices	as needed	as needed	
Tomato, wedges	as needed	as needed	
Scallion, chopped	as needed	as needed	
Cilantro leaves, whole	as needed	as needed	
Fish sauce with lemon and chilies (see recipe)	1 small side dish	1 small side dish	

See color insert for photograph of recipe

Fried Rice with Shrimp

YIELD: 10-12 SERVINGS

Rice, jasmine, cooked	2 lb	900 g	Cook rice one day in advance and reserve.
Shrimp, shelled, and deveined	1 1/2 lb	700 g	Clean shrimp and toss in a small amount of lime juice. Place in refrigerator and reserve. Cut the white sections of the scallions into 1 1/2-in. (4-cm) pieces and reserve for garnishing. Chop the remaining green sections and reserve for cooking.
Lemon juice, fresh squeezed	as needed	as needed	
Scallions	12	12	

TO PREPARE AN INDIVIDUAL SERVING

Oil, vegetable	2 tsp	10 ml	Heat wok or heavy skillet over high heat. Add the oil and distribute evenly over the pan. Stir-fry the garlic until it just begins to brown. Add the shrimp and continue to stir-fry until they just begin to turn pink.
Garlic, minced	1 tsp	5 g	
Shrimp	2–3 oz	60–90 g	
Onion, sliced	1 oz	30 g	Add the onion, fish sauce, and sugar. Stir-fry to combine well, then taste and adjust seasonings if necessary.
Fish sauce	2 tsp	10 ml	
Sugar	1 tsp	5 g	
Rice, cooked, room temperature	1 1/2 cups, approx.	1 1/2 cups, approx.	Add rice and mix well. When heated through, remove and reserve in a warm place, or, move rice/shrimp mixture to the side of the pan.
Egg, beaten	1 small	1 small	If pan is dry, add a little oil. Add the egg and the chopped scallion and scramble. When the egg is set, combine it with the rice/shrimp mixture and heat through. When done, place in the center of a warm plate.
Scallion, chopped green sections	2 tsp	2 g	
Coriander leaves, fresh	as needed	as needed	Garnish with a sprinkling of coriander leaves and black pepper, scallion, and cucumber slices. The fish sauce condiment or other condiment, such as chili sauce, can be served in a small dish on the side.
Pepper, black	as needed	as needed	
Cucumber slices	as needed	as needed	
Scallion, white section	as needed	as needed	
Fish sauce with lemon and chilies	as needed	as needed	

Fried Rice with Shrimp and Sausages

YIELD: 12 SERVINGS

FLAVORING SAUCE

Chicken stock	4 oz	120 ml	*Combine ingredients and reserve.*
Oyster sauce	3 oz	90 ml	
Soy sauce, light	1 tbsp	15 ml	
Sesame oil	2 tsp	10 ml	

RICE

Rice, long grain	2 lb	900 g	*Rinse rice 2–3 times using fresh water each time. When the water remains clear, drain and place the rice in a pot with enough water to cover by several inches. Soak the rice for 2 hours.*

Chinese sausages	1 lb	450 g	*Wash sausages. Drain the rice. Place rice, water, and sausages in a pot that has a tight-fitting lid. Cook rice according to standard procedures (soaking has already caused the rice to absorb some water). When the rice is done remove the sausages, cover the pot with an absorbent towel, and replace the lid. Allow the rice to cool. Cut the sausages in half lengthwise, then slice thinly. Reserve.*
Soaked rice			
Water	2 qt	1.9 lt	

SHRIMP

Shrimp, shelled and deveined, cut into 1/4-in. (0.75-cm) pieces	1 lb	450 g	*Prepare shrimp. Combine the remaining ingredients and pour over shrimp. Toss well to coat shrimp evenly. Allow to marinate for 15–20 minutes before using.*
Oyster sauce	1 tbsp	15 ml	
Rice wine or dry sherry	1 tbsp	15 ml	
Gingerroot, peeled and grated	1 tbsp	12 g	
Soy sauce	1 tbsp	15 ml	
Sugar	2 tsp	10 g	
Pepper, white	1 tsp	2 g	

(Continued on facing page)

Egg

Oil, vegetable	*1 tbsp*	*15 ml*
Eggs, lightly beaten with 2 tbsp (30 ml) water	*6 large*	*6 large*

Heat wok or heavy skillet over medium to high heat. Add oil. When oil is hot, stir-fry eggs until they are firm. Remove eggs from pan, cut into small pieces, and reserve.

To complete

Oil, vegetable	*2 tbsp*	*30 ml*
Gingerroot, minced	*1 tbsp*	*15 g*
Garlic, minced	*1 tbsp*	*15 g*
Reserved sausage		
Reserved shrimp		

Heat wok or heavy skillet over high heat. Add oil. When oil is hot add the ginger, garlic, and cooked sausages and stir-fry until the sausages begin to lightly brown, about 1 minute. Add the shrimp with the marinade and stir-fry briefly until the shrimp turn pink.

Cooked rice		
Reserved flavoring sauce		
Reserved eggs		
Scallions, chopped	*as needed*	*as needed*
Cilantro leaves, chopped	*as needed*	*as needed*

Add the rice and the flavoring sauce and continue to stir-fry until heated through. Garnish each serving with a sprinkling of chopped scallions and cilantro.

Rice with Two Chilies, Pork, and Shrimp

YIELD: 10 SERVINGS

Oil, vegetable	1 tsp	5 ml	*In a skillet heat oil, then scramble eggs until they are set but still moist. Reserve.*
Eggs, lightly beaten	3 large	3 large	
Oil, vegetable	3 oz	90 ml	*Heat wok or heavy skillet over high heat. Add oil and distribute over pan. Stir-fry the onion and chili peppers until they begin to soften. Add the curry paste and continue to stir-fry until the oil begins to separate from the mixture.*
Onion, fine dice	1 lb	450 g	
Chili peppers, red and green, seeds and ribs removed, then sliced thin	1 tbsp each or to taste	1 tbsp each or to taste	
Curry paste, red (see recipe or use commercially prepared)	3 tbsp	50 g	
Pork, ground	12 oz	340 g	*Add the pork and stir-fry until the pork is cooked through.*
Shrimp, small, peeled and deveined	2 lb	900 g	*Add the shrimp and stir-fry until they turn pink. Add the rice and mix to blend thoroughly.*
Rice, cold, cooked	10–12 cups	10–12 cups	
Reserved egg			*Add the scrambled egg and stir-fry over high heat to blend all ingredients and heat through. When serving, garnish each portion with a sprinkling of sliced scallion and cilantro leaves.*
Scallion, white and green sections, sliced thin	as needed	as needed	
Cilantro leaves, fresh, chopped	as needed	as needed	

Rice Dumplings with Ground Pork

YIELD: 10-12 SERVINGS

DOUGH

Rice flour	1 lb	450 g
Water, hot	as needed	as needed

Use an electric mixer with the dough hook attached. Place flour in bowl and mix on medium speed, adding hot water a little at a time. Mix until the dough is smooth and elastic. Amount of water you will need will vary. When done, cut dough into four equal pieces. Wrap each piece in plastic wrap and let rest for 1–2 hours.

FILLING

Pork butt, ground with a small amount of the fat	1 lb	450 g
Stock, chicken	4 oz	120 ml
Soy sauce, dark	1 oz	30 ml
Sesame oil	1/2 oz	15 ml
Salt, kosher	2 tsp	10 g
Pepper, white	1 tsp	2 g

Combine ingredients and mix until the ingredients just hold together. Do not overmix. Place in the refrigerator and chill before using.

(Continued on next page)

Reserved dough	*as needed*	*as needed*
Reserved filling	*as needed*	*as needed*

Remove one piece of the dough and knead lightly until it becomes soft and elastic. Divide this into 10 equal pieces. To stuff, place a piece of the dough on your palm and make a depression in the center with the thumb of your other hand. Fill with 1–2 tsp of the pork filling. Hold the filling in place with your thumb and work the dough over the filling. Remove your thumb and pinch the opening closed. The finished dumpling will be shaped like a slightly irregular, pointed ball. Place on a tray covered with plastic wrap or parchment paper that has been lightly dusted with flour, and continue until all of the dough and filling have been used. Dumplings may then be refrigerated until needed or frozen for future use.*

TO SERVE

Prepared dumplings	*3–4 per serving*	*3–4 per serving*
Chicken stock or water	*8 oz*	*240 ml*

Place stock in a small saucepan and bring to a boil over high heat. Add the dumplings one at a time. Cook for 8–10 minutes. Place in a heated bowl with enough of the cooking liquid to cover. Serve immediately.

*If frozen, defrost in refrigerator before using.

Rice with Red Cooked Pork

YIELD: 10 SERVINGS

CHILI CONDIMENT

Vinegar, white distilled	8 oz	240 ml	*Combine ingredients and reserve.*
Soy sauce, dark	1 tbsp	30 ml	
Sugar	6 oz or to taste	170 g or to taste	
Salt	1 tsp or to taste	5 g or to taste	
Chilies, fresh, red, green and yellow, seeds and ribs removed, thinly sliced	6 oz	170 g	
Pork, loin, or tenderloins, trimmed	2 lb	900 g	*Cut pork into 5 x 2 in. (13 x 5 cm) square strips. If using small tenderloins 8–12 oz (220–340 g), leave whole. Combine the remaining ingredients and marinate the pork for 1 hour.*
Tomato catsup or tomato sauce	4 oz	120 g	
Soy sauce, light	2 oz	60 ml	
Soy sauce, dark	1 tbsp	15 ml	
Sugar	1 tbsp	15 g	
Stock, chicken or beef	12 oz	350 ml	*Place marinated pork, the marinade, and the stock in a small saucepan and bring to a boil over medium heat. Lower heat and simmer, partially covered, until the pork is very tender. Remove pork and reserve. Reserve the liquids in the pot.*

(Continued on next page)

SAUCE

Reserved pot liquids		
Soy sauce, light	*2 oz*	*60 ml*
Fish sauce	*1 oz*	*30 ml*

Add ingredients to the pot liquids and return to a simmer over medium heat. Taste and adjust seasonings if necessary to achieve a good sweet/salty balance.

Flour, all-purpose	*1 oz*	*30 g*
Water	*as needed*	*as needed*

Dissolve the flour in enough water to make a thin paste. Add this to the other ingredients in the pot and cook until the liquids thicken and the flour is well cooked.

TO PREPARE AN INDIVIDUAL SERVING

Rice, cooked	*4 oz*	*115 g*
Cooked pork, warmed	*3 oz*	*90 g*
Sauce, heated	*thin film*	*thin film*
Cucumber slices	*as needed*	*as needed*
Scallion, julienne	*as needed*	*as needed*
Cilantro leaves	*as needed*	*as needed*
Reserved chili condiment	*as needed*	*as needed*

Place a bed of warm rice on a heated plate. Cut the pork into bite-sized slices and place them in an attractive arrangement over the rice. Top with a film of the sauce. Garnish plate with cucumbers, scallion, and cilantro leaves. Serve a small side dish of the reserved chili condiment on the side.

Fried Rice with Shrimp Served in a Pineapple

YIELD: 4 SERVINGS

Pineapple, ripe	*1 large*	*1 large*	*Wash the pineapple and remove any discolored leaves. Place the pineapple on its side and remove the upper third in one slice. Remove as much of the meat as possible from both sections of the pineapple. Cut into small cubes. Reserve both the pineapple meat and the shells. The lower section will be used as the serving container, the upper section will serve as a lid.*
Oil, vegetable	*1 tbsp*	*15 ml*	*Heat oil in a wok or heavy skillet. When just below the smoking point, add ingredients and stir-fry until the shrimp begin to turn pink.*
Shrimp, peeled and deveined, tail section of peel left on	*6 oz*	*170 g*	
Sausages, Chinese, cut into thin slices	*3 oz*	*90 g*	
Cashew nuts	*2 oz*	*60 g*	
Pineapple meat			
Rice, cooked	*as needed*	*as needed*	*Use enough cooked rice which, when added to the other ingredients, will fill the cavity of the deeper pineapple shell to overflowing. Add ingredients and stir-fry until heated through and thoroughly combined. Adjust seasonings if necessary.*
Raisins	*2 oz*	*60 g*	
Ham, smoked	*2 oz*	*60 g*	
Soy sauce, light	*1 tbsp or to taste*	*15 ml or to taste*	
Salt	*to taste*	*to taste*	
Pineapple shell, deeper section			*Fill the shell to overflowing with the rice/shrimp mixture. Place on a small sheet pan and bake in a 250°F (120°C) oven for 5 minutes.*
Lettuce leaves, Bibb or red leaf	*as needed*	*as needed*	*Remove pineapple from heat and place on a bed of lettuce leaves. Garnish the top of the rice mixture with strips of fresh chili arranged in an attractive pattern. Place a small bouquet of cilantro leaves in the center. Cover the top, placing the remaining pineapple shell slightly askew.*
Red chili pepper, fresh, long, cut into very thin strips	*4–5 strips*	*4–5 strips*	
Cilantro leaves	*as needed*	*as needed*	
Pineapple section, for lid			

Rice Vermicelli with Shrimp and Bok Choy

YIELD: 2 SERVINGS

FLAVORING MIXTURE

Chicken stock	2 oz	60 ml	*Combine ingredients and reserve.*
Soy sauce	2 tsp	10 ml	
Rice wine or dry sherry	2 tsp	10 ml	
Garlic, minced	1 tsp	5 g	
Gingerroot, minced	1 tsp	5 g	
Salt	pinch	pinch	
Rice vermicelli	4 oz	115 g	*Soak noodles in boiling water for 10 minutes. Drain and reserve.*
Chinese cabbage (bok choy)	4 oz	115 g	*Wash leaves. Cut into thin strips slicing across the stem. Reserve.*
Oil, vegetable	2 tsp	10 ml	*Heat a wok or heavy skillet over high heat. Add the oil and distribute it over the pan. When oil is just below the smoking point, stir-fry the shrimp until they just turn pink. Remove from pan and reserve in a warm place.*
Shrimp, peeled and deveined	6 oz	170 g	
Reserved cabbage			*Return the pan to high heat adding a little oil if necessary. Stir-fry the cabbage until it is hot but still very crisp.*
Reserve flavoring mixture			*Add ingredients to the pan. Lower heat, cover, and cook until the vermicelli is tender.*
Reserved noodles			
Reserved shrimp			*Add the shrimp, return heat to high, and stir-fry until heated through.*

Fried Rice, Vegetarian

YIELD: 10-12 SERVINGS

Ingredient	US	Metric
Rice, long grain	1 1/2 lb	680 g
Water	1.75 qt	1.8 L
Oil, vegetable	1 tbsp	15 ml
Onion	12 oz	340 g
Bamboo shoot, sliced	6 oz	170 g
Scallions, chopped, white and green parts	6	6
Mushrooms, Chinese, black, soaked, caps diced, stems discarded	10	10
Green peas	6 oz	170 g
Corn kernels, fresh	6 oz	170 g
Eggs, lightly beaten with 2 tbsp (30 ml) water	6 large	6 large

Cook rice according to standard procedure. When done, remove lid, cover with an absorbent towel, return the lid, and let cool. Reserve.

Heat wok or heavy skillet over high heat. Add oil. When oil is hot, stir-fry ingredients until the onions are soft. Remove from pan and reserve.

Using the same pan, add half the beaten egg and spread it over as much of the surface of the pan as possible to create a thin pancake. When eggs have set, turn them to the other side and cook briefly. Remove egg from pan, roll into a cylinder, then slice into very thin strips. Repeat this process with the remaining egg. Reserve.

TO COMPLETE

Ingredient	US	Metric
All of the above ingredients		
Vegetable stock	4 oz	120 ml
Soy sauce, light	3 tbsp	45 ml
Sesame oil	2 tbsp	30 ml

Combine the cooked rice, vegetables, egg strips, stock, soy sauce, and sesame oil. Stir-fry over medium heat until the rice is well coated and heated through.

Basmati Rice and Vegetable Pilaf

YIELD: 10-12 SERVINGS

Basmati rice, washed and soaked	1 1/4 lb	570 g
Water	1 1/2 qt	1.4 L

To wash rice, place in mixing bowl filled with water. Pour off the water and refill the bowl. Do this as many times as necessary until the water runs clear. Soak the rice in 1 1/2 qt (1.4 L) of cold water for 1/2 hour. Drain rice and reserve the water. Place the reserved water in a pot with a tight-fitting lid. Bring to a boil, then add the rice. Stir gently until the water returns to a boil. Lower heat and simmer, partially covered, until all of the water has been absorbed. Place a clean kitchen towel over the top of the pot and replace the lid. Cover completely. Let sit for 5 minutes. While the rice is cooking, prepare the following.

Clarified butter	3 oz	90 ml
Onion, sliced thin	8 oz	230 g
Carrot, small dice	4 oz	115 g
Mushrooms, white, sliced thin	4 oz	115 g
Garam masala	1 tsp	2 g
Cayenne pepper	pinch or to taste	pinch or to taste

Heat the clarified butter over medium heat in a heavy skillet. Fry the onions until they begin to brown lightly. Add the carrot, mushrooms, garam masala, and cayenne. Stir well and cook for another minute. Remove pan from heat and reserve.

Potatoes, cut into small cubes	4 oz	115 g
Cauliflower, small florets	4 oz	115 g
Peas	4 oz	115 g

Blanch vegetables in boiling water for 2 minutes. When done, plunge in iced water and reserve.

Cooked rice	
Reserved onion/ mushroom mixture	
Reserved blanched vegetables	

Gently fold the onion/mushroom mixture and the blanched vegetables into the rice. Cover and keep warm in a cool to moderate oven until needed. Serve garnished with cashew nuts that have been sautéed in oil and chopped fresh cilantro leaves.

NOODLES

It is interesting to speculate on the reasons for the emergence of noodles as an important part of the Asian diet. Playing much the same role as rice, a foundation upon which small amounts of flavorful meats, fish, poultry, or vegetables are added, noodles are enjoyed for the most part in savory dishes in almost every Asian country with the possible exception of India. Noodles probably originated in the colder geographical regions of Asia where wheat and millet, two grains that are well suited to its manufacture, could be readily grown. Scarcity of fuel may have been an important reason for the creation of this vital staple. In an area of the world where energy sources have always been in short supply, the reduction in cooking time needed for grains in the form of noodles from that required for whole grains was significant. Noodles, in addition to being energy-efficient, were easy to prepare and store. Further, as a platform upon which an infinite variety of dishes could be created, they had the wonderful capacity to rapidly assuage a hungry appetite with a myriad of tastes and flavors. While all of these reasons undoubtedly played a part in the emergence of the noodle as a mainstay in the daily diet of so many of the world's people, it is probably the sheer delight noodles bring, as well as the healthful qualities they possess, that accounts for their ever-growing popularity over hundreds of generations.

The extensive variety of noodles available to us from the Asian kitchen, both dried and fresh, is based less on differences in shape, as in the pastas associated with Europe, than on the kind of grain or other food substances used to make them. Like European pasta, Asian noodles are made from water-based pastes of flour ground from wheat, buckwheat, millet, rice, or mung beans. These pastes are kneaded into a dough, then either extruded or rolled and cut into round or flat elongated ribbons of varying thicknesses and widths. Other food substances such as agar-agar and soy beans (for bean curd noodles), while not as common, are also used to make noodles. Some noodles contain egg and a small amount of food coloring to enrich the color; others use tea, shrimp, or vegetables to create flavorful variations. Asian noodles are available either dried or fresh and usually come in some form of long strands. Packaged in twisted, portion-sized bundles, in stick form, or bundled in larger quantities, they are most often cooked in boiling water, rinsed thoroughly to remove any traces of excess starch, then reheated in some manner before serving. Bean thread or cellophane noodles, made from mung bean flour, are an exception to this procedure; they must be soaked before cooking except when they are added to soups or other boiling liquids. Today, some varieties of noodles are available in the marketplace precooked, requiring no advance preparation.

Noodles can be incorporated into most of the stir-fried dishes presented in this book. If noodles are used as an integral part of the recipe, suggested quantities of meat, fish, vegetables, etc., as well as sauces or condiments, should be adjusted accordingly.

Some of the most commonly found Asian noodles are as follows:

BEAN-THREAD VERMICELLI   Also known as cellophane, bean-thread, glass, or transparent noodles. Made from a mixture of mung bean flour and water, they are cooked directly in soups, braised dishes, and can also be deep-fried. When used in stir-fried dishes, they must first be soaked in water until soft, then cut to desired lengths. Also used in sweet dishes combined with coconut milk, syrups, flower essences, sweet potatoes or yams.

BROAD-BEAN   Wide bean-thread noodles that must be soaked to soften before using.

EGG NOODLES   Available dried in a variety of widths and thicknesses, but most commonly served as thin round strands. Made from a mixture of wheat flour, water, and eggs, they are packaged in portion size or larger bundles. Best soaked in hot water to soften and untangle. Cooking time will vary according to the thickness of the strand. Also available fresh, these noodles are used in soups, stir-fries, or are sometimes deep-fried to form an attractive, crunchy, tangled mass.

PLAIN NOODLES   Made the same way as egg noodles, but without the egg.

SOBA NOODLES   Flat, square-shaped, ribbon noodles made from a mixture of buckwheat and wheat flours and water. Light brown in color and in flat sticks 7–10 in. (18–25 cm) long, soba are cooked in boiling water, rinsed under cold, running water, then drained. To serve, they are reheated by immersing in boiling water or by incorporating them during the cooking process with other foods. Also available made with green tea (cha-soba).

SOMEN NOODLES   Thin, white noodles made from a mixture of hard wheat flour, water, and salt, similar in shape to soba noodles.

UDON NOODLES   Thick noodles made from a mixture of hard wheat flour, water, and salt, used in soups and stews.

RICE NOODLES   Also known as rice sticks, or rice vermicelli, these dried noodles are white to cream in color and come in a variety of thicknesses. Rice noodles are brittle and must be soaked before using, except when deep-fried. Fresh rice noodles, either extruded in strands or in partially cooked sheets which may be cut into ribbons of any width or used with fillings, are also available.

WHEAT FLOUR NOODLES   Also known as lo-mein, these are available both dried and fresh and are used in soups and fried noodle dishes.

Noodles with Ginger Garlic Beef Broth

YIELD: 10-12 SERVINGS

Ingredient	US	Metric	Method
Beef, top round, cut into 1-in. (2.5-cm) cubes	2 lb	900 g	*Place meat in a pot of boiling water and blanch for 2–3 minutes. Drain and reserve.*
Water, boiling	as needed	as needed	
Oil, peanut	3 oz	90 ml	*Heat oil in a wok or heavy saucepan over moderate to high heat. Add ingredients and stir-fry for 20–30 seconds. Add the blanched beef and continue to stir-fry until the meat is lightly browned.*
Scallions, white and green parts cut into 1/2-in. (1.25-cm) pieces	4–5	4–5	
Gingerroot, peeled and chopped	2 tbsp	25 g	
Garlic, chopped	2 tsp	10 g	
Soy sauce, light	6 oz	180 ml	*Combine ingredients and add to the beef. Stir-fry for another minute or until thoroughly mixed.*
Rice wine or dry sherry	2 oz	60 ml	
Soy sauce, dark	1 oz	30 ml	
Sugar	3 tbsp	45 g	
Soy bean paste	1 1/2 oz	40 g	
Stock, beef	2 qt	2 L	*Add the beef stock and the star anise. Bring to a boil and partially cover. Lower heat and simmer until the meat is tender, about 1 hour. Skim broth, as needed.*
Star anise	4, whole	4, whole	

(Continued on next page)

Carrot, 1/2-inch (1.5-cm) cubes	8 oz.	230 g
Sesame oil	1 tbsp	15 ml
Pepper, black, fine ground	to taste	to taste

Add ingredients and continue to simmer for another 5 minutes or until the carrots are cooked through but still firm. Adjust seasonings if necessary. Let cool and reserve. Degrease when cold.

TO PREPARE AN INDIVIDUAL SERVING

Egg noodles, wide	3–4 oz per serving	90–115 g per serving
Meat and broth, reheated to a boil	as needed	as needed
Scallions	as needed	as needed

Cook noodles in briskly boiling water until tender. When done, drain and place in a warm, deep bowl. Spoon a portion of meat and broth on top. Garnish with chopped scallion.

Beggar's Noodles

Scallion, chopped	1 medium	1 medium	*Combine ingredients and reserve.*
Soy sauce, light	2 tsp	10 ml	
Vinegar, rice	2 tsp	10 ml	
Noodles, wheat	3 oz	90 g	*Cook noodles in a generous amount of briskly boiling water until tender. Drain and place in a warm bowl.*
Peanut butter	1 tbsp	15 g	*Add the peanut butter and sesame paste and toss to coat noodles. Pour the scallion mixture on top and serve.*
Sesame paste	2 tsp	10 g	
Reserved scallion mixture			

Braised Bean-Thread Noodles with Mushrooms and Shrimp

YIELD: 10-12 SERVINGS

Ingredient	US	Metric	Method
Bean-thread noodles	1 1/4 lb	570 g	*Soak noodles in hot water for 3–4 minutes then drain. Reserve.*
Mushrooms, Chinese, black, dried	10	10	*Soak mushrooms in hot water until soft and plump. Discard stems, then julienne caps. Reserve.*
Shrimp, dried	1 oz	30 g	*Soak dried shrimp in hot water until tender, about 5 minutes. Reserve*
Scallions, green and white sections	6	6	*Cut the scallions and gingerroot into julienne similar in size to the mushroom slices. Reserve.*
Gingerroot, peeled	1 1/2 oz	50 g	

TO PREPARE

Ingredient	US	Metric	Method
Oil, vegetable	1 tbsp	15 ml	*Heat wok or heavy skillet over high heat. Add oil and distribute evenly over pan. Stir-fry ingredients until the ginger becomes aromatic.*
Reserved mushrooms			
Reserved shrimp			
Reserved gingerroot			
Roasted pork, small dice	8 oz	230 g	
Reserved scallions			*Add ingredients and bring to a boil. Lower heat, cover, and simmer for 5–6 minutes.*
Stock, chicken	1 qt	1 L	
Soy sauce, light	3 oz	90 ml	
Reserved noodles			*Add ingredients and mix well. Simmer for 5 minutes more.*
Vinegar, rice	2 oz or to taste	60 ml or to taste	
Salt	to taste	to taste	
Pepper, black	to taste	to taste	

Chicken in Black Bean Sauce over Egg Noodles

YIELD: 10 SERVINGS

Egg noodles, thin	2 lb	900 g	*Cook noodles in a generous amount of briskly boiling, lightly salted water. When done, drain, then rinse in cold water. Toss in a small amount of oil to keep the strands separated. Reserve.*
Oil, vegetable	as needed	as needed	
Chicken, leg meat, trimmed and deboned	1 1/2 lb	680 g	*Cut meat into 1 x 1 1/2 in. (2.5 x 4 cm) pieces. Marinate in the remaining ingredients for 15–20 minutes.*
Soy sauce	2 tbsp	30 ml	
Rice wine	2 tbsp	30 ml	
Cornstarch	2 tsp	8 g	
Fermented black soy beans	4 oz	115 g	*Rinse the soy beans under running water, drain well, then chop fine. Combine with the garlic and reserve.*
Garlic, minced	1 tbsp	15 g	

SAUCE

Stock, chicken	20 oz	600 ml	*Combine ingredients and reserve.*
Soy sauce, light	3 tbsp	45 ml	
Sesame oil	2 tsp	20 ml	
Cornstarch	1 tbsp	10 g	

(Continued on next page)

TO PREPARE AN INDIVIDUAL SERVING

Oil, vegetable	*for deep-frying*	*for deep-frying*	Deep-fry the chicken at 320°F (160°C) until cooked through and lightly browned.
Chicken	2 oz	60 g	
Oil, vegetable	2 tsp	16 ml	Heat wok or heavy skillet over high heat. Add oil and distribute it evenly over the surface of the pan. Add the black bean/garlic mixture and stir-fry briefly until it becomes aromatic. Add the green pepper and onion and continue to stir-fry until they are hot but still crisp.
Black bean/garlic mixture	1 tsp	10 g	
Green bell pepper, diced	1 oz	30 g	
Onion, diced	1 oz	30 g	
Reserved sauce	2 oz	60 ml	Add the reserved sauce and stir-fry until well mixed and the sauce has thickened slightly. Add the noodles, heat through, and serve. Or, place noodles in a strainer basket and plunge into boiling water to reheat. Drain, then place noodles on a warm plate and top with the chicken sauce.
Cooked noodles*	3 oz	90 g	

*Some dried egg noodles available in Asian markets have been precooked.

Chicken with Cellophane Noodles

YIELD: 10-12 SERVINGS

Noodles, cellophane (bean-thread)	10 oz	280 g	*Place noodles in a bowl and soak for 15 minutes in a generous amount of boiling water. Drain and cut into 2-in. (5-cm) lengths. Reserve.*
Water, boiling	as needed	as needed	
Oil, vegetable	2 tbsp	30 ml	*Heat a wok or heavy skillet over high heat. Add oil and distribute it over the surface of the pan. Stir-fry the chicken and scallions until the chicken becomes white.*
Chicken, breast meat, skinned, boned, cut into bite-sized pieces	3 lb	1.3 kg	
Scallions, white and tender green sections, cut into thin slices	6–8 depending on size	6–8 depending on size	
Stock, chicken	12 oz	350 ml	*Add ingredients and bring to a boil.*
Fish sauce	3 oz	90 ml	
Soy sauce	2 oz	60 ml	
Pepper, black, ground	1/2 tsp or to taste	1 g or to taste	
Reserved cellophane noodles			*Add noodles, lower heat and cover pan. Simmer for 3–4 minutes or until the chicken is cooked through and the noodles are tender. Serve with tomato and onion salad served on the side.*

See color insert for photograph of recipe

Hot and Sour Soup with Noodles

YIELD: 10-12 SERVINGS

Ingredient	US	Metric	Instruction
Pork, lean	12 oz	340 g	*Chill pork well, then cut into fine julienne. Mix the soy sauce with the cornstarch until all of the cornstarch has dissolved. Place the pork strips into a mixing bowl and toss until the meat is well coated. Stir-fry in a hot, oiled wok or heavy skillet until slightly crisp. Reserve.*
Soy sauce, light	2 oz	60 ml	
Cornstarch	2 tbsp	20 g	
Oil, vegetable	2 tbsp	30 ml	
Mushrooms, Chinese, black, dried	8	8	*Soak mushrooms until soft and plump. Remove stems and discard. Slice caps into fine julienne. Reserve.*
Water, hot			
Bamboo shoot, canned, whole	8 oz	220 g	*Slice bamboo shots and bok choy into fine julienne. Reserve.*
Bok choy	6 oz	170 g	
Oil, vegetable	2 tbsp	30 ml	*In a small soup pot, heat the oil over medium high heat. Add the bean paste and scallions and stir-fry briefly.*
Red bean paste, hot	2 tbsp or to taste	40 g or to taste	
Scallions, green and white parts, chopped	4	4	
Stock, chicken	2 1/2 qt	2.5 L	*Add ingredients, mix well, and bring to a boil. Lower heat and simmer for 5 minutes. Add salt to taste.*
Soy sauce	2 oz	60 ml	
Fried pork strips			
Reserved bamboo shoot			
Reserved mushrooms			
Reserved bok choy			
Salt	to taste	to taste	

(Continued on facing page)

Wheat or soaked cellophane noodles; or, rice sheets*	4 oz	4 oz

Add noodles to pot and bring to a boil. Cook until the noodles are soft. Cooking time will vary depending on which noodles are used. Remove from heat and reserve.

TO SERVE

Soup	as needed	as needed
Vinegar	splash	splash
Sesame oil	a few drops	a few drops
Pepper, black, ground	pinch	pinch

Reheat soup as needed. Pour into heated bowls and add a splash of vinegar, a few drops of sesame oil, and a pinch of black pepper to each bowl.

If using rice sheets, fold in half, then continue to fold until they are about 2 in. (5 cm) wide. Cut into 1/2-in. (1.5-cm) noodles and add to soup.

Noodles with White and Black Sesame Seeds

YIELD: 10 SERVINGS

NOODLE SAUCE

Oyster sauce	5 tbsp	75 ml	*Combine ingredients and reserve.*
Soy sauce, light	4 tbsp	60 ml	
Soy sauce, dark	2 tbsp	30 ml	
Vinegar, white	1 tbsp	15 ml	
Oil, sesame	1 tsp	5 ml	
Sugar	2 tbsp	30 ml	
Garlic, minced	1 1/2 tsp.	8 g	
Pepper, white	1 tsp.	2 g	
Sesame seeds, white, toasted	4 tsp	8 g	*Place the seeds in a dry, heavy skillet and toast on the stovetop over low heat for about 10 minutes, stirring occasionally. Reserve.*
Sesame seeds, black, toasted	4 tsp	8 g	
Chinese egg noodles, thin	2 lb	900 g	*Cook noodles in a generous amount of boiling water until tender but still firm. Place in a colander and rinse under cold running water for 2–3 minutes. Drain well.*
Cold cooked noodles			*Combine the noodles, the reserved sauce, and the scallion oil. Add the sesame seeds and mix well to coat the noodles evenly. Serve cold, or at room temperature.*
Reserved sauce			
Scallion oil (see recipe)	2 oz	60 ml	
Reserved sesame seeds			

Noodles with Curried Beef

YIELD: 10-12 SERVINGS

GARNISHES

Bean sprouts, trimmed and blanched	*1 1/4 lb*	*570 g*
Bean curd, steamed and diced	*8 oz*	*230 g*
Shallots, sliced and fried crisp	*8 oz*	*230 g*
Peanuts, roasted and ground fine	*8 oz*	*230 g*
Garlic, sliced and fried until a light golden color	*4 oz*	*115g*
Scallions	*10*	*10*
Lemon wedges	*10*	*10*
Hard-cooked eggs, cut in quarters (use 2 quarters per serving)	*5–6*	*5–6*
Coriander leaves, fresh, whole	*as needed*	*as needed*

Prepare garnishes and reserve each in a separate container. When needed, use in appropriate amounts. Serve at room temperature.

CURRY MIXTURE

Lemon grass, white tender section	*2 tbsp*	*12 g*
Red pepper flakes	*1 tbsp*	*6 g*
Coriander seeds	*2 tsp*	*4 g*
Galangal, minced	*1 tsp*	*5 g*
Cumin, ground	*2 tsp*	*4 g*
Curry powder	*2 tsp*	*4g*
Cardamom, ground	*1 tsp*	*2 g*
Nutmeg, ground	*1/2 tsp*	*1 g*

Using a mortar and pestle, pound ingredients to a smooth mass. Reserve.

(Continued on next page)

Beef,* top or bottom round, trimmed of all fat, cut into bite-sized pieces	2 lb	1 kg	*Using a wok or heavy saucepan, simmer the beef in the coconut milk until it is very tender. Remove from heat and reserve. Remove 4 oz (120 ml) of the coconut milk and place it in a small saucepan.*
Coconut milk, thin (see recipe)	2 qt	2 L	
Reserved coconut milk			*Bring the coconut milk to a boil over medium heat. Add the curry mixture and stir to blend thoroughly. Cook for 1 minute. Return this mixture to the pot containing the beef, then add the thick coconut milk. Mix well and bring to a boil. Season with fish sauce and sugar to taste and remove from heat. Reserve.*
Reserved curry mixture			
Coconut milk, thick (see recipe)	4 oz	120 ml	
Fish sauce	to taste	to taste	
Sugar, palm or light brown	to taste	to taste	

TO PREPARE AN INDIVIDUAL SERVING

Noodles, rice or egg	3 oz per serving	90 g per serving	*Cook noodles until done as desired. Drain well, then place them in the center of a warm plate. Pour the reheated beef and curry sauce over the top of the noodles.*
Cooked beef in curry sauce	2–3 oz per serving	60–90 g per serving	
Reserved garnishes			*Surround the edge of the plate with an attractive arrangement of the garnishes.*

Pork or chicken may be substituted.

Noodles with Coconut Sauce Served Cold

YIELD: 10-12 SERVINGS

DRESSING

Fish sauce	6 oz	180 ml	*Combine ingredients and reserve.*
Lime juice, fresh squeezed	4 oz	120 ml	
Sugar	3 oz	90 g	
Wheat noodles, thin	1 1/2 lb	680 g	*Cook noodles in a generous amount of briskly boiling water until tender. Drain, then rinse under cold running water. When cool, drain thoroughly. Place in a mixing bowl and add the dressing. Toss to distribute evenly and reserve.*
Reserved dressing			
Coconut milk, thin	12 oz	350 ml	*Place the coconut milk in a heavy-bottomed saucepan and bring to a boil over low to medium heat. Add the shrimp and simmer briefly until the shrimp just begin to turn pink. Remove from heat and cool.*
Shrimp, peeled and deveined	1 1/2 lb	680 g	
Pineapple, fresh, chopped	8 oz	170 g	*Combine ingredients. Reserve.*
Garlic, minced	4 oz	90 g	
Gingerroot, shredded	3 oz	90 g	

TO SERVE

Reserved noodles	as needed	as needed	*Mound a portion of noodles in the center of a chilled plate. Arrange 2 oz (60 g) of the shrimp and the coconut milk on top. Sprinkle some of the pineapple mixture around the edges of the noodles. Garnish with several fresh cilantro leaves, small amounts of very thinly sliced red bell and red chili peppers, and a wedge of fresh lime.*
Reserved shrimp and sauce	as needed	as needed	
Reserved pineapple mixture	as needed	as needed	
Cilantro leaves, fresh	as needed	as needed	
Peppers, red bell	as needed	as needed	
Peppers, red chili	as needed	as needed	
Lime wedges	as needed	as needed	

Noodles with Crab Meat in Broth

YIELD: 10 SERVINGS

Noodles, egg, wide	2 lb	900 g	*Cook noodles in a generous amount of briskly boiling, lightly salted water. When done, drain, then rinse in cold water. Toss in a small amount of oil to keep the strands separated. Reserve.*
Crab meat, cooked	1 1/2 lb	680 g	*Marinate crab meat for 15–20 minutes in the ginger/rice wine mixture. Reserve.*
Water	4 oz	120 ml	
Rice wine or dry sherry	2 oz	60 ml	
Gingerroot	4 thin slices	4 thin slices	

TO PREPARE AN INDIVIDUAL SERVING

Oil, vegetable	2 tsp	20 ml	*Heat wok or heavy skillet over high heat. Add oil and distribute evenly over the surface of the pan. Add the scallions and gingerroot and stir-fry until aromatic.*
Scallions, white and green parts cut into 2-in. (5-cm) lengths	2, trimmed	2, trimmed	
Gingerroot, fine julienne	1 slice	1 slice	
Mushroom caps, dried, black, Chinese, soaked and sliced thin, or fresh mushrooms	2	2	*Add the mushrooms and crab meat and sauté briefly.*
Crab meat	2 oz	60 g	
Stock, fish or chicken	6 oz	180 ml	*Add ingredients and bring to a boil. Adjust seasonings if necessary.**
Soy sauce, light	2 tsp	10 ml	
Rice wine	2 tsp	10 ml	
Sugar	1/2 tsp	3 g	
Salt	to taste	to taste	
Pepper, fine ground	to taste	to taste	
Reserved noodles	3 oz	90 g	*Add the noodles and heat through. Pour into heated bowl and garnish with a few drops of sesame oil.*
Sesame oil	a few drops	a few drops	

*Broth may be thickened at this point with 1 tsp (3 g) of cornstarch mixed with just enough cold water to make a thin paste.

Fried Noodles and Spicy Beef

YIELD: 10-12 SERVINGS

BEEF SAUCE

Soy sauce, light	2 oz	60 ml
Soy sauce, dark	1 oz	30 ml
Pepper, black, ground	2 tbsp	15 g
Beef, minced	2 lb	1 kg

Combine ingredients thoroughly and let marinate for 20 minutes.

Oil, vegetable	2 tbsp	30 ml
Onion, finely diced	1 lb	450 g
Garlic, minced	2 oz	60 g
Beef, marinated		
Scallion, green sections, cut into fine julienne	2 oz	60 g
Fish sauce	2 tbsp or to taste	30 ml or to taste
Sugar	2 tbsp or to taste	30 g or to taste

Heat wok or heavy skillet over high heat. Add oil and distribute evenly over the surface of the pan. Stir-fry the onion and garlic until lightly browned. Add the beef and continue to stir-fry until the meat has browned. Add the scallion, fish sauce, and sugar to taste.

Stock, beef	12 oz	350 ml
Tapioca flour, mixed with enough cold water to make a thin paste	2 oz	60 g

Add the stock, lower heat, and simmer for 10 minutes, stirring occasionally. Adjust seasonings if necessary. Add the tapioca paste, mix well, and cook until the liquids begin to thicken. Remove from heat and reserve.

TO PREPARE AN INDIVIDUAL SERVING

Noodles, fresh, wide, rice	3–4 oz per serving	90–115 g per serving
Soy sauce, dark	2 tsp	10 ml
Oil, vegetable	2 tbsp	30 ml

In a mixing small bowl just large enough to hold the noodles, add the soy sauce and mix to coat the noodles evenly. Heat oil in a wok or skillet over medium to high heat and fry the noodles until done. Transfer to a warm plate.

Beef mixture, reheated as needed	4–5 oz per serving	115–140 g per serving

Place the reheated beef mixture on top.

Singapore Style Noodles

YIELD: 10 SERVINGS

GARNISHES

Eggs, lightly beaten	5	5	Combine the eggs with salt and pepper to taste. Prepare three or four thin pancake-like omelets in a lightly oiled or nonstick skillet. Turn out onto a plate to cool. Roll each separately and slice into thin ribbons. Reserve.
Salt	to taste	to taste	
Pepper, black, ground	to taste	to taste	
Oil, vegetable	as needed	as needed	
Garlic, chopped	2 tbsp	30 g	Rinse garlic in cold water. Dry in absorbent towel, then fry until very lightly browned. Rinse the black beans, then mash them with the garlic. Reserve.
Salted black beans*	2 tbsp	30 g	
Scallions, white and tender green sections, chopped	10	10	Prepare garnishes and reserve.
Coriander leaves, chopped	5 sprigs	5 sprigs	
Chilies, red fresh, sliced thin	as needed	as needed	
Rice noodles, dried, thin	2 lb	1 kg	Place the rice noodles in boiling water. As the noodles begin to soften, separate the strands. When soft, about 30–40 seconds, drain in a colander. Cool the noodles gradually by placing them on a tray and lifting them gently to release heat. Add a small amount of oil and toss. Cover and reserve.
Water, boiling	8 qt	8 L	
Oil, vegetable	as needed	as needed	

(Continued on facing page)

Roast pork, shredded	1 1/4 lb	570 g
Shrimp, small, peeled and deveined	1 1/4 lb	570 g
Bean sprouts, trimmed	10 oz	280 g
Celery, chopped fine	10 oz	280 g

Prepare ingredients. Reserve each in a separate container.

TO PREPARE AN INDIVIDUAL SERVING

Oil, vegetable	2 tsp	10 ml
Reserved garlic/bean mixture	1/2 tsp	6 g
Reserved pork	2 oz	60 g
Reserved shrimp	2 oz	60 g
Stock, chicken	2 oz	60 ml
Reserved bean sprouts	1 oz	30 g
Reserved celery	1 oz	30 g
Reserved noodles	3 oz	90 g

Heat wok or heavy skillet over high heat. Add the oil and distribute over surface of pan. Add the garlic/bean mixture and pork. Stir-fry briefly until the mixture becomes aromatic. Add the shrimp and continue to stir-fry until they just begin to turn pink.

Add ingredients and stir-fry until the beans and celery are heated through.

Add noodles to the pan. Combine all ingredients thoroughly and heat through.

TO SERVE

Reserved garnishes	as needed	as needed

Garnish the noodle mixture with strands of the egg pancake, scallion, coriander leaves, and sliced chili.

Spicy Noodle Sauté with Chicken

YIELD: 1 SERVING

Noodles, rice, fresh, wide*	4 oz	115 g
Soy sauce, dark	2 tsp	10 ml

Cook noodles briefly in rapidly boiling water so that they are slightly underdone. Rinse under cold water, drain well, then place in a small mixing bowl. Add the soy sauce and toss to distribute over the surface of the noodles. Reserve.

CHILI MIXTURE

Garlic, sliced	1 tbs or to taste	15 g or to taste
Chilies, small hot, fresh	2–3 or to taste	2–3 or to taste

Using a mortar, pound ingredients together to make a paste.

Oil, vegetable	2 tsp	10 ml
Garlic chili mixture		
Chicken, breast meat, skinned and boned, cut into small, bite-sized pieces	3 oz	90 g
Tomatoes, cherry, cut in halves	4	4

Heat wok or heavy skillet over high heat. Add oil and distribute evenly over the surface of pan. Add the garlic/chili mixture and stir-fry briefly until it becomes aromatic. Add the chicken and stir-fry until the chicken is just barely cooked through. Add the cherry tomatoes.

Catsup	2 tsp	10 ml
Fish sauce	2 tsp	10 ml
Vinegar	1 tsp	5 ml
Sugar	1 tsp	5 g

Add these ingredients and continue to stir-fry until heated through. Taste pan liquids, and adjust seasonings, if necessary, to achieve a good balance between the sour, sweet, and salty flavors.

Reserved rice noodles		
Chili pepper, fresh, sliced very thin	as needed	as needed

Add the cooked noodles and stir-fry until heated through. Serve on a bed of lettuce leaves and garnish with thin strips of fresh, red, hot chili peppers.

*Other varieties of noodles may be substituted.

Szechwan Noodles

YIELD: 10-12 SERVINGS

Rice noodles, thin	2 lb	900 g	*Cook noodles in briskly boiling water until tender. Drain and rinse under cold water. When cool, drain again, then add oil. Toss to coat strands evenly. Reserve.*
Vegetable oil	1 tbsp	15 ml	
Mushrooms, Chinese, black	12	12	*Soak mushrooms in just enough hot water to cover. When soft and plump, discard tough stems and julienne the caps. Reserve.*
Dried shrimp	4 tbsp	4 tbsp	*Soak shrimp in hot water until tender. Reserve.*
Stock, chicken	1 1/2 qt	1.5 L	*Place ingredients in saucepan and bring to a simmer over low heat, stirring occasionally. Simmer for 5 minutes, then remove from heat and reserve.*
Peanut butter	2 oz	60 g	
Sesame paste	1 oz	30 g	
Chili oil	1 tbsp or to taste	30 ml or to taste	
Salt	to taste	to taste	

SAUCE

Oil, vegetable	1 tbsp	15 ml	*Heat wok or heavy skillet over high heat. Add oil and distribute evenly over the surface of the pan. Stir-fry ingredients for about 1 minute.*
Chili peppers, small, red, dried	4 or to taste	4 or to taste	
Onion, diced	12 oz	340 g	
Reserved mushrooms			
Reserved shrimp			

(Continued on next page)

Pork, ground	1 lb	450 g	*Add pork and stir-fry until lightly browned. Add the soy sauce, bean paste and chili sauce and continue to stir-fry for another 2 minutes.*
Soy sauce, light	1 1/2 oz	50 ml	
Bean paste, yellow	2 oz	60 g	
Chili sauce	1 oz	30 g	
Cornstarch	2 tbsp	20 g	*Dissolve the cornstarch in a small amount of water and add. Cook, stirring, until slightly thickened. Reserve.*
Water	as needed	as needed	

TO PREPARE AN INDIVIDUAL SERVING

Reserved stock	4 oz	120 ml	*Bring stock to a boil. Reheat noodles briefly in the stock, then pour both the noodles and stock into a heated bowl. Top with the meat sauce, a sprinkle of chopped scallion, and a few drops of sesame oil.*
Reserved noodles	2 oz	60 g	
Meat sauce, heated	2 oz	60 g	
Scallion, chopped	as needed	as needed	
Sesame oil	as needed	as needed	

Rice Noodles with Pork Curry

YIELD: 10-12 SERVINGS

CHILI PASTE

Chilies, small dried	2 tsp red pepper flakes	7 g red pepper flakes
Shallots, sliced thin	2 oz	60 g
Garlic, sliced thin	1 1/2 oz	40 g
Shrimp paste	1 tbsp	20 g
Turmeric, ground	1 tbsp	7 g
Salt	1 tsp.	5 g
Spareribs, pork	1 1/2 lb	700 g
Water	as needed	as needed
Oil, vegetable	1 tbsp	15 ml
Reserved chili paste		
Pork, ground	1 1/2 lb	700 g
Tomatoes, cherry	1 1/2 lb	700 g

Combine ingredients in a mortar and pound into a paste. A blender may also be used. Reserve.

Saw or chop the ribs across the bone into 2-in. (5-cm) lengths, then separate the ribs along the bone. Place in a pot with just enough water to cover. Bring to a boil, then lower heat to a simmer. Partially cover pot and cook until the meat is tender, skimming the liquid until it is clear and free of fat. When done, remove from heat and reserve the meat in the liquid.

Heat wok or heavy skillet over high heat. Add the oil and heat to just below the smoking point. Add the chili paste and stir-fry until it becomes fragrant. Add the pork and stir-fry until cooked through and lightly browned. Add the tomatoes and stir-fry briefly. When done, add these ingredients to the pot containing the spare ribs and bring to a simmer.

(Continued on next page)

Fish sauce	*2 oz*	*60 ml*
Fermented soybeans	*2 oz*	*60 g*
Sugar	*1 1/2 tbsp*	*25 g*
Garlic, sliced thin, then stir-fried in oil until lightly browned	*3 oz*	*90 g*
Scallion	*2 oz*	*60 g*
Coriander, stems and leaves, finely chopped	*2 oz*	*60 g*

Add ingredients and mix well. Remove from heat and reserve until needed.

TO PREPARE AN INDIVIDUAL SERVING

Rice noodles, thin	*4 oz per serving*	*115 g per serving*
Reserved pork curry	*as needed*	*as needed*

Cook noodles until tender. Drain, then top with a reheated portion of the pork curry.

Udon Noodles in Broth

BROTH

Dashi (see recipe)	2 qt	2 L
Soy sauce, dark	2 oz	60 ml
Soy sauce, light	2 oz	60 ml
Mirin	1 oz	30 ml
Sugar	2 tbsp	30 g
Salt	2 tsp or to taste	10 g

Combine ingredients and bring to a boil over medium heat. Keep hot over low heat if using immediately. Or, lower heat and simmer for 4–5 minutes. Let cool, then refrigerate. Reheat as needed.

TO PREPARE AN INDIVIDUAL SERVING

Udon noodles	4 oz	115 g
Noodle broth* (see recipe), heated	as needed	as needed
Scallions, white and tender green parts, sliced thin		
Shichimi**		

Place noodles in rapidly boiling water and cook until tender. Remove the noodles and rinse immediately in cold water, then drain. To reheat, plunge noodles briefly into boiling water, then place noodles in a deep, warm bowl and add enough hot noodle broth to just cover. Sprinkle with the sliced scallions. Serve shichimi on the side.

VARIATIONS

The scallion may be eliminated and substituted with a slice of lightly fried tofu that has been pressed first to remove some of the liquid content. Or, a raw egg can be placed whole into the bowl along with the steaming broth and noodles and cooked in the bowl. Garnish this version with a sprinkling of nori seaweed that has been crumbled.

See color insert for photograph of recipe

*If a thicker consistency is desired, the noodle broth can be thickened with a small amount of a cornstarch/cold water mixture before pouring over hot noodles.

**Shichimi is a general-purpose condiment that is used to add extra flavor to a wide variety of dishes. It is a blend of seven different ingredients including red pepper, dried mandarin orange peel, seaweed, black hemp seeds, Sichuan pepper corns, and white sesame seeds. The mixture is processed into tiny flakes. It can be purchased through commercial sources under the name "Seven-spice powder" and is packed in shaker containers suitable for placement on the table.

Shanghai Noodles with Bean Sprouts

YIELD: 10 SERVINGS

SEASONING SAUCE

Chicken stock	1 pt	470 ml	*Combine ingredients and mix until the sugar and cornstarch are completely dissolved. Reserve.*
Soy sauce, light	3 oz	90 ml	
Soy sauce, dark	1 oz	30 ml	
Sesame oil	1 oz	30 ml	
Rice wine or dry sherry	1 tbsp	15 ml	
Cornstarch	1 tbsp	10 g	
Garlic, minced	2 tsp or to taste	10 g or to taste	
Salt	1 tsp or to taste	5 g or to taste	
Pepper, white	1 tsp or to taste	2 g or to taste	
Egg noodles, thin	2 lb	900 g	*Cook egg noodles in lightly salted water until tender. Rinse under cold running water, then drain. Toss the noodles lightly with a small amount of oil to keep them from sticking together. Reserve.*
Oil, vegetable	as needed	as needed	

TO PREPARE AN INDIVIDUAL SERVING

Oil, vegetable	2 tsp	10 ml	*Heat a wok or heavy skillet over high heat. Add the oil and heat until just below the smoking point. Stir-fry the bean sprouts and scallions for 20–30 seconds. Add the seasoning sauce, mix well, then add the noodles. Lower heat and stir-fry until the noodles are heated through and have absorbed all of the pan liquids.*
Bean sprouts, washed and trimmed	1 1/2 oz	40 g	
Scallion or chives, sliced thin	1 tbsp	6 g	
Seasoning sauce	2 oz	60 g	
Reserved noodles	3 oz	90 g	

See color insert for photograph of recipe

Desserts

CHAPTER TEN

DESSERTS

The western dessert course in its many guises—simple to complex, elaborate, artfully arranged and oft times much decorated—provides a culmination to the dining experience that we have grown to anticipate and love. Unfortunately, this course does not play a major role in the Asian dining experience. While every Asian cuisine boasts of representative sweet dishes, these are usually reserved for special occasions, or eaten as snacks rather than as a dessert. The desire for an appropriate concluding course, however, seems to be universal. To satisfy that need, a majority of the Asian cultures bring the meal to a close by serving a wide variety of fresh fruits which are available in great abundance. Rather than present desserts that have been invented for western tastes or those that attempt to mimic western preparations using other than traditional ingredients, I have chosen instead to include some representative sweet dishes that may be used for that purpose.

Lychee Sauce for Fresh Fruit

YIELD: VARIABLE

Lychee nuts, canned	2, #2 cans*	2, #2 cans*	Drain can, reserving the lychees and the liquid in which they were packed, separately.
Cornstarch	1 tbsp	10 g	Mix cornstarch with the water to make a smooth paste. Place the reserved liquid in a small saucepan and bring to a boil. Lower heat to a simmer and add the cornstarch. Cook until the mixture thickens. Remove from heat and pour into the bowl of a food processor fitted with the steel blade.
Water	1 tbsp	15 ml	
Reserved liquid			
Reserved lychees			Add ingredients and puree. Refrigerate until needed. Use as a sauce for fresh fruits.
Ginger, candied, chopped fine	4 oz	115 g	
Lime juice, fresh squeezed	3 oz	90 ml	
Cream, heavy or evaporated milk (optional)	2 oz	60 ml	

*No. 2 cans: 20 fluid oz (590 ml), drained weight, 12 oz (355 ml).

Spring Snow with Mixed Fruits

YIELD: 10-12 SERVINGS

Agar-agar*	*1/2 oz*	*15 g*
Water	*1 qt*	*950 ml*
Sugar	*10 oz*	*300 g*
Egg whites	*2*	*2*
Reserved agar-agar and water		
Lemon juice	*1 oz*	*30 ml*
Ramekins, 3 oz (90 ml) or molds	*as needed*	*as needed*
Fresh fruits, strawberries, kiwi, grapes, lemon slivers, candied fruit, etc.	*as needed*	*as needed*

Place the agar-agar in a small saucepan, add the designated amount of water, and simmer until it has dissolved.

Add the sugar and simmer, uncovered, stirring occasionally, until the liquid becomes slightly thickened. Reserve.

Whip egg whites until stiff. Gradually add the agar-agar and water while still warm. Add the lemon juice and mix well.

*Cut fruit into small attractive pieces. Moisten the insides of the ramekins with water. Place an equal amount of the mixed fruits into each of the ramekins or similar sized molds. Fill to the tops with the agar-agar mixture. Let cool, then refrigerate until needed.***

If using agar-agar in powdered form, place in a saucepan containing the water and bring to a boil. Lower heat and simmer until it is dissolved. If using filaments, also known as "agar-agar strips," or sheets, break them into small pieces and soak in water to cover for 20 minutes. After soaking, squeeze to remove any water that has not been absorbed and follow procedure in step one.

Agar-agar preparations set up at room temperature and will remain firm without refrigeration. A chilled serving temperature simply makes this recipe more refreshing. Agar-agar mixtures also tend not to cling to whatever kind of vessel they are poured into. They can, therefore, be unmolded very easily with no advance preparation.

See color insert for photograph of recipe

Saffron Rice Dessert with Raisins and Almonds

YIELD: 10 SERVINGS

Rice, long grain, Basmati	1 lb	450 g
Water	1 qt	1 L
Milk, hot	8 oz	240 ml
Saffron, ground	1 tsp	2 g
Raisins, golden, select	1 oz	30 g
Butter, clarified	4 oz	120 ml
Cinnamon, ground	1 tsp	2 g
Cardamom, ground	1/2 tsp	1 g
Clove, ground	1/2 tsp	1 g
Reserved milk with saffron and raisins		
Sugar, confectioner's	8 oz	230 g
Reserved rice		

Rinse rice until the water remains clear. Place rice in a saucepan and bring to a boil. Cover pot with a tight fitting lid and reduce heat to a simmer. Cook until the rice is tender, but still firm. Drain, if any excess water remains. Reserve.

In a small, heavy-bottomed saucepan, heat milk to just below the boiling point. Remove from heat and add the saffron and raisins. Cover pot and let sit until the raisins are plump and the saffron has dissolved.

Heat butter over low to medium heat, then add the spices. Cook, stirring, until they are well mixed and aromatic.

Add the milk, sugar, and rice, and bring to a simmer. Cover pot and cook over very low heat until the rice is very tender and all of the liquid has been absorbed. Divide the rice equally into individual ramekins and garnish with an arrangement of slivered almonds on top.

Ginger in Honey

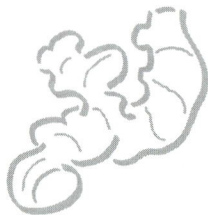

Gingerroot, very fresh	1 lb	450 g	*Peel the gingerroot, then cut it on the diagonal into very thin oval slices. Place in a saucepan with the water and bring to a boil over high heat. Continue to boil rapidly for 10 minutes. Drain the gingerroot, reserving the liquid for other uses.*
Water	1 1/2 qt	1.5 L	
Honey	8 oz	230 g	*Combine honey and water in a heavy-bottomed sauce pan and bring to a boil. Add the ginger and reduce heat. Simmer, uncovered, for 30–40 minutes, or until the liquids have been reduced by half. Serve cold or at room temperature, alone or as a garnish for other desserts.*
Water	8 oz	240 ml	

Broiled Banana with Fresh Apricot/Apple Puree

YIELD: 10 SERVINGS

Apricots, fresh, ripe	1 1/2 lb	680 g
Apple juice	4 oz	120 ml
Sugar, light brown	to taste	to taste

Wash apricots, split them in two, and discard pits. Place in blender or food processor fitted with the steel blade and puree. Add the apple juice and sugar. Pulse a few times to blend. Reserve refrigerated.

BASTING MIXTURE

Orange juice	8 oz	240 ml
Lemon or lime juice, fresh squeezed	3 oz	90 ml
Cardamom	1/2 tsp or to taste	1 g or to taste
Nutmeg or cinnamon	1/2 tsp or to taste	1 g or to taste

Combine ingredients and reserve.

TO PREPARE AN INDIVIDUAL SERVING

Banana, split down the middle lengthwise	1 medium, slightly underripe	1 medium, slightly underripe
Clarified butter	as needed	as needed
Basting mixture	1 tbsp	30 ml
Maple or dark brown sugar	as needed	as needed

Brush both sides of the banana with clarified butter and place in an heat-proof individual serving dish. Spoon a small amount of the basting sauce on top, then sprinkle lightly with sugar. Place under broiler flame until lightly browned.

Almond slices, toasted	as needed	as needed
Reserved apricot sauce, room temperature	as needed	as needed

When done, sprinkle a small amount of almond slices over the bananas. Top with several spoonfuls of the apricot puree.

Songaya

YIELD: VARIABLE, DEPENDING ON SIZE OF MOLDS

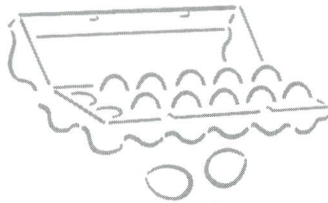

Sugar, dark brown	3/4 lb	340 g	*Combine ingredients and stir until the sugar is completely dissolved. Taste, and adjust seasonings if necessary.*
Coconut milk, thick	1 1/2 pt	700 ml	
Jasmine or orange flower water	2 oz or to taste	60 ml or to taste	
Eggs, large, beaten	5	5	*Add the eggs, mix well, then strain the mixture through a fine sieve.*
Oil, vegetable	as needed	as needed	*Lightly oil the ramekins, then fill with the custard mixture. Place ramekins in a pan containing enough hot water to reach halfway up the sides. Bake in 325°F (160°C) oven for 40–50 minutes or until mixture is set. When cool, place in refrigerator. Unmold to serve and garnish with fresh orange slices.*
Ramekins, 3 oz (90 ml) or other similar molds	as needed	as needed	

Water Chestnuts in Coconut Milk

YIELD: 10-12 SERVINGS

Water chestnuts, fresh or canned*	1 1/2 lb	680 g
Lightly acidulated water	as needed	as needed

If fresh water chestnuts are available, select those that are very firm with no traces of soft spots. Wash, then boil for 10 minutes, drain and let cool. Peel the layers of thin, light brown leafy layers that cover the nut. Slice and reserve in lightly acidulated water to cover.

Coconut milk, thin	30 oz	900 ml
Sugar	8 oz or to taste	230 g or to taste

Heat coconut milk over low to medium heat until very warm. Add sugar and stir until it is thoroughly dissolved. Let cool and reserve.

Reserved water chestnuts	2 oz	60 g
Reserved coconut milk	3 oz	90 ml
Small ice cubes	2 tbsp	2 tbs.

Drain the water chestnuts. Combine with the coconut milk and refrigerate. When serving, place a portion of the water chestnuts and coconut milk in a small, deep bowl and add 2 tbsp of small ice cubes.

*Jackfruit, or Longan, a close relative of the lychee, both of which are readily available canned, can be substituted or used in combination with the water chestnut. Garnish with a small amount of colorful berries in season.

Steamed Peaches in Honey

YIELD: 10 SERVINGS

Peaches, large, freestone, slightly under ripe	10	10	
Mint, fresh	4–5 sprigs	4–5 sprigs	

Wash peaches and remove stems, if any. Place in a pot with boiling water for 6–8 seconds to loosen skins. Peel, then cut the peaches in half starting from the stem end. Discard the pits. Distribute the mint sprigs over a steamer rack, then arrange the peach halves, cut side down, on top. Steam over boiling water until the peaches are tender. Cooking time will vary depending on size of peaches and degree of ripeness. When done, discard the mint sprigs and place the peach halves cut side down, in a stainless steel pan just large enough to hold them.

Sugar	4 oz	115 g
Honey	2 oz	60 g
Rosewater	1 tbsp	15 ml
Water	8 oz	240 ml
Mint leaves, fresh	as needed	as needed

Combine ingredients in a small saucepan and bring to a boil over medium heat. Lower heat and simmer until the syrup thickens. Distribute the honey syrup evenly over the peach halves. Serve 2 halves per portion. Garnish with fresh mint leaves.

Milk Pudding with Citrus Fruit

YIELD: 10 SERVINGS

Rice, basmati	1 oz	30 g
Milk	2 oz	60 ml
Milk	2 qt	2 L
Sugar	4 oz or to taste	115 g or to taste
Orange flower water	2 tsp or to taste	10 ml or to taste

Soak rice overnight. Drain, then place in a blender with the milk and puree.

In a heavy-bottomed saucepan, preferably nonstick, bring the milk to a boil over medium heat. Reduce heat to a simmer. Add the milk/rice mixture and cook, stirring occasionally, until reduced to 1 qt (1 L).

Add the sugar and cook briefly, stirring until the sugar has completely dissolved. Add the orange flower water, stir, and remove from heat. Place in a blender or mixer and whip until no lumps remain. When cool, refrigerate until needed.

TO SERVE

Citrus fruit, orange, tangerine, small grapefruit	3–4 oz per serving	90–115 g per serving
Reserved reduced milk	3 oz per serving	90 g per serving
Berries, fresh, in season	as needed	as needed

Use fruit segments singly or in combination. Mix gently with reduced milk and serve in chilled stemware or small bowls. Garnish with fresh berries in season.

Mango with Rabadi

Y I E L D :   1 0   S E R V I N G S

RABADI*

Milk	2 1/2 qt	2.5 L
Sugar, granulated	4 oz	115 g

Pour milk into a shallow, heavy-bottomed saucepan, preferably nonstick. Bring the milk to a boil over low to medium heat, stirring occasionally, to prevent the milk from sticking to the pan. Lower heat to a simmer and cook for about 1 hour or until the milk has been reduced to one-fourth of the original volume. Scrape the sides of the pan and stir frequently to break up any skin that forms on the top. When done, add the sugar, place in a blender or mixer, and whip until smooth. If preferred, Rabadi can be left in its lumpy state. Allow to cool, then refrigerate until needed.

Mango, flesh, ripe fresh preferred; canned acceptable	1 1/2 lb	680 g
Pistachios, undyed and unsalted	6 oz	170 g

Cut mango flesh into uniform slices or dice. Blanch the pistachios in boiling water for a few minutes if the thin skin covering the nut is still attached. Drain thoroughly, then chop fine. Sprinkle over the mango and chill.

TO PREPARE AN INDIVIDUAL SERVING

Mango and pistachios	3 oz	90 g
Reserved Rabadi	2 oz	60 ml

Arrange the mango/pistachio mixture in the center of a chilled dessert plate. Top with Rabadi, or, place a pool of Rabadi on the plate, then arrange the fruit and nuts on top.

*Rabadi, simply, a sweetened reduction of whole milk, can be used as a sauce for any number of fresh fruits. It can also be served with or without the chopped nuts.

See color insert for photograph of recipe

Semolina and Raisin Halwa

YIELD: 12 SERVINGS

Sugar	10 oz	300 g	*Place sugar and raisins in a mixing bowl. Bring water to a boil. Let sit for 1–2 minutes, then pour over the sugar and raisins. Stir to dissolve the sugar. Reserve.*
Raisins, black, select	3 oz	90 g	
Water, boiling	1 1/4 qt	1.2 L	
Clarified butter	8 oz	240 ml	*Heat clarified butter in a large, heavy-bottomed skillet, preferably nonstick, over medium heat. Add the semolina and stir to incorporate the butter. Fry, stirring until the flour is lightly browned.*
Flour, semolina (farina)	8 oz	230 g	
Reserved sugar/raisin mixture			*Slowly add the sugar, raisin, and water mixture to the flour, stirring rapidly to avoid lumps. Bring to a boil, lower heat and simmer, stirring frequently, until the liquid is completely absorbed and the flour is cooked through.*
Cardamom, ground	1/2 tsp or to taste	1 g or to taste	*Add the cardamom and mix. Taste, and adjust flavorings if necessary. Pour into individual goblets and top with 1 tbsp (15 ml) of heavy cream added just before serving. May be served warm or at room temperature.*

Coconut Custard Flavored with Rosewater Essence

YIELD: 12 SERVINGS

Eggs, beaten	6	6	*Using a wire whisk, combine ingredients.*
Coconut milk, thin	1 qt	950 ml	
Cardamom, ground	1 tsp	2 g	
Mace, ground	1/2 tsp	1 g	
Nutmeg, ground	1/2 tsp	1 g	
Rose water	2 tbsp or to taste	30 ml or to taste	
Sugar, light brown	6 oz	170 g	*Add the sugar. Pour into a heavy-bottomed saucepan and warm over low heat, stirring, until the sugar is dissolved completely. Pour into 3-oz (90-ml) ramekins or other similar molds. Place in a pan containing enough hot water to reach halfway up the sides of the containers. Bake in a 325°F (160°C) oven until set. Let cool, then refrigerate. Garnish with berries in season.*

Coconut Gelatin Flavored with Rose Water

YIELD: 12 SERVINGS

Agar-agar,* powdered, or in strand or sheet form	1 1/2 oz	40 g
Water	1 qt	950 ml
Coconut milk, thin	1 qt	950 ml
Sugar	8 oz or to taste	230 ml or to taste
Rose water	1 tbsp	15 ml
Salt	pinch	pinch

Place the agar-agar in a small saucepan, add the designated amount of water, and simmer until it has dissolved.

*Add ingredients and simmer, uncovered, stirring frequently, for 15–20 minutes. Pour into a pan to a depth of 1 1/2–2 in. (4–5 cm) and cool until set, then refrigerate. The coconut milk will separate and rise to the top, making two distinctive layers. When firm, cut into elongated rectangular pieces. For individual servings, this preparation may also be poured into ramekins or other single-serving-sized molds.***

*If using agar-agar in powdered form, place in a saucepan containing the specified amount of water and bring to a boil. Lower heat and simmer until it is dissolved. If using filaments, also known as "agar-agar strips," or sheets, break them into small pieces and soak in water to cover for 20 minutes. After soaking, squeeze to remove any water that has not been absorbed and follow procedure and quantities in step one.

**Agar-agar preparations set up at room temperature and will remain firm without refrigeration. A chilled serving temperature, however, makes this dessert more refreshing. Agar-agar mixtures also tend not to cling to whatever kind of vessel they are poured into. They can, therefore, be unmolded very easily with no advance preparation.

Coconut Rice Cake with Mango

YIELD: 10-12 SERVINGS

Rice, short grain	1 lb	450 g

Soak rice overnight in a generous amount of water. Drain, then steam until rice becomes tender and the grains stick together easily when pressed.

Coconut milk, thick	1 qt	950 ml
Syrup, sugar	8 oz or to taste	240 ml or to taste

Combine the coconut milk and sugar syrup. Gently mix 10 oz (300 ml) of this mixture with the rice taking care not to crush the grains. Reserve the remaining coconut milk mixture.

Oil, vegetable	as needed	as needed

Divide the rice equally among 3-oz (90-ml), lightly oiled ramekins or similar molds, filling each to the top. Press lightly but firmly, to compact the rice evenly. Cover and chill for 2–3 hours before serving.

TO PREPARE FOR SERVING

Mango, ripe	2–3 oz per serving	60–90 g per serving
Reserved coconut milk mixture	2–3 oz per serving	60–90 ml per serving

Peel and slice or dice mangos. Unmold ramekins on to the centers of chilled dessert plates. Pour the reserved coconut milk mixture over and around the rice. Garnish with slices or diced pieces of mango placed on top and/or around the molded rice.

Candied Apple

YIELD: 2 SERVINGS

Sugar	10 oz	280 g	*Combine ingredients and bring to a boil over high heat. Do not stir. Cook until the syrup reaches 325°F (162°C). If a thermometer is not available, when the sugar has become a rich golden color, remove it from the heat and place a drop of the syrup into iced water. If the syrup hardens into a ball immediately upon contact with the water, it has reached the correct temperature. Reserve over low heat.*
Water	2 oz	60 ml	
Egg white	1 large egg	1 large egg	*Mix the egg white and water with enough corn- starch to make a thin batter.*
Water	1 tbsp	15 ml	
Cornstarch	as needed	as needed	
Apples, medium size, firm tart, peeled and cored	2	2	*Cut the apples into eight wedges each and coat with the cornstarch batter.*
Oil, vegetable	for deep- frying	for deep- frying	*Deep-fry the apple wedges at 375°F (190°F). When golden brown, remove the apple wedges from the oil and dip them first into the hot syrup then immedi- ately into the iced water to harden the coating. Serve while the apple is still warm.*
Reserved syrup			
Iced water	small bowl	small bowl	

Banana Fried
in a Coconut/Tapioca Batter

YIELD: VARIABLE

BATTER

Flour, rice	6 oz	170 g	*Blend ingredients.*
Flour, tapioca	2 oz	60 g	
Coconut, grated	2 oz	60 g	
Sugar	2 oz	60 g	
Salt	2 tsp	10 g	
Water	*approx. 16 oz*	*approx. 470 ml*	*Add water in small increments to make a batter the consistency of very thick cream.*

TO PREPARE AN INDIVIDUAL SERVING

Banana, medium sized, slightly underripe	*1 per serving*	*1 per serving*	*Slice banana into three or four slices, lengthwise. If banana is very long, cut first into two halves, cross-wise. Dip banana pieces into the batter to coat well. Deep-fry at 350°F (175°C) until golden brown. Drain on absorbent towel and serve on a warm plate sprinkled with a light layer of finely grated coconut.*
Oil, vegetable	*for deep-frying*	*for deep-frying*	
Coconut, grated, fresh or dried			

Banana in Coconut Milk

YIELD: 10 SERVINGS

Bananas, small, slightly underripe	10	10
Coconut milk, thin	1 qt	1 L
Sugar	8 oz or to taste	230 g or to taste
Salt	1/2 tsp	3 g

Cut bananas in half, lengthwise, then cut each half in two to create four pieces. Place the coconut milk, sugar, and salt in a heavy-bottomed saucepan and bring to a boil over moderate heat. Add the bananas, and, when the liquid has returned to the boil, lower heat and simmer for 2–3 minutes. Serve banana pieces together with approximately 3 oz (90 ml) of the coconut milk in a small, shallow bowl. May be served hot or cold.

Apple Kheer

YIELD: 10-12 SERVINGS

Apples, tart, firm	2 1/2 lb	1.2 kg	*Peel and core the apples, then grate them directly into a saucepan containing lightly acidulated water to cover. Bring to a boil over high heat. Lower heat and simmer for 2–3 minutes. Drain into a strainer and press to remove as much water as possible.*
Water and lemon juice	as needed	as needed	
Clarified butter	4 oz	120 ml	*In a heavy-bottomed saucepan, heat butter over medium heat. Add the apples and cook, stirring, until the apples begin to brown lightly.*
Grated apples			
Milk	2 qt	2 L	*In a deep saucepan, preferably nonstick, bring the milk to a boil over medium heat. Add the apples and sugar. Cook, uncovered, stirring occasionally, until the mixture is thick.*
Sugar	1 lb	450 g	
Almonds, sliced, toasted	2 oz	60 g	*Add ingredients and mix well. Lower heat and simmer, stirring, until the mixture has a creamy texture. May be served hot or cold. Serve with spiced cookies or wafers.*
Raisins, golden, select	2 oz	60 g	
Cardamom, ground	1/2 tsp or to taste	1 g or to taste	

Suggested Readings

Aksomboon, Kwanruan and Somchai, with Diana Hiranaga. *Thai Cooking from the Siam Cuisine Restaurant.* Berkeley, Calif.: North Atlantic Books, 1989.

Alejandro, Reynaldo. *The Philippine Cookbook.* New York: Perigee Books, 1982.

Art Culinaire, 8th edition, Spring 1988. "Japan: Master Chefs from the Far East." Atlanta, Ga.: Culinaire, Inc., 1988.

Brennan, Jennifer. *The Original Thai Cookbook.* New York: Perigee Books, 1981.

Brennan, Jennifer. *The Cuisines of Asia.* New York: St. Martin's Press, 1984.

Detrick, Mia. *Sushi.* San Francisco: Chronicle Books, 1981.

Devi, Yamuna. *The Art of Indian Vegetarian Cooking.* New York: E.P.Dutton, 1987.

Duong, Binh and Marcia Kiesel. *Simple Art of Vietnamese Cooking.* New York: Simon & Schuster, 1991.

Fu, Pei Mei. *Pei Mei's Best Selections Chinese Cuisine.* Taipei: Pei-Mei Fu, with T&S Industrial Co., Ltd., 1987. (Imported by Summit Import Corp., New York.)

Haydock, Yukiko and Bob. *Japanese Garnishes: The Ancient Art of Mukimono.* New York: Holt, Rinehart and Winston, 1980.

Hiang, Lie Sek. *Indonesian Cookery.* New York: Bonanza Books, 1963.

Huang, Elizabeth. *Healthful Cooking.* Taipei: Wei-Chuan Publishing.

Huang, Su-Huei. *Chinese Appetizers & Garnishes.* Taipei: Wei-Chuan Publishing, 1982.

Huang, Su-Huei. *Chinese Snacks.* Taipei: Wei-Chuan Publishing, 1985.

Huang, Su-Huei. *Chinese One Dish Meals.* Taipei: Wei-Chuan Publishing, 1987.

Kahrs, Kurt. *Thai Cooking.* New York: Gallery Books, 1990.

Kongpan, Sisamon and Pinyo Srisawat. *The Elegant Taste of Thailand: Cha Am Cuisine.* Berkeley/Hong Kong: SLG Books, 1989.

Konishi, Kiyoko. *Japanese Cooking for Health and Fitness.* Woodbury, New York: Barron's Educational Series, 1984.

Konishi, Kiyoko. *Entertaining with a Japanese Flavor.* Tokyo: Kodansha International, 1990.

Lee, Calvin B. T. and Audrey Evans Lee. *The Gourmet Chinese Regional Cookbook.* Secaucus, N.J.: Castle Books, 1976.

Lee, Florence C. and Helen C. Lee. *Kimchi: A Natural Health Food.* Elizabeth, N.J.: Hollym Corp., Publishers, 1988.

Lin, Florence. *Florence Lin's Complete Book of Chinese Noodles, Dumplings and Breads.* New York: William Morrow, 1986.

Lin, Lee Hwa. *Noodles: Classical Chinese Cooking.* Taipei: Chin Chin Publishing.

Lo, Eileen Yin-Fei. *New Cantonese Cooking.* New York: Viking Penguin, 1988.

Lo, Kenneth. *Chinese Vegetable and Vegetarian Cooking.* London: Faber and Faber, 1974.

Lo, Kenneth. *New Chinese Cooking School.* Tucson, Arizona: HP Books, 1985.

Marks, Copeland. *The Exotic Kitchens of Indonesia: Recipes from the Outer Islands.* New York: M. Evans and Company, 1989.

Ngo, Bach and Gloria Zimmerman. *The Classic Cuisine of Vietnam.* New York: Plume/Penguin Books USA, 1986.

Noh, Chin-hwa. *Healthful Korean Cooking: Meats and Poultry.* Elizabeth, N.J.: Hollym Corp. Publishers, 1985.

Noh, Chin-hwa. *Traditional Korean Cooking: Snacks and Basic Side Dishes.* Elizabeth, N.J.: Hollym Corp. Publishers, 1985.

Oriental Cooking Class Cookbook. Lincolnwood, Ill.: Publications International, Ltd., 1990.

Passmore, Jacki. *The Encyclopedia of Asian Food and Cooking.* New York: Hearst Books, William Morrow and Co., 1991.

Passmore, Jacki. *The Noodle Shop Cookbook.* New York: Macmillan, 1994.

Passmore, Jacki and Daniel P. Reid. *The Complete Chinese Cookbook.* New York: Exeter Books, 1982.

Poladitmontri, Panurat, Judy Lew and William Warren. *Thailand: The Beautiful Cookbook.* San Francisco, Calif.: Collins Publishers, 1992.

Rossant, Colette. *Colette's Japanese Cuisine.* New York: Kodansha International Ltd., 1985.

Sahni, Julie. *Classic Indian Cooking.* New York: William Morrow, 1980.

Simonds, Nina. *Classic Chinese Cuisine.* Shelburne, Vt.: Chapters Publishing, Ltd., 1994.

Singh, Manju Shivraj. *Royal Indian Cookery: A Taste of Palace Life.* New York: McGraw-Hill, 1987.

So, Yan-kit. *Yan-kit's Classic Chinese Cookbook.* New York: Dorling Kindersley, 1993.

Solomon, Charmaine. *The Complete Asian Cookbook.* Rutland, Vt.: Charles E. Tuttle Co., 1992.

Songkhla, Wandee Na. *The Royal Favourite Dishes (from the "Hunger Diary" of King Rama V of Thailand).* Bangkok. (Publisher and date not translated.)

Spayde, Jon. *Japanese Cooking.* Secaucus, N.J.: Chartwell Books, 1984.

Taik, Aung Aung. *Under the Golden Pagoda: The Best of Burmese Cooking.* San Francisco: Chronicle Books, 1993.

Tropp, Barbara. *The Modern Art of Chinese Cooking.* New York: William Morrow, 1982.

Tsuji, Shizuo. *Japanese Cooking: A Simple Art.* New York: Kodansha International Ltd., 1980.

Van Holzen, Heinz and Lother Arsana. *The Food of Indonesia: Authentic Recipes from the Spice Islands.* Singapore: Periplus Editions (HK) Ltd., 1995.

Ven, Shin Chih. *Cheng Wei Vegetarian Dessert Cuisine.* Taipei: Mei-Ching Co., 1989.

Yan, Martin. *The Well-Seasoned Wok.* Emeryville, Calif.: Harlow & Ratner, 1993.

Glossary

Agar-Agar	A natural gelatin derived from seaweed which dissolves in boiling water, sets at room temperature, and does not require refrigeration to remain firm. Available in stick form, sheets, or as a powder, its gelling capacity is much greater by volume than animal-product-based gelatin. It is used in savory as well as sweet dishes. Products using agar-agar as a gelling agent unmold easily, without the need for immersion in hot water.
Anise, star	(see Star anise)
Asparagus bean, long bean, yard-long bean, long-podded cow peas	Harvested when young and approximately 15 in. (38 cm) in length, this legume is particularly suited to stir-frying, braising, and as a component in curry dishes. Its flavor and texture are enhanced when combined with assertive flavors. Two varieties with slightly different characteristics are marketed—a pale green and a dark green; the dark green variety is thinner and has a firmer texture. Easily perishable, these beans can be stored under refrigeration for several days if received when very fresh.
Bamboo shoots	One of the most popular ingredients in Asian cooking, the young, tender shoots of the mature bamboo plant are used in a wide variety of dishes. Fresh shoots, which are available occasionally, contain a toxin and must be parboiled before using in combination with other foods. Canned shoots, packed in water, are readily available and are marketed either sliced or whole. After draining, a 15-oz (425-g) can will yield 8 1/2 oz (240 g) of usable product.
Bean curd (Tofu)	A semi-firm food product of Chinese origin made by combining a setting agent with ground boiled soybeans and water. Usually found formed into squares and stored or packed in water, bean curd has practically no flavor of its own but readily absorbs those of other foods and sauces. Best to purchase in sealed containers that have been kept under refrigeration and are date-stamped to indicate freshness, bean curd is an important source of protein in many Asian cuisines. Store refrigerated, in water that is changed on a daily basis.
Bean pastes; bean sauces	Ancient flavoring products whose primary ingredient is fermented soybeans. A mixture of mashed soybeans, spices, garlic, chili, and salt, these products are available in a variety of consistencies and flavors, the latter ranging from hot to mild. Their distinctive and pungent flavor is found in the foods of China as well as of most other Asian countries. The popular condiment, Hoisin sauce, is a product of this group of flavorings. Also in this family of pastes and sauces is a sweet red bean paste, which is used as a filling for buns, pastries, and cakes. Available in cans, jars, or bottles. Also known as black bean sauce, chili bean paste, hot black bean sauce, soybean paste.

Beni shoga (ginger, pickled)	Gingerroot, cut into paper-thin slices and pickled in a rice vinegar, sugar, and salt brine. Colored pink to light red, it is used as a condiment particularly with sushi and sashimi.
Black beans, fermented	Soy beans that have been cooked, salted, and fermented. Used mashed, chopped, or whole, they are a popular flavoring agent used in a wide variety of steamed, stir-fried, and braised dishes.
Bok choy, Chinese cabbage	A leafy vegetable with spinach-like leaves and thick, white stems. The entire plant may be used, resulting in little waste. One pound (450 g) yields 14 oz of usable product. Crunchy stalks, which take a bit longer to cook than the leaves, are juicy and have a slightly sweet taste. One of the most popular Asian vegetables, it is used in stir-fried dishes, braised dishes, and soups. It is also pickled with chili and garlic and served as a condiment or accompaniment. For stir-frying, select bok choy with thinner, narrower leaves.
Caraway seeds	Commonly used in conjunction with other seeds and spices to flavor Indian and Burmese dishes.
Cardamom	The second most expensive spice after saffron. The pods, either pale green or dark brown, are gathered by hand. Available either in the pod or as seeds, the most flavorful form of ground cardamom is obtained by opening pods and grinding the seeds on an as-needed basis.
Chili-flavored oil	A very hot flavoring oil made by infusing hot vegetable oil with crushed, dried red chili flakes or pods. Can be obtained through commercial sources or easily prepared in the kitchen (see recipe).
Chili bean paste	A convenient form of seasoning to impart hot chili flavor which can vary greatly in degree of "heat," consistency, and flavor. Made from ground chilies, salt, vinegar, garlic, and fermented soybeans to produce a very strong-flavored mixture.
Chili peppers	Indigenous to the Americas and one of the oldest known cultivated plants, chilies were introduced to the world of gastronomy by Christopher Columbus. Thousands of varieties are grown and enjoyed in a wide range of dishes. The flavors and heat properties of chili peppers can vary enormously from one variety to another. Not all chili peppers possess a fiery nature. Many of these varieties are available fresh year round, as well as dried, canned, or in bottles. Fresh chilies tend to be more flavorful than dried. The effect of peppers can be intensified by the inclusion of the ribs and seeds, which tend to contain more of the "heat" than the flesh of the pepper. It is generally held that the smaller the pepper, the hotter the flavor, but as this is not always the case, it is best to taste for "hotness" before using. Great care should be taken when

working with chili peppers, as capsaicin, the agent responsible for the characteristic "heat," can cause severe irritation.

Chili powder	Finely ground, dried red chilies. Available in a wide range of flavor, from mild to intensely hot.
Chili sauce	Available in a wide variety of textures and flavors depending on national origin. The Chinese version has a thick texture and is available medium to very hot. It is used both as a flavoring agent and as a dipping sauce. Other versions, such as those found in Vietnam and Thailand, vary from intensely hot to sweet.
Chinese red date, jujube	Used in northern Chinese and some Korean dishes, both savory and sweet. A small red, firm-fleshed, fibrous fruit with a slightly wrinkled skin similar in texture to the black date. Available ripe and dried, having a strong date-plum flavor. Soften in boiling water before using. Also available green, pickled in brine. Used in soups, braised dishes, and sweets. Available fresh in some markets from fall to early spring.
Chojang sauce	(see Chapter 8, Flavorings and Condiments)
Choy sum	A leafy vegetable with long, medium thick stems and rounded, light green leaves. Closely resembles the small, center leaves of bok choy. Stems, when thick, should be peeled before cooking.
Cilantro leaves	(see Coriander)
Cinnamon	The peeled, rolled, and sun-dried bark of a member of the Lauraceae family, an evergreen tree native to Sri Lanka. Available in two forms, rolled sticks and ground, it is an essential ingredient in spice mixtures for curries.
Cloud ear fungus (wood ear fungus)	An "ear-shaped" lichen with a distinctive woodsy flavor and slightly crunchy texture. Available dried, it increases four to five times in volume when soaked. After soaking, discard its hard stems and chop the remainder into appropriate sizes. Readily absorbent of flavorings, it is used in stir-fried dishes, soups, and braised dishes.
Coconut milk, thick or thin	(see Chapter 8, Flavorings and Condiments)
Coriander, cilantro, Chinese parsley	An indispensable flavoring herb used throughout Asia with the exception of Japan, its fresh leaves are used as a garnish, a flavoring for curry, and chopped in combination with other foods. Available fresh year round, all parts of the plant, leaves, roots, stems, and seeds are used in a wide variety of recipes. An essential part of curry mixtures, the seeds are marketed as "coriander."

Cornstarch	Commonly used in Asian cooking as a coating for fried foods, a binding agent, and thickener. Dissolves quickly when mixed with cold water. When added in small amounts to hot pan liquids in stir-fried dishes, it produces a shiny, transparent sauce. If cooked too long it has a tendency to separate or break down. As a rule-of-thumb measurement, 1 tbsp (10 g) of cornstarch to 1 tbsp (15 ml) of cold water will lightly thicken 8 oz (240 ml) of liquid. It is also used to produce light-textured cakes and pastries.
Cumin	Available as seeds or ground, an essential component of curry spice mixtures and a basic flavoring for garam masala. Similar to caraway seed in appearance, its flavor is markedly different. For best results when using ground cumin, toast seeds until they pop, then grind to a powder.
Curry paste	(see Chapter 8, Flavorings and Condiments)
Curry powder	A traditional blend of spices containing a number of different spices and other flavoring agents. Many regional varieties exist. Most commonly found ingredients are cumin seeds, black mustard seeds, fenugreek seeds, curry leaves, coriander seeds, dried chili pepper, and turmeric. Also used are black pepper, cinnamon, and cloves which are toasted, ground, and blended on an as-needed basis. Curry powders are readily available from commercial sources in a variety of flavors. While convenient to use, most of these products lack the intensity of flavor found in freshly toasted, ground, and blended mixtures.
Daikon, giant white radish	An important vegetable throughout Asia, found in a variety of sizes and shapes. It is used in condiments and eaten as a vegetable raw, cooked, or pickled. A versatile vegetable, it can be sliced or grated for salads and dipping sauces. It is also used in soups and stews. A fundamental ingredient in Japanese cooking, it is best to use when the plant has reached a length of 8–10 in. (20–25 cm).
Dashi	A basic soup stock used in Japanese cooking (see Chapter 3, Soups).
Dried bonito flakes (hana-katsuo)	The flesh of the bonito or frigate mackerel, dried to a rock-like consistency then shaved into flakes. It is an essential ingredient in the making of Dashi. The shaved pieces are also used to enrich the flavor of sauces. Available packaged in various sizes, seasoned dried bonito flakes are also sold in disposable infusion bags similar to tea bags.
Fennel seeds	Used in spice mixes in India, Indonesia, Thailand, and Sri Lanka, the seeds are somewhat sweet and have an anise-like flavor.
Fish sauce, Nam Pla (Thailand), Nuoc Mam (Vietnam)	A pungent sauce made from fermented fish and salt. Color ranges from amber to dark brown. Essential to the foods of Thailand and Vietnam,

fish sauce is used as a cooking ingredient. It is also served as a condiment with the addition of finely sliced or chopped hot, fresh chilies and chilies and lime juice.

Five-spice powder	A combination of finely ground star anise, fennel seeds, cloves, Szechwan pepper corns, and cinnamon. Commercial brands use these spices in different proportions. Taste and aroma, therefore, will vary.
Flour, chickpea, gram flour	Used for Indian recipes, it is made from chickpeas which have been roasted then ground into flour. If this flour is not available, spread a thin layer of unroasted chickpea flour in a pan and place in a moderate oven until lightly toasted.
Galanga, Galangal, Siamese ginger, Ka (Thailand), Laos (Indonesia and Vietnam)	A ginger-like rhizome with a creamy white flesh and pink shoots, available fresh, frozen, dried, and ground. Fresh and frozen are interchangeable. Increase amount by one-third if using dried. Indispensable in Thai cuisine. While many substitute ginger when galanga is unavailable, there is no real substitute for galanga.
Garam masala	A spice mix associated with Indian foods (see Chapter 8, Flavorings and Condiments).
Ginger, juice	(see Chapter 8, Flavorings and Condiments)
Ginger, pickled	(see Beni shoga)
Gingerroot	A rhizome with a slightly coarse gray-tan skin, gingerroot is one of the most prevalent flavoring agents in Asian cooking. Available fresh year round, ginger should be peeled before using. It is used sliced, chopped, grated, shredded or minced, squeezed for juice or infused to make ginger wine. Large amounts can add considerable "heat" to a dish. Ginger is also sliced paper thin and pickled in sweetened vinegar to make "beni shoga," a popular condiment served with sushi and sashimi. Dried or powdered ginger is not a good substitute.
Ginkgo nuts	Available canned year round; fresh in the fall. If fresh nuts are used, they must be cracked open, the hard shell discarded, and the soft, creamy-white nut placed in very hot water to soften the inner skin, which can then be removed.
Golden needles	(see Lily bulbs)
Hana-katsuo	(see Dried bonito flakes)
Hoisin sauce	(see Bean paste)
Japanese eggplant	A wide variety available both in shape and size. Compared to the vari-

ety familiar to Europeans and Americans, Japanese eggplants tend to be firmer textured, sweeter, with a more pronounced flavor. One of the most commonly found varieties is long and slender with a light to dark purple skin; it does not have the slightly acrid taste usually associated with eggplants, and is usually available fresh in the spring and summer months.

Japanese mustard	Available powdered in small cans and in tubes.
Jujubes	(see Chinese red dates)
Kaffir lime	A variety of lime about the same size as the lime commonly found in the market. Grown in Southeast Asia, it has a textured, knobby, dark green skin rich in fragrant oils. The leaves and rind are available fresh or dried and are used with greater frequency than the juice. The dried leaves and rind must be soaked for an hour or two before using. They provide a characteristic flavoring associated with Thai and other Asian cuisines. The aromatic zest is also frequently used, added to curries, soups, and stews. A combination of citrus leaves and fresh lime zest can be used as a substitute.
Konbu, sea kelp, sea tangle	A giant sea kelp used to make Dashi (see recipe), the stock that is central to many Japanese dishes and to sushi rice. It imparts a distinctive flavor reminiscent of the sea. Konbu may be wiped lightly with a damp cloth (but never soaked) before using. The light grayish-white mold found on the surface contributes to the flavor it imparts. It may be scored lightly to release flavor and can be used several times before all of the flavor has been released. Shredded, it can be stir-fried or deep-fried.
Lemongrass, citronella	Available fresh and dried, a grass-like plant which imparts a lemon-like flavor. Resembling the scallion, this fragrant grass has a long pale green-to-whitish bulb which is the part most commonly used in cooking. The upper leaves are dried and used for making a tea. The bulb-like tender sections are sliced thin and used in curries and salads. When used in soups or braised dishes, the bulb section is crushed and removed when the cooking is completed.
Lily bulbs, golden needles, dried lily flowers, lotus buds	Dried buds of the tiger lily, used to add a delicate, musky flavor to many dishes. Before using, they must be reconstituted in water for at least 30 minutes or until they become tender. When reconstituted, cut to appropriate size.
Long beans, asparagus beans	(see Asparagus beans)
Malt sugar, maltose	A sweet extract of wheat similar in consistency to molasses. Used for sweetening, glazing meats and duck (Peking Duck).

Mirin, sweet cooking rice wine, Japanese sherry	A sweetened, golden-colored sake used for cooking purposes only and not for drinking. Used to glaze grilled foods and add flavor to basting sauces. The alcohol content, which is very low, is usually cooked off by boiling the liquid, leaving the sweet residual flavor.
Miso	A fermented soybean-based paste blended with other ingredients. Miso is a staple in the Japanese kitchen, used as a soup base, for pickling, in salad dressings, soups, and stews. Also used as a condiment, it is marketed in a number of forms, each with its own distinctive flavor and aroma and with applications in a wide variety of dishes. The popular Miso Soup contains the bean paste combined with Dashi and various small garnishes. Available in tubs, jars, and plastic bags. After opening containers, miso must be refrigerated but stores well.
Mushrooms, black Chinese	The most common mushroom used in Asian cooking is more tan to dark brown than black. Marketed in dried form which heightens the flavor, these mushrooms must be soaked until plump and soft before using. Only the caps are used; tough stems are discarded. The soaking liquid can be incorporated into other dishes. Other mushrooms, such as the shiitake, matsutaki, straw, and oyster, are also used and are available either fresh or dried.
Mustard, powdered, hot	Ground mustard seeds mixed with water or vinegar to desired consistency. Used as a dipping sauce.
Mustard seeds, black	Used in curries, sauces, pickles, and relishes. Toast in a dry pan until they begin to pop before using.
Nigella seeds	A small, plump, black seed used to make pickles and as an ingredient for curry spice mixes.
Noodles	(see Chapter 9, Rice and Noodles)
Nori seaweed	Also known as laver, nori seaweed is used as a wrapping for sushi. Should be refreshed by a light toasting before using.
Nuoc cham	(see recipe in Chapter 8, Flavorings and Condiments)
Oil, peanut	A popular cooking oil that imparts a slightly nutty flavor. Its ability to withstand high cooking temperatures makes it ideal for stir-frying.
Oil, sesame	A rich, amber-colored oil extracted from toasted sesame seeds and used primarily as a flavoring agent. If used for frying it is usually combined with another, less flavorful vegetable oil. Sesame oil has a low burning point. Sesame oil extracted from untoasted sesame seeds is also available. This oil is not used in Asian cuisine.

Oils, cooking	Vegetable oils pressed from peanuts, soybeans, coconut, sunflower seeds, and oils extracted from tropical palms are used for cooking purposes. Generally bland in flavor, their ability to withstand high temperatures without burning makes them highly desirable for stir-frying. Other oils, such as sesame and mustard, as well as oils derived from animals, such as lard, chicken, and duck fat, are used more as flavoring or finishing agents.
Orange peel, dried	Contrary to the name, this dried peel is made from the rind of the tangerine or mandarin. It is used to impart a slightly tart, citrus flavor to sauces, soups, and braised dishes.
Oyster sauce	A dark brown, thick sauce made from dried oysters, soy sauce, and brine. Used as a flavoring and coloring agent in stir-fried and other braised dishes as well as a table condiment.
Pine nuts	Most often grown in Korea, usually available dried. Used as a garnish and in sweet dishes. If unavailable, use chopped, untoasted cashews.
Ponzu sauce	(see Chapter 8, Flavorings and Condiments)
Poppy seeds, white, black	A very tiny seed that imparts a nutty flavor. When ground to a paste-like consistency, they are used as thickeners and as a flavoring agent in curries, rice, and vegetarian dishes.
Red curry paste	A flavorful blend of herbs and spices whose color is determined by the color of the primary chili pod used in the preparation and an essential ingredient in the preparation of Thai curry dishes. Most popular is red curry paste, followed by green curry paste, all of which have intense, hot flavors.
Rice	(see Chapter 9, Rice and Noodles)
Sake, Japanese rice wine	Made from fermented rice and usually drunk warm from small cups, Sake is one of the most important ingredients in the Japanese kitchen. It is used extensively in cooking where it acts as a food tenderizer, a modifier of salty flavors and when combined with other ingredients such as soy sauce and sugar in sauces and marinades; it also helps to produce rich glazes.
Shichimi	A general-purpose Japanese condiment used to add extra flavor to a wide variety of dishes. It is a blend of seven different ingredients including red pepper, dried mandarin orange peel, seaweed, black hemp seeds, Sichuan pepper corns, and white sesame seeds. The mixture is processed into tiny flakes. Can be purchased through commer-

cial sources under the name "seven-spice powder" and is packed in shaker containers suitable for placement on the table.

Shaohsing, Shao Hsing wine	In continuous production for over 2,000 years this wine is made from rice, millet and a yeast mold. It is considered to be one of the best of the Chinese wines and is used in stir fried dishes and marinades. If unavailable, dry sherry or Japanese sake could be used as a substitute.
Shrimp, dried	Dehydrated, small shrimp used as a flavor enhancer in soups and fillings. Orange to pink in color, they should be soaked before using. They may also be deep-fried and served with a chili dipping sauce.
Shrimp paste	Used in many southeast Asian countries, it is made from pounded shrimp and salt. Best quality has a smooth texture and is not very salty. Available in jars.
Soybean paste	(see Bean pastes)
Soy sauce	The traditional seasoning of Asia. Made from fermented soybeans combined with roasted wheat, barley, or rice and a yeast mold and salt for further fermentation. Available in two basic forms: light soy sauce, used primarily for stir-frying, as a basis for dipping sauces, and in stocks, and for dishes such as seafood and poultry to enhance, not mask, delicate flavors; and dark soy sauce which is richer in color, thicker and is used to add color and a more intense flavor. Sometimes marketed as "mushroom soy."
Star anise	A seed pod resembling an eight-pointed star. It imparts a strong anise or licorice flavor. An essential ingredient in Chinese five-spice powder it is available whole or in powder form. In braised dishes the seeds pods can be used whole or in part.
Sugar, malt (maltose)	(see Malt sugar)
Szechwan chili paste	(see Chapter 8, Flavorings and Condiments)
Szechwan peppercorn	Not a true peppercorn, this reddish brown seed from a variety of ash tree, has a sharp, distinct flavor. Ground into a powder it is used in combination with other ground spices. When toasted, ground, and mixed with salt it is used as a dipping powder for fried foods. It is also an essential ingredient in the Japanese condiment known as shichimi.
Tamarind, juice, pulp	An essential ingredient in the food of India, Malaysia, and Indonesia, it is the flesh of the seed pod of the Tamarind tree. Available fresh, in jars, in concentrate form, as well as dried. It is used to impart a sweet-tart flavor to sauces, soups, and curries. It is also used in chutneys. In marinades it is used as a flavoring and tenderizing agent.

Tangerine peel	(see Orange peel, dried)
Teriyaki sauce	(see Chapter 8, Flavorings and Condiments)
Tofu	(see Bean curd)
Turmeric	The essential ingredient responsible for the vivid, yellow colors associated with curried dishes. Used extensively in India, Thailand, Indonesia, Malaysia, and Burma. It is occasionally available fresh, but most often is found ground. Must be used sparingly because of its strong flavor.
Vinegar, rice	A mild-flavored condiment that adds tartness to salads and other dishes. Flavored varieties are also available. Wine vinegar, which has a much stronger flavor, is not a good substitute.
Wasabe, Wasabi	Available in powdered form which when mixed with water produces a fiery paste. Indigenous to Japan, Wasabi is served as an accompaniment to sushi and sashimi dishes.
Water chestnut	The dark brown bulb of a water plant, its white flesh has a crisp texture and a slightly sweet flavor. Available canned and, at times, fresh. Used commonly in stir-fried dishes, it can also be eaten as a snack.
Wonton wrappers	Thin pastry wrappers, available fresh or frozen.
Wood ear fungus (black fungus; cloud ear fungus; tree ear)	(see Cloud ear fungus)
Yakitori sauce	(see Chapter 8, Flavorings and Condiments)

Purveyors of Asian Food Products

The acquisition of Asian food products is no longer difficult in most regions, particularly in areas which are in close proximity to urban population centers. Increased immigration from a host of Asian countries has fostered not only a significant increase in public eating establishments but also in the market network necessary for their support. In addition to ethnic markets, many supermarkets now carry a complete line of authentic Asian food products as well as a wide selection of specialty fresh produce items and other perishables. A majority of the establishments listed below deal on the retail level. Many of these retail outlets, however, will sell wholesale providing the quantities are sufficient. For the small scale restaurant operator, if needed quantities are not large, this may be the most economical way to purchase. For buyers who purchase in larger quantities, most of the items needed to complete the recipes in this volume can be obtained through major wholesale purveyors.

A separate listing of wholesale distributors follows the retail list.

ARIZONA

Oriental Food Store
408 West Main St.
Jacksonville, AZ 72076

Kimbong Market
502 Dobson St.
Meza, AZ 85202

Siam Import Market
5008 West Northern Ave.
No. 3
Glendale, AZ 85301

CALIFORNIA

May Wah Trading Co.
1230 Stockton St.
San Francisco, CA 94133

Viet Nam Thuc Phan
Menlo Park, CA 94025

Dobashi Co.
240 East Jackson St.
San Jose, CA 94112

Yaohan USA Corp.
2121 West 182nd St.
Torrance, CA 90504

Wa Heng Doufu Soy Sauce
2451 26th Ave.
Sacramento, CA, 95822

Uoki Sakai
1656 Post
San Francisco, CA 94101

Simex International
331 Clement St.
San Francisco, CA 94101

Lorenzana Food Corp.
4921-25 Santa Monica
Blvd.
Los Angeles, CA 90028

Bankok Market, Inc.
4804-6 Melrose Ave.
Los Angeles, CA 90029

Pacific Coast Sprout Farm
5640 Warehouse Way
Sacramento, CA (916)
381-6054

Mekong Oriental
Supermarket
1301 Broadway
Sacramento, CA 95818

A Dong Thuc Pham
6001 Eldercreek
Sacramento, CA 95824

Hillcrest Oriental Food
Center
426 University Ave.
San Diego, CA 92103

K. Sakal Co.
1656 Post St.
San Francisco, CA 94115

Que Huong
9087 Bolsa Ave.
Westminster, CA 92683

Philippine Grocery
4929 Mission St.
San Francisco, CA 94101

M & M Oriental Foods
635-B East Arrow Highway
Azusa, CA 91702

Canton Food Inc.
1100 East 5th St.
Los Angeles, CA 90013

Bezjian's Grocery, Inc.
4725 Santa Monica Blvd.
Los Angeles, CA 90029

COLORADO

Pacific Mercantile Grocery
1925 Lawrence St.
Denver, CO 80202

Far East Flavors
8547 East Arapahoe Rd.
Suite J205
Greenwood Village, CO
80111

Kim Young Oriental
1444 Chester St.
Aurora, CO 80010

Thai Binh Market
1445 Dayton St.
Denver, CO 80231

Oriental Food Market
2707 Arapahoe Ave.
Boulder, CO 80302

Park's Oriental Market
229 North Academy Blvd.
Colorado Springs, CO
80909

CONNECTICUT

Thai Binh Market
1445 Dayton St.
Denver, CO 80231

Oriental Food Market
2707 Arapahoe Ave.
Boulder, CO 80302

Park's Oriental Market
229 North Academy Blvd.
Colorado Springs, CO
80909

East-West Trading Co.
68 Howe St.
New Haven, CT 06105

Vietnam House
242 Farmington Ave.
Hartford, CT 06105

FLORIDA

Oriental Imports
1118 South Orange Ave.
Jacksonville, FL 32801

Tomiko's Oriental
441 Bryn Athyn Blvd.
Mary Esther, FL 32569

Trung My
8737 South West 72nd St.
Miami, FL 33173

Indian Grocery Store
2342 Douglas Road
Miam Beach, FL 33134

Misako's Oriental Foods
129 New Warington Road
North Pensacola, FL
32406

Asian Market
3214 9th St.
St. Petersberg, FL 33704

Asia Market
1241 East Colonial Drive
Orlando, FL 32803

South and Eastern Food
Supply
6732 N.E. 4th Ave.
Miami, FL 33138

GEORGIA

Asian Trading Co.
2581 Piedmont NE
Atlanta, GA 30324

Daido Foods
2390 Carroll Ave.
Chamblee, GA 30341

Dong A Oriental Food
3331 Buford Hwy.
Atlanta, GA 30260

Makoto
1067 Oaktree Rd.
Decatur, GA 30033

Oriental Trading
8415 Cresthill Ave.
Savannah, GA 31406

Thai Oriental Market
676 Highway 85
Riverdale, BA 30274

Satsuma-ya
5271-B Buford Hwy.
Doraville, GA 30340

ILLINOIS

Ah Joo Oriental Food
9210 N. Waukegan Rd.
Morton Grove, IL 60053

Diamond Trading Co.
913 W. Belmont Ave.
Chicago, IL 60657

Bangkok Grocery
1003-5 W. Leland Ave.
Chicago, IL 60640

Far East Trading Co.
2837 N. Western Ave.
Chicago, IL 60618

Far East Food Co.
105 S. Fifth St.
Champaign, IL 61820

Furuya, & Co.
5358 N. Clark St
Chicago, IL 60616

Ginza & Co.
315 E. University
Champaign, IL 61820

India Gifts and Foods
1031 W. Belmont Ave.
Chicago, IL 60650

India Groceries
5010 N. Sheridan Rd.
Chicago, IL 60640

Kam Shing Co.
2246 S. Wentworth St.
Chicago, IL 60616

Oriental Food Market and
Cooking School
2801 Howard St.
Chicago, IL 60645

Korea Market
2606 W. Lawrence Ave.
Chicago, IL 60625

Kyotoya Corp. Food & Craft
1182 S. Elmhurst
Mt. Prospect, IL 60056

Lee Wah Co.
2246 S. Wentworth Ave.
Chicago, IL 60615

Lin's International Inc.
1537 S. State St.
Chicago, IL 60605

New Quon Wah
2515 Wentworth Ave.
Chicago, IL 60616

New Way Trading, Inc.
3328 N. Clark St.
Chicago, IL 60657

Philippine Food Corp.
4547 N. Ravenswood
Chicago, IL 60625

Sun Hing Co.
2239 S. Wentworth Ave.
Chicago, IL 60616

Tong Yang Market
5131 N. Western Ave.
Chicago, IL 60625

Wah May Food Products
Co.
2401 S. Wentworth Ave.
Chicago, IL 60616

IOWA

Tokyo Foods
1005 Pierce St.
Sioux City, IA 51105

Jung's Oriental Food Store
913 East University Ave.
Des Moines, IA 50316

Lucky Dragon, Inc.
319 East Main St.
Ottumwa, IA 52501

LOUISIANA

Kim Thanh
3003 Florida Blvd.
Baton Rouge, LA 70803

Korea House
615 Orange St.
New Orleans, LA 70130

Oriental Merchandise Co.
2636 Edenborn Ave.
Metairie, LA 70002

Tien Nha Trang
1804 Baratario Blvd.
Marrero, LA 70072

MARYLAND—WASHINGTON, D.C.

Da Hua Foods Inc.
617 I St. NW
Washington, D.C. 20001

House Of Hanna
7838 Eastern Ave.
Washington, D.C. 20012

Mee Wah Lung Co.
608 H St. NW
Washington, D.C. 20001

Mikado
4709 Wisconsin Ave. NW
Washington, D.C. 20016

Spices and Foods
Unlimited, Inc.
2018A Florida Ave. NW
Washington, D.C. 20009

Wang's Co.
800 7th St. NW
Washington, D.C. 200001

Arirang House
7918 Georgia Ave.
Silver Spring, MD 20910

Asian Foods Inc.
2301 University Blvd. West
Wheaton, MD 20902

Asia House Grocery
2433 Saint Paul St.
Baltimore, MD 21218

India Emporium
68-48 New Hampshire Ave.
Tacoma Park, MD 20912

Indian Sub-Continental
Store
908 Philadelphia Ave.
Silver Spring, MD 20910

MASSACHUSETTS

Joyce Chen Unlimited Inc.
172-174 Massachusetts Ave.
Arlington, MA 02174

India Tea and Spice, Inc.
453 Common St.
Belmont, MA 02178

Mirim Trading Co., Inc.
152 Harvard Ave.
Allston, MA 02134

See Sun Co.
36 Harrison Ave.
Boston, MA 02111

Sun Sun Co.
34 Oxford St.
Boston, MA 02111

Tung Hing Lung
5 Hudson St.
Boston, MA 02111

Wing Wing Imported
Groceries
79 Harrison Ave.
Boston, MA 02111

Yoshinoya
36 Prospect St.
Cambridge, MA 02139

New Sun Market
154 Brighton Av.
Brighton, MA 02135

Chung Wah Hong Co.
55 Beach St.
Boston, MA 02111

MICHIGAN

Mt. Fuji Oriental Foods
22040 W. 10 Mile Rd.
Southfield, MI 48075

Phil-Asian Tropical Food
Mart
4638 Woodward
Detroit, MI 48233

Gabriel Importing Co.
2461 Russell St.
Detroit, MI 48207

India Grocers
35-46 Cass Ave.
Detroit, MI 48201

Rafal Spice Company
2521 Russell St.
Detroit, MI 48207

Oriental Food Store
18919 W. 7 Mile Rd.
Detroit, MI 48219

MINNESOTA

International House
75 W. Island Ave.
Minneapolis, MN 55401

Phil-Oriental Imports, Inc.
476 Lexington Parkway
St. Paul, MN 55104

United Noodle Corp.
2015 E. 24th St.
Minneapolis, MN 55404

Vietnam & Hong Kong
Int'l
419 W. Broadway
Minneapolis, MN 55411

Thai Store
1304 Eastlake St.
Minneapolis, MN 55407

Kwong Tung Noodle Manu.
Co.
326 Cedar Ave.
Minneapolis, MN 55404

MISSOURI

Kim's Mart
6692 Enright Ave.
St. Louis, MO 63114

King's Trading
3736 Broadway
Kansas City, MO 64111

Seema Enterprises
10612 Page Ave.
St. Louis, MO 63132

Quality International
3228 Ivanhoe
St. Louis, MO 63139

West Quon Wah
1651 S. Grand St.
St. Louis, MO 63104

Jay Asia Food
3232 S. Grand St.
St. Louis, MO 63118

NEBRASKA

Asian Market
2413 Lincoln Rd.
Bellevue, NE 68005

Oriental Market
611 North 27th St.
Lincoln, NE 68503

Oriental Trading Co.
10525 J St.
Omaha, NE 68127

NEW JERSEY

Aki Oriental Food Co.
1635 Lemoine Ave.
Fort Lee, NJ 07024

Daido International
1385 16th St.
Fort Lee, NJ 07024

Bombay Bazaar
797 Newark Ave.
Jersey City, NJ 07306

India Bazaar
204 Hudson St.
Hoboken, NJ 07030

Krishna Grocery Store
103 Broadway
Passaic, NJ 07057

Mira-San Oriental Food
Store
530 Newark Ave.
Jersey City, NJ 07306

Fil-Am Food Mart, Inc.
685 Newark Ave.
Jersey City, NJ 07306

Sam Bok
3012-18 Edwin Ave.
Fort Lee, NJ 07024

Sammi Oriental Grocery
Store
444 Broad Ave.
Leonia, NJ 07605

NEW YORK

House of Spices
76-17 Broadway
Jackson Heights, Queens,
NY

Duang
75-17 37th Ave.,
Jackson Heights, Queens,
NY

American India Traders
139 Division St.
New York, NY 10002

India Spice Store
110 Lexington Ave.
New York, NY 10012

Dean and Deluca
560 Broadway
New York, NY 10012

Sahadi Importing Co. Inc.
187 Atlantic Ave.
Brooklyn, NY 11201

Thailand Food Corp.
2445 Broadway
New York, NY 10012

Mabuhay
524 Ninth Ave.
New York, NY 10018

Thuan Nguyen
82 Mulberry St.
New York, NY 10013

Cathay Food Products
115 Broadway
New York, NY 10004

Wing Fat Co.
33-35 Mott St.
New York, NY 10013

Chinese-American Trading
Co.
91 Mulberry St.
New York, NY

Aphrodisia Products
282 Bleeker St.
New York, NY 10014

Foods of India
120 Lexington Ave.
New York, NY 10016

Annapurna
127 E. 28th St.
New York, NY 10016

Kalustyan Orient Export
Trading Co.
123 Lexington Ave.
New York, NY 10016

Mr. Spiceman
615 Palmer Rd. Dept.705
Yonkers, NY 10314

Bangkok Market
106 Park St.
New York, NY 10013

Tanaka and Co.
326 Amsterdam Ave.
New York, NY 10023

Kim Man Food
200 Canal St.
New York, NY 10013

Wing Woh Lung Co.
50 Mott St.
New York, NY 10013

C.T.Yang
2830 West Henrietta Rd.
Rochester, NY 14620

NEW MEXICO

Yonemoto Bros.
8725 4th St.
Albuquerque, NM 87114

Fremont Fine Foods
556 Coronado Center N.E.
Albuquerque, NM 110

OHIO

Bayanihan Food, Inc.
625 Bolivar
Cleveland, OH 44101

Dayton Oriental Foods
812 Xenia Ave.
Dayton, OH 45410

International House of
Foods
712 Washington Avle. SE
Columbus, OH 43206

Oriental Food & Gifts
500 W. Main St.
Fairborn, OH 45324

Soya Food Products Inc.
2356 Wyoming Ave.
Cincinnati, OH 45214

Bangkok Grocery
3277 Refugee Rd.
Columbus, OH 43227

Far East Co.
247 W. McMillan St.
Cincinnati, OH 45219

Kim's Mart
1400 Beaverton Dr.
Dayton, OH 45429

Sam Wah Rick Kee Co.
2146 Rockwell Ave.
Cleveland, OH 44114

Thai Grocery
108 E. Main St.
Columbus, OH 43215

OKLAHOMA

Indian Foods and Spices
13125 El. 36th St.
Tulsa, OK 74134

Viet Nam Market
2702 E. 15th St.
Tulsa, OK 74104

Japan Imported Foods
808 N.W. 6th St.
Oklahoma City, OK 73106

OREGON

Anzen Japanese Foods &
Imports
736 Northeast Union Ave
Portland, OR 97232

Porter's Foods
125 West 11th St.
Eugene, OR 97410

Albertson's
5415 S.W. Beaverton-
Hillsdale Hwy.
Portland, OR 97221
(Other locations in area)

Fred Meyer's Stores
100 N.W. 20th
Portland, OR 97209
(Other locations in area)

PENNSYLVANIA

Chinese & Oriental Food
Product
   Research Inc.
117 N. 10th St.
Philadelphia, PA 19107

Asia Products Corporation
226 North 10th St.
Philadelphia, PA 19107

House of Spices of New
York
4101 Walnut St.
Philadelphia, PA 19104

The Oriental Ltd.
804 South 12th St.
Philadelphia, PA 19147

Wing On
1005 Race St.
Philadelphia, PA 19107

Phil-Am Food Mart
5601 Camac
Philadephia, PA 19104

Penn Herbs
603 North 2nd St.
Philadelphia, PA 19123

Hong Kee
935 Race St.
Philadelphia, PA 19107

Bombay Emporium
294 Craft Ave.
Pittsburgh, PA 15213

India Bazaar
3358 Fifth Ave.
Pittsburgh, PA 15213

TEXAS

Asiatic Imports
821 Chatres
Houston, TX 77003

Hoa Binh
2800 Pravis St.
Houston, TX 77006

Eastern Foods
8626 1/2 Long Point
Houston, TX 77003

Tachibana
4886 Hercules Ave.
El Paso, TX 79904

Korea Super Market
6427 Bissonet
Houston, TX 77074

Tan Viet Market
10315 Ferguson Drive
Dallas, TX 75228

Dragon Gate Market
3524 East Lancaster
Ft. Worth, TX 76103

Chung Hing Co.
815 Chatres
Houston, TX 77003

Dockee Import
817 Chatres
Houston, TX 77003

Nippon Daido International
1138 Westheimer
Houston, TX 77042

Oriental Import-Export Co.
2009 polk St.
Houston, TX 78209

Vietnam Plaza
2200 Jefferson St.
Houston, TX 77003

American-Asian Foods
6866 Shady Brook Lane
Dallas, TX 75231

Oriental Market
502 Pampas Drive
Austin, TX 78752

Laos Grocery
5813 Amarillo Blvd. East
Amarillo, TX 97107

Suvanee's Oriental
7403 Highway 80
West San Antonio, TX
78227

UTAH

Royal Thai Market
860 West Riverdale Rd.
Riverdale, UT 84403

K & K International Market
7046 South State St.
Midvale, UT 84047

Viet Nam Food
610 South State St.
Salt Lake City, UT 84111

Sage Farm Market
1515 South Main St.
Salt Lake City, UT 84115

VIRGINIA

China Grocery Inc.
3509 S. Jefferson St.
Baileys Crossroad, VA
22041

Tokyo Market
5312 Va. Beach Blvd.
Virginia Beach, VA 23462

Viet-My Corporation
1007 St. Stephen Road
Alexandria, VA 22304

Manila Mart
3610 Lee Highway
Arlington, VA 22207

Bankok Oriental
3832 Mt. Vernon Ave.
Alexandria, VA 32305

Oriental House
4816 Richmond Hwy.
Alexandria, VA 22306

Vietnam Imports
922 W. Broad Street
Falls Church, VA 22046

Mekong Center
3107 Wilson Blvd.
Arlington, VA 22201

Super Asian Market
2719 Welson Blvd.
Arlington, VA 22306

Backlick Oriental
6681-82 Backlick Rd.
Springfield, VA 32305

WASHINGTON

Specialty Spice House
Pike Place Market
Seattle, WA 98105

Uwajimaya
519 6th Ave. South
Seattle, WA 98104

Angor Wat Market
5912 196th St.
Lynwood, WA 98036

The Philippine Best
10303 Greenwood North
Seattle, WA 98103

Saigon Market
1034 South jackson St.
Seattle, WA 98104

Asian Market
10855 N.E. 85th St.
Bellevue, WA 98004

WISCONSIN

Chadda Imports
1450 E. Brady St.
Milwaukee, WI 53202

India Groceries and Spices
4733 W. North Ave.
Milwaukee, WI 53208

International House of
Foods
440 W. Gorham St.
Madison, WI 53703

Spice House
1048 N. Old World 3rd St.
Milwaukee, WI

Vientiane Market
12205 16th St.
Milwaukee, WI 53204

CANADA

S. Eakin, Inc
1203 St. Lawrence
Montreal, Quebec H2X
2S6
Canada

Filipino Market
4 Irwin St.
Toronto, Ontario
Canada

Kohinoor International
Foods
1438 Gerrard St. East
Toronto, Ontario M4L
1Z8
Canada

Mihamaya
392 Powell St.
Vancouver, British
Columbia VGA 1G4
Canada

Iwaki Japanese Food Store
2627 Yonge St.
Toronto, Ontario M4P 2J6
Canada

India Food Center
802 Somerset St.
Ottawa, Ontario K1R 6R5
Canada

Chinamart Trading Co.
210 Spadina Ave.
Toronto, Ontario
Canada

House of Spice-Kensington
Market
190 Somerset St. West
Toronto, Ontario M5T 2L6
Canada

Chung Mee Trading Co.
437 Dundas St. West
Toronto, Ontario M5T
1G6
Canada

MAJOR WHOLESALE DISTRIBUTERS

Sysco Corporation
Corporate Headquarters
1390 Enclave Parkway
Houston, TX 77077-2099
(713) 584-1390
FAX: (713) 584-1737

Alliant Foodservice, Inc.
Clayton, Dubilier & Rice, Inc.
One Parkway North
Deerfield, IL 60015-2545
(847) 405-8500
FAX: (847) 405-8980

Marriott Distribution
Services
One Marriott Dr.
Dept. 984.45
Washington, DC 20058
(301) 380-2517
FAX: (301) 380-2233

Nugget Distributor
Cooperative of America, Inc.
4226 Coronado Av.
Stockton, CA 95204
(209) 948-8122
FAX: (209)546-0770

Pocahontas Foods, USA
7420 Ranco Rd.
P.O. Box 9729
Richmond, VA 23228
(804) 262-8614
FAX: (804) 261-4394

Monarch, Inc.
P.O. Box 1328
Greenville, SC 29609
(803) 676-8600
FAX: (803) 676-8756

U.S. Food Service
1065 Highway 315
Suite 101
Wilkes Barre, PA 18702
(717) 831-7500
FAX: (717) 822-0909

Comsource, Independent
Food Service Companies,
Inc.
Suite 400
280 Interstate North
Parkway
Atlanta, GA 30339
(770) 952-0871
FAX: (770) 952-0872

Japan Food Canada, Ltd.
540 Forbes Blvd.
So. San Francisco, CA
94080
(415) 871-1660
FAX: (415) 952-3272

Japan Food Canada, Ltd.
1880 Bonhill Rd.
Mississaga, Ontario L5T 1C4
(905) 564-5511
FAX: (905) 564-6644

Dole & Bailey, Inc.
16 Conn St.
Woburn, MA 01801
(617) 935-1234
FAX: (617) 935-9085

Index

VAN NOSTRAND REINHOLD ▮VNR▮

Your Name_____   Address_____
Title_____   City/State/Zip_____
Function_____   Phone_____
Company_____   Fax_____
Date of book purchase_____   E-Mail_____

Thank you for your interest in Van Nostrand Reinhold publications. To enable us to keep you abreast of the latest developments in your field, please complete the following information.

1. With respect to the topic of this book, are you a:
   a. student in this field
      name of your institution: _____
   b. working professional in this field
   c. hobbyist in this field

2. For how many years have you worked/studied in this field?
   _____

3. Of which professional associations are you a member?
   _____
   _____
   _____

4. To which industry or general food-related publications/resources do you subscribe for important information?
   _____
   _____
   _____

5. Describe your professional title:
   a. chef   h. sommelie
   b. caterer   i. consulting services
   c. restaurant owner/manager   j. government
   d. food and beverages manager   k. librarian
   e. student   l. education/research
   f. professor/teacher   m. other (please specify)
   g. pastry chef   _____

6. How/where was this book purchased? (circle one)
   a. bookstore
   b. publisher's outlet
   c. through offer in mail
   d. through book club
   e. other _____

7. How/where do you usually purchase professional books?
   (please circle all that apply)
   a. bookstore
   b. publisher's outlet
   c. through offer in mail
   d. through book club
   e. other_____

8. Do you own or have access to a computer with a modem?
   a. yes   b. no

9. To which electronic on-line services do you have access?
   (please circle all that apply)
   a. America On-Line   e.   World Wide Web
   b. Prodigy   f.   other (please specify)
   c. Compuserve   _____
   d. Internet   g.   none

10. Do you own or have access to a computer with a CD-ROM reader?
    a. yes   b. no

11. Would you purchase updates, supplements and/or additional chapters to this book in an electronic format?
    a. yes   b. no

12. Which format would you prefer?
    a. disk (circle one)   Mac   Dos   Windows
    b. CD-ROM
    c. online
    d. other_____

13. What was the primary reason for purchasing this book?
    a. professional enrichment
    b. academic coursework
    c. personal interest/hobby
    d. other_____

14. Would you be interested in or subscribe to a Professional Chef's Newsletter? a. yes   b. no
    If yes, which do you prefer?
    a. online   b. print

15. In which of the following areas would you be interested in new books?
    a. International cuisine   e. buffets
    b. catering   f. wines
    c. baking and pastry   g. other (please specify)
    d. beverage management   _____

VNR is constantly evaluating its services and products in order to improve them to better meet your needs.

If you need further information please do not hesitate to contact us by fax at 212-475-2548.

BE SURE TO VISIT US AT OUR WEB SITE
http://www.vnr.com/vnr.html

Gelber/Asian Cooking 0-442-31942-8   *an International Thomson Publishing company* I⟨T⟩P

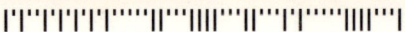

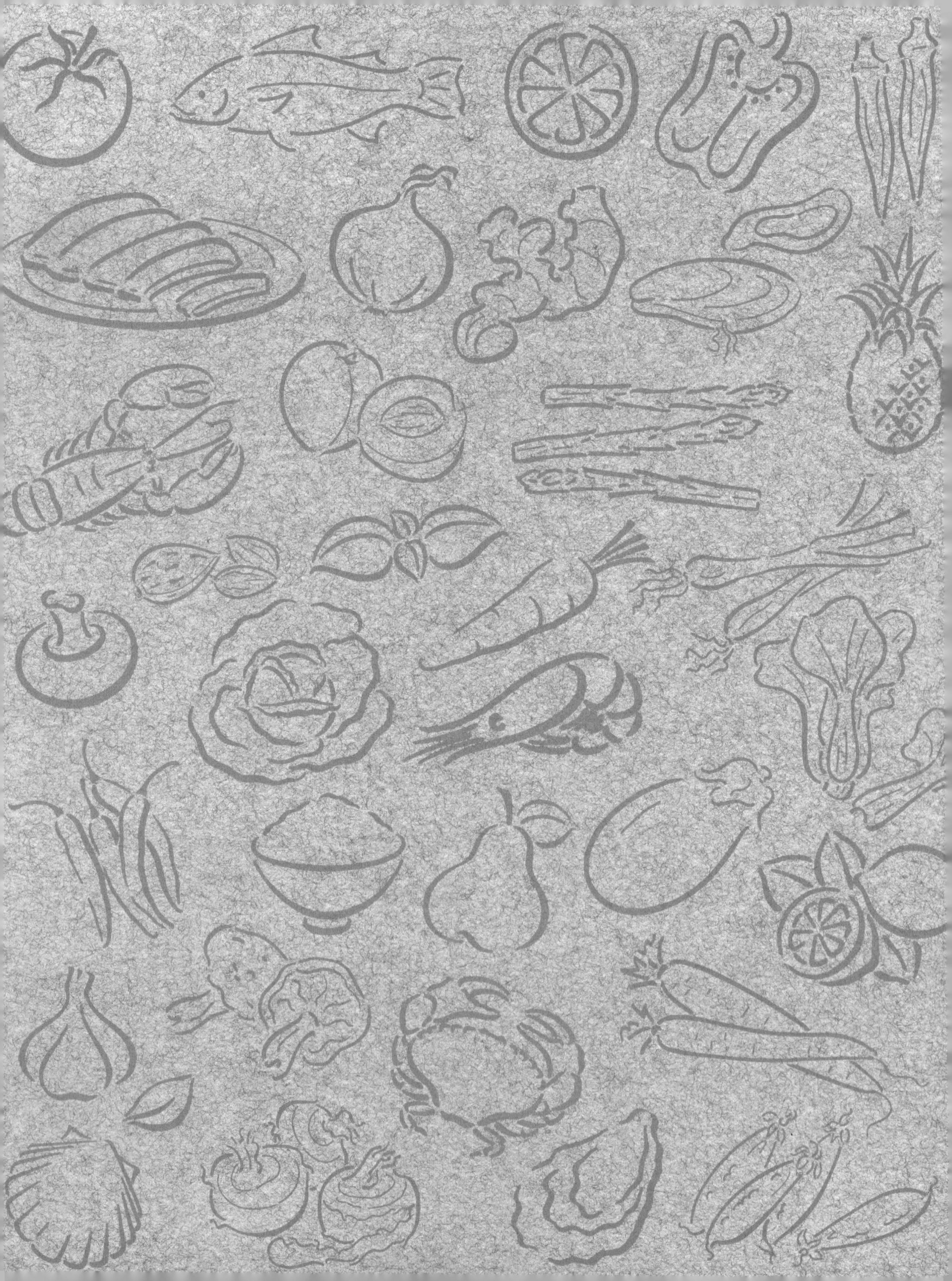